JOHN LA FARGE

IN PARADISE:

THE PAINTER AND HIS MUSE

John La Farge
The Muse of Painting
(Decorative Panel. Seated Figure in Yellow. Study for The Muse of Painting)
1870   Oil on canvas   49 1/2 x 38 1/4 in. (125.7 x 97.2 cm.)
The Metropolitan Museum of Art,   New York, Gift of J. Pierpont Morgan and Henry Walters, 1909 (09.176)

JOHN LA FARGE IN PARADISE:
THE PAINTER AND HIS MUSE

James L. Yarnall

WILLIAM VAREIKA FINE ARTS
NEWPORT, RHODE ISLAND

This book was published on the occasion of the exhibition *John La Farge in Paradise: The Painter and His Muse*, held from March 31-May 31, 1995 at the gallery of William Vareika Fine Arts, Newport, Rhode Island.

Designers: Donna S. Maytum and Craig A. Newell
Editor: Susanne Owens Koenig
Mechanical Production: Micrographix, Newport, Rhode Island

Color Separations: Elite Color Group, Providence, Rhode Island

Printed and bound in the U.S.A. by Meridian Printing, East Greenwich, Rhode Island under the supervision of Fern Malouin

Published by William Vareika Fine Arts, Newport, Rhode Island

Library of Congress Catalog Card Number: 95-060588

ISBN: 1-887265-00-7

Cover: John La Farge
    The Last Valley—Paradise Rocks, 1867
    Oil on canvas
    32 x 41 1/2 in. (81.3 x 105.4 cm)
    Private Collection
    (see fig. 167)

Table of Contents

Foreword by William Vareika   i

Prelude   1

I.   The Topography of Paradise: Then and Now   3
     Ridges and Ponds   4
     Rivers and Brooks   14
     Farms and Forests   15
     Hanging Rocks Road   16
     Beaches   18

II.   La Farge Before Paradise, 1835-1860   19

III.   La Farge at Paradise, 1861-1864   27
     The Puddingstone Ledge and the Sacred Grove, 1862   33
     With John Bancroft at Paradise, 1863   42
     Maurice Stadtfield and Photography, 1863-1864   49

IV.   A Year of Transition, 1864-1865   56

V.   La Farge in Paradise, 1865-1871   63
     Oils and Watercolors   67
     Cronies and Colleagues   96
     Paradise Valley, 1866-1868   102
     The Last Valley, 1867-1868   114
     Views over Bishop Berkeley's Rock   121
     Paradise "At A Blow," 1868-1871   124

VI.   Paradise as Allegory and Memory   135
     Allegory and Illustration   138
     Easel Paintings and Decorative Work   151
     Studio Memories   167

Postlude   173

Notes   176

Maps   183

Chronology   192

Dictionary of People and Places   195

Appendices I - III   204

Bibliography   208

Index   212

FOREWORD
William Vareika

*What is the peculiar sensation, what is the peculiar quality of pleasure, which
his work has the property of exciting in us, and which we cannot get elsewhere?
For this, especially when he has to speak of a comparatively unknown artist, is
always the chief question which a critic has to answer.* — Walter Pater

In 1971, when a perceptive professor quoted this late nineteenth century critic in his grading comments of a college term paper on John La Farge, this artist was known to a serious degree by only a few scholars and a handful of knowledgeable collectors.

But to a nineteen-year old Boston College pre-law sophomore, the words proved compelling and prophetic, and I pursued this enigmatic and fascinating artist until my career plans and even my place of residency were significantly altered. A new world opened for me—the world of John La Farge, a rich and multi-faceted one.

William Vareika Fine Arts evolved out of my interest in La Farge and other major artists who thrived in the picturesque natural setting, rich intellectual background, and exclusive social climate of Newport, Rhode Island. La Farge has always been my personal favorite, and in the last ten years I have had the honor of owning a great many works by him, including some that I had long admired from the literature on La Farge. The thrill of rediscovering in person such works, often lost for decades, is the best reward that I could ask.

The changing reputation of John La Farge is a barometer of the aesthetic mood of our nation. In his day, he was dubbed "our sole 'Old Master'" and ranked alongside the most distinguished American artists, such as Homer and Whistler. The tide of modernism in the early twentieth century all but eclipsed his name, and for decades he was dismissed as overly eclectic or too European in character for a true American artist. Yet in the last twenty years, La Farge has enjoyed a Renaissance of scholarly appreciation, and today his works are considered in the mainstream of the most marketable works on the American scene.

I am still surprised to find individuals with great artistic sensitivity who understand only the more familiar aspects of La Farge's art, such as his work in stained glass. Fortunately, many others have embraced him as one of our country's most innovative and influential cultural figures who made contributions in an unparalleled array of genres: landscape, still life, and figure painting; mural decoration; stained-glass design and production; book illustration; art instruction; and the writing of art criticism, travelogues, and cultural history. His enduring impact was felt by the notables of his time: Stanford White, Henry James, Henry Hobson Richardson, Julia Ward Howe, Henry Adams, and Augustus Saint-Gaudens—to name just a few.

With great pleasure and pride, my wife Alison and I publish this book and present an exhibition to coincide with its publication. In both projects, we explore one of the lesser known periods of the artist's career, the years during and after the Civil War when La Farge worked primarily in Paradise, a scenic coastal region of Middletown, Rhode Island, just a few miles from downtown Newport. Some of us feel that during this time in Paradise La Farge produced the most beautiful and inspired artworks of his long and diverse career. It also excites us that so many of the works of art in both the book and the exhibition are being shown and published for the first time.

The Director of the La Farge Catalogue Raisonné, Dr. James L. Yarnall, is a well-known contributor to La Farge scholarship, and his devotion to *John La Farge in Paradise: The Painter and His Muse* reflects the thoroughness that is characteristic of his work. Jim began with intensive and original documentation of the history, art, and geology of Paradise before launching into a voyage of discovery into the places where La Farge lived and worked. He spent months in the field—literally—exploring and photographing the hills, ledges, valleys, ponds, streams, groves, meadows, and beaches that inspired our favorite artist in that very special place by the sea. Jim approached the topic with insight, enthusiasm, and professionalism—notwithstanding encounters with skunks, guard dogs, muck and mud, treacherous cliffs, and icy ledges.

I personally am very grateful to Mary A. La Farge for her counsel and assistance on the project, and for making the resources of the La Farge Catalogue Raisonné, including the archival photographs and files of her late husband, Henry A. La Farge, available to this undertaking. I am also grateful to other members of the La Farge family who provided assistance and who have continually supported ongoing research on the artist.

I join Jim Yarnall in thanking the following individuals who aided us in the preparation of the book and exhibition: Mary Bland, Gladys Bolhouse, Dr. and Mrs. Howard Browne, Mr. and Mrs. William Buell, Mike Corcoran, Posy and Charlie Dana, Anne and Jeff Dunn, Martha Fleischman of Kennedy Galleries Inc., Lawrence Frank, Mrs. Robert H.I. Goddard, Mr. and Mrs. David A. Gray, Dick Grosvenor, Mr. and Mrs. Jim Hodges, Anthony F. Janson, Charles W. Kellett, Mr. and Mrs. Donald King, Ann Kirby, Mr. and Mrs. Jim Kirby, Margaret D. Lockwood, Mr. and Mrs. John P.C. Mathews, Sean M. McNally, Natalie N. Nicholson, Senator Claiborne Pell, Ralph Sabetta, Richard N. Sayer, Ned Sherman, Margo Hawes Stapleton, Greg and Luise Strauss, Tim Sturtevant, Capt. and Mrs. Leroy Taylor, Mr. and Mrs. John A. van Beuren, Mr. and Mrs. George Warren, John Wilmerding, Douglas and Kathy Wilson, and John Winslow. In addition, we appreciate the help of Julian Francis ("Dede") Peckham Jr., Julian (Jay) Peckham III, and Mr. and Mrs. George H. Tolderlund for access to and information on the Peckham Brothers Quarry.

We owe a great debt to the staff and board members of the art, history, and research facilities on Aquidneck Island, especially the following individuals: Stanley Grossman and Natalie N. Nicholson, Middletown Historical Society; Arnold Cogswell Jr. and Mark J.J. Simmons, The Newport Art Museum; Daniel Snydacker, Bertram Lippincott III, and M. Joan Youngken, The Newport Historical Society; Paul Miller and Armin Allen, The Preservation Society of Newport County; C. Matthews Dick, The Redwood Library and Athenaeum. We also thank the staffs of the Newport Public Library, Middletown Public Library, Newport City Hall, and Middletown Town Hall. In addition, we appreciate the gracious help of Annemarie Houston, St. Mary's Church, in finding baptismal records of La Farge's children.

In Providence, we thank: Allison Cywin, the Rhode Island Historical Society, Graphic Arts Department; J. Stephen Grimes, Rhode Island Supreme Court Judicial Records Center; and Robin McLaren, Rhode Island State Archives. In Boston, thanks go to: Erica Hirschler, Carol Troyen, and Theodore E. Stebbins Jr., Museum of Fine Arts; Timothy Brigard, Fogg Art Museum; and Robert C. Vose Jr. and Vose Galleries.

Special thanks are extended to the many individuals and institutions that loaned works and provided photographs for use in the book, and to their staff and board members who assisted us: Addison Gallery of American Art, Phillips Academy; Janet Parks, Avery Architectural and Fine Arts Library, Columbia University; Katharine J. Watson, Bowdoin College Museum of Art; Mr. and Mrs. Willard G. Clark; Linda Simmons, The Corcoran Gallery of Art; Charles A. Dana III; Susan M. Taylor and Lisa McDermott, Davis Museum and Cultural Center, Wellesley College; Rob Lancefield, Davison Art Center, Wesleyan University; Elizabeth Gambosi, Fogg Art Museum, Harvard University Art Museums; Vance Jordan and Tom Parker, Jordan-Volpe Gallery Inc.; H. Barbara Weinberg, Peter Kenny, John K. Howat, and Deanna Cross, The Metropolitan Museum of Art; Natalie N. Nicholson and Stanley Grossman, Middletown Historical Society; Mary L. Sluskonis, Museum of Fine Arts, Boston; Kathy Fieramosca, The National Academy of Design; National Museum of

American Art, Smithsonian Institution; Mel Ellis, The New Britain Museum of American Art; Arnold Cogswell Jr. and Mark J.J. Simmons, Newport Art Museum; M. Joan Youngken, The Newport Historical Society; Paul Miller and Anne Moore, The Preservation Society of Newport County; Alan Rosenbaum, Barbara Ross, and Karen E. Richter, The Art Museum, Princeton University; Angela Brown Fischer and Judith Richardson Silvia, The Redwood Library and Athenaeum; John Dryfhout and Gregory C. Schwarz, the Saint-Gaudens National Historic Site; David W. Steadman and Patricia J. Whitesides, The Toledo Museum of Art; Susan E. Strickler and Joan Elizabeth Reid, Worcester Art Museum; Jules Prown, Richard Field, and Susan Warner, Yale University Art Gallery. We also appreciate the contributions of anonymous private collectors who loaned works of art and supplied photographs.

In the production of the book, I thank Fern Malouin, Deborah Roy-Albanese, and the staff at Meridian Printing and Elite Color Group; Jack and Donna Maytum, Bob Raymond, Marlene Horan, Rodney Davis, and Nancy Thomas of Micrographix.

At my gallery, I thank Marianne Vareika, Carol Nunes, Peter Dutra, and the rest of the staff.

Finally, to my wife Alison and our children Timothy, Christian, and Hope, for their support, understanding, and shared love of John La Farge.

William Vareika
Newport, Rhode Island
March 1995

I join Bill in thanking the private individuals and public institutions that abetted this complex undertaking. I also thank Bill and Alison Vareika and the staff of William Vareika Fine Arts for the support of this project, manifested in more ways than can be counted, on more occasions than I can remember. Bill was instrumental in providing the contacts needed to explore sites at Paradise, and himself went on many expeditions of discovery. We all owe the greatest debt to the late Henry A. La Farge, whose lifelong work on a catalogue raisonné of his grandfather's works provides the groundwork for any such undertaking. His widow, Mary A. La Farge, is the continuing link to his work through the headquarters she maintains to house the photographs and correspondence that compose his massive archives, and that is now known as the La Farge Catalogue Raisonné Inc. Mary A. La Farge and Oliver La Farge Hamill have also provided an administrative structure that makes continuing her late husband's work possible and fruitful.

I owe a personal debt to Natalie N. Nicholson, a great-granddaughter of Stephen P. Barker, who consulted on the Barker family and Paradise Avenue, providing many bibliographic citations used throughout this study. In addition, I owe special thanks to: Francine Corcione, the project's research associate; the John Nicholas Brown Center for the Study of American Civilization for a fellowship, office space, and library access at Brown University; the Center's Director, Joyce Botelho; Mr. and Mrs. Willard G. Clark; Stephen M. Lovette for monetary conversions; Marjory B. Hinman and Eve Daniels, Broome County Historical Society; Colleen Hennessey, Archivist of the Freer Gallery of Art and Arthur M. Sackler Gallery, Smithsonian Institution, Washington, D.C.; Ralph Sabetta, a Newport horticulturist; Paul A. Miller of The Preservation Society of Newport County; the staff of The Newport Historical Society; Donna and Jack Maytum for use of a darkroom; and Susanne Owens Koenig who patiently edited the manuscript under tremendous time constraints.

James L. Yarnall
Middletown, Rhode Island
March 1995

PRELUDE

John La Farge and his brother Louis,
c. 1843
Daguerreotype
4 x 6 in. (10.2 x 15.2 cm.)
Private Collection

Shortly before his twenty-fourth birthday on March 31, 1859, John La Farge (1835-1910) made the momentous decision to become an artist. The choice led him to Newport, Rhode Island, where Paradise—that discrete section of nearby Middletown on the southeastern tip of Aquidneck Island (map 1A-1B)—became a special source of his artistic inspiration.[1]

Paradise had long played the muse for creative souls marooned there by choice or circumstance. Expansive farmlands, rolling hills, jutting cliffs, a dramatic coastline with barren stretches of dune grass and sparkling acres of beach sand—these ingredients were as conducive to the meditations of poets as to the picturesque formulations of artists. The ethos of Paradise very appropriately takes its tone from **Reverend George Berkeley** (1684/5-1753), an Irish prelate who came to Rhode Island in 1729 while raising funds for a proposed college in Bermuda. Though his plans came to naught, Berkeley produced a significant philosophical treatise during the two years that he lived in a colonial farmhouse that he built in Middletown. Legend has it that the Bishop wrote while seated in the cleft of the most prominent topographical oddity of Paradise, Hanging Rocks (fig. 1). This dramatic rock formation takes several of its many names from this apocryphal episode: **Bishop Berkeley's Rock**, Berkeley's Chair, and the Bishop's Seat.

Since the time of Berkeley, Paradise has remained a place apart even as its topography has changed dramatically. La Farge's pictures of Paradise preserve forever the former aspect of the pastoral countryside. His story moreover is a remarkable one, tinged with romance as it chronicles the making of a great artist.

A Dictionary of People and Places *found on pp. 195-203 provides biographical notes and other explanations for those terms appearing in bold type.*

1.
Unidentified Photographer
Bishop Berkeley's Rock, c. 1900
Postcard
3 3/8 x 5 3/8 in.
(8.3 x 13.2 cm.)
William Vareika Fine Arts, Newport

CHAPTER I

THE TOPOGRAPHY OF PARADISE: THEN AND NOW

Despite changes to Paradise over time, we can still find many of the specific sites depicted by La Farge. A rapid survey of the prominent landmarks and topographical features of the area forms an essential prelude to this study, especially for those who have never been to Paradise.

Paradise comprises about one square mile of Middletown bordered by **Second Beach**, **Paradise Avenue**, **Green End Avenue**, and **Third Beach Road**. Middletown originally was part of Newport, and the island on which the towns are located was once called Rhode Island. In 1743, the Colony of Rhode Island and Providence Plantations set aside Middletown as a separate entity.[2] Now Newport, Middletown, and their neighbor to the north, Portsmouth, constitute Aquidneck Island, one of several islands in the State of Rhode Island's Narragansett Bay.

The name Paradise reflects the idealism of the eighteenth century, to which we also owe names like "Providence Plantations"—still part of the official name of Rhode Island—and "The Eden of America," a nickname for the state.[3] Like these other theological appellations, Paradise evokes Biblical beneficence without declaring a specific religious affiliation, much in the spirit of Roger Williams.

Paradise also has its own quaint mythology, explained by reference to **Purgatory Chasm**, a gaping cleft in the **Purgatory Rocks** to the west of Second Beach (fig. 2). Fourteen feet wide and fifty feet deep, this fracture is the most

2.
The Heliograph Co., New York
Purgatory Chasm, c. 1900
Postcard
3 3/8 x 5 3/8 in.
(8.3 x 13.2 cm.)
William Vareika Fine Arts, Newport

G 925 "Purgatory", Newport, R. I.

awesome of many similar fissures at Paradise.[4] Once said to open into bottomless ocean depths, it inspired belief in a "Devil's Chasm" where Lucifer tempted unsuspecting maidens from the rocks to their doom. Another nickname, "Lover's Leap," derives from an oft-told legend that also postulates the origin of the names Purgatory and Paradise. In olden times, the daughter of the owner of the bluffs challenged her beau to prove his love by vaulting over the chasm. Once accomplished, he realized the folly of risking his life to satisfy her adolescent vanity. Exclaiming that to cross the abyss was to journey from Purgatory to Paradise, he abandoned the maiden, much to her lasting regret.[5]

Purgatory Chasm remains much as it was in those more mythic times, though topped today by a tree growing on its brink that all but blocks the view once so famous (fig. 3). Like many of the places that La Farge knew and loved at Paradise, it is both immutable and mutable. As we tour Paradise in words and images, our study will include a look at what has changed and what has not—and the many shades of gray in between.

3.
Purgatory Chasm, Looking East
Photograph by the author
(Nov. 1994)

RIDGES AND PONDS

Paradise is crossed from north to south by a series of seven puddingstone ridges that were thoroughly studied over a century ago by a local scientist who became a professor of geology at Williams College, **T. Nelson Dale** (1845-1937) (map 3).[6] The ridges run like fingers towards the sea, often submerged beneath land but at times rising into miniature mountains called the **Paradise Hills** or Paradise Rocks. Dale analyzed puddingstone as quartz, mica schist, slate and other stone

4.
St. George's School, Looking West from
the Dike of Gardiner's Pond
Photograph by the author
(Jan. 1995)

that had been fused into a concrete-like mix during the metamorphic pre-history of the planet. He concurred with earlier scientists that the characteristic texture of puddingstone resulted from two great natural forces: ocean pressure that had smoothed the conglomerated rock; and glacial erosion that had created deep faults in the rock masses.[7] He classified the ridges with Roman numerals, a system that still proves useful in providing an orientation to the various geographical features of the area.

Ridge I is the rise now occupied by St. George's School (fig. 4), a complex begun in 1901 that came to be dominated by a chapel designed by Ralph Adams Cram (1863-1942), completed in 1928. The south end of this ridge forms **Easton's Point** and encompasses Purgatory Rocks and Purgatory Chasm. The north end includes Honyman's Hill, crossed by Green End Avenue. Paradise Avenue, the main route running from north to south through Paradise, lies at the base of this ridge. The road was lined with plane trees (fig. 5) and called Swamp Road until about 1865 when it became Paradise Road. After paving in the early twentieth century, it became Paradise Avenue.

5.
Unidentified Engraver
Paradise Near Newport, R.I.
(Paradise Avenue), c. 1840
Wood engraving on paper
1 1/2 x 2 1/4 in.
(3.4 x 5.5 cm.)
Private Collection

6.
Peter's Rock from Paradise Farm,
Looking East
Photograph by the author
(Nov. 1994)
*Note the blunted end of the rock,
quarried beginning in 1893.*

Much of La Farge's life at Paradise centered around this road and Ridge II, which runs parallel and to the east of Paradise Avenue. Near the north end of this ridge is the lofty **Peter's Rock** (fig. 6), named for Peter Barker (1787-1875), who once owned the ridge and farm in front of the rock. In former times, this was also called Great Rock due to its visibility from **First Beach** in Newport (fig. 7). This high spine once was considered "the best point of view on the island," and the vista from its summit over the **Sakonnet River, Flint Point,** and **Sachuest Point** earned the nickname "**Paradise Lost**" (fig. 8).[8] Quarrying of Peter's Rock goes back to colonial times, but grew into a serious business after 1893 when the local **Peckham Brothers** set up a stone crusher just north of Peter's Rock (fig. 9).[9] A large section of the ridge has now been consumed, with much of the stone crushed into bedrock for Rhode Island's highway system. The blunted end of Peter's Rock barely preserves the former high point in the long ridge, but from a distance Peter's Rock still has its distinctive broad profile. Quarrying of Peter's Rock has temporarily ceased, resuming at a new stone crusher set up just to the north near **Sachuest Way.**

7.
Unidentified Photographer
First Beach, Newport, c. 1900?
Postcard
3 3/8 x 5 3/8 in.
(8.3 x 13.2 cm.)
Middletown Historical Society,
Middletown

8.
"Paradise Lost"
View from Peter's Rock Looking Southeast
Photograph by the author
(Dec. 1994)

9.
Peckham Brothers Quarry and The Stone
Crusher; from Peter's Rock, Looking North
Photograph by the author
(Nov. 1994)

Ridge II contains an unusual gap behind Peter's Rock no longer readily apparent due to overgrowth. This gap is a sort of gradated natural roadway that once provided ready communication to the valley on the other side, as well as to the summit of Peter's Rock, which descends gradually into the gap. The gap was an especially vital point in the ridge during the American Revolution, when the land was owned by Isaac Barker (1752-1834), who served as a spy for the American cause during British occupation of his farm. As seen in an old photograph showing Isaac's great-great granddaughter, Amy Barker (1890-1984) (fig. 10), a crotched bar-way once spanned the gap to control the passage of farm animals. The fence continued up to the summit of Peter's Rock where Isaac Barker would arrange the crotches as a signal to the Americans, headquartered across the Sakonnet River at Little Compton, to pick up communiques left in a secret hiding place by the coast.[10]

On the other side of the ridge of Peter's Rock, a gentle valley slowly descends to the Atlantic Ocean. Known for much of this century as the estate of **Gray Craig**, this valley is the scene depicted by La Farge in one of his most famous paintings, *Paradise Valley* (see fig. 154). La Farge's close friend, the celebrated writer Henry James (1843-1916), described this place as "back of the second beach, looking down on the ocean at the south."

> *The place itself will be familiar only to those rare pedestrians who, not contented with enjoying the scenery from the seat of a barouche, have strolled at will among the lovely meadows, where in the most primeval solitude it is possible to get far-reaching views of the sea, or to find fascinating little nooks among hills and valleys whose very existence is hardly known to the ordinary summer visitor. One great charm of Newport scenery is its modesty: it has no massive cliffs that extort wonder and admiration, its hills are hardly more than gentle undulations; it has no rich abundance of trees growing at the water's edge, there is nothing but a stretch of yellow meadow grass rolling gently to the water, with here and there a softly rising hill. It is like a grand landscape in miniature.*[11]

10.
Unidentified Photographer
The Gap behind Peter's Rock
with Amy Barker at the Bar-Way,
c. 1910
Photograph
3 5/8 x 4 5/8 in.
(8.9 x 11.4 cm.)
Private Collection

8

The dramatic effect of the Gray Craig estate upon the topography of this part of Paradise merits a digression to explain its history. In 1891, the local Barker family sold the farming valley to the east of Peter's Rock to millionaire banker O.H.P. Belmont (1858-1908) for use as a get-away from Belcourt Castle, his mansion on Bellevue Avenue in Newport. Belmont mapped the land in 1892, calling the estate "Gray Crag" (map 5). In 1902, Belmont sold the land to Mr. and Mrs. J. Mitchell Clark, who erected a crenelated mansion called "Gray Crag" just above **Nelson's Pond** at the south end of the valley (fig. 11). Mr. and Mrs. Jordan Mott purchased the mansion in 1914 and renovated it for five years. On the eve of reopening in June 1919, the house burnt to the ground. The property was then purchased by Mary and Michael M. van Beuren who built the present "Gray Craig" on the site in 1926 (fig. 12). The gardens and outbuildings for the new house running northward through the valley soon altered the topography and vistas of the farmlands that La Farge had known as "Paradise Valley."

As Ridge II continues past Gray Craig, it forms a picturesque cliff along the west side of Nelson's Pond (fig. 13). The cliff was just a few minutes walk from the houses where La Farge stayed on Paradise Avenue and became one of his favorite painting spots. From a puddingstone ledge on top of the cliff, the view of Nelson's Pond, Second

13.
Cliff and Puddingstone Ledge of Nelson's Pond, Looking West from the Peninsula
Photograph by the author
(Nov. 1994)

Beach, Purgatory Rocks, and the eastern ridges of the Paradise Hills is diverse and dramatic. Hugging the base of the cliff, a native oak-hickory forest became La Farge's "Sacred Grove," a special place to paint woodland scenes that later became backgrounds for his mythological and religious paintings.

Ridge III is the least clearly defined of the ridges. It runs along the valley north of the Gray Craig mansion as a series of hillocks and puddingstone eruptions. More eruptions surface on the Gray Craig front lawn. These lead to a rock peninsula jutting into Nelson's Pond (fig. 14), an island at the southeast side of Nelson's Pond, and a large puddingstone formation now buried beneath the southernmost tip of its dike. These also became some of La Farge's favorite places to set up his easel to paint.

Ridge III merges with three prominent spines that are now enclosed by the **Norman Bird Sanctuary**. The first spine, Ridge IV, borders a stream bed that runs along the Gray Craig estate into Nelson's Pond, forming a precipitous canyon-like wall (fig. 15). Ridges V and VI form **The Last Valley** (fig. 16), so-called because it is the last major valley encountered before the tidal plain bordering the Sakonnet River. The Last Valley was a favorite tourist site in the nineteenth century and went by many names, including the "Lost Valley" and "Happy Valley" (fig. 17). It became the subject of numerous pictures by La Farge, including one of his largest and most famous paintings (see fig. 167). The valley floor, then a verdant meadowland used for picnics, is now an impassable cattail marsh. Ridge V, the west wall of the valley, descends to an inconspicuous pond hugging its side that goes by the name **Paradise Pond**.[12] Ridge VI, the east wall, is the most dramatic and picturesque ridge in Paradise. Rising at its loftiest point to seventy feet above sea level, it features a faceted inner wall of eroded puddingstone (fig. 18) and terminates in Bishop Berkeley's Rock.

17.
Unidentified Engraver
Happy Valley
(The Last Valley), before 1884
Wood engraving on paper
(Engraver: "Reid")
1 7/8 x 2 3/8 in. (4.6 x 5.8 cm.)
From Frank G. Harris,
History of the Re-Union of the Sons and Daughters of Newport, R.I., July 4th, 1884
(Newport: Davis & Pitman, 1885), p. 171

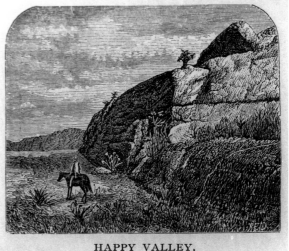

HAPPY VALLEY.

14.
The Peninsula at Gray Craig from the
Lawn, Looking Southeast
Photograph by the author
(Jan. 1995)

15.
"Canyon," by the Gray Craig Estate,
Looking North
Photograph by the author
(Jan. 1995)

16.
The Last Valley,
Looking South from the East Wall
Photograph by the author
(Dec. 1994)

18.
Inner Wall of The Last Valley,
Looking Northeast
Photograph by the author
(Dec. 1994)

19.
Gabrielle De Veaux Clements (1858-1934)
Bishop Berkeley's Seat, c. 1890
Etching on light brown paper
Image: 2 3/4 x 4 1/4 in.
(6.2 x 10.2 cm.)
Private Collection

These three prominent ridges are flanked by two ponds, both greatly expanded in the 1880s and after as components of the **Newport Water Works** system.

To the east is Nelson's Pond, discussed above in relation to the lawn of the Gray Craig estate. The northern contours of the pond are only slightly changed from La Farge's day, at least when the water table is low during the dry season and the peninsula jutting from the north creates the distinctive Large and Small Basins. The southern and western sides were dredged and diked beginning in 1882, making the pond wider and deeper than it was originally (map 2). A beach along the west side, lining the cliffs and rocky shoreline, has all but disappeared except in the driest weather, making the pond about fifty feet wider in many places. The dike not only assures that these areas will flood in wet weather, but also alters the former relationship of the pond to the beachfront by creating a sharp visual barrier. This expansion has also eliminated swampy marshes that once constituted much of the east side of the pond. The teeming water lily patches that provided La Farge with one of his favorite and most characteristic subjects to paint have been replaced by channels of dark water.

East of the Last Valley, where the ridges give way to the Sakonnet River plain, is **Gardiner's Pond**. This originally was an irregularly shaped pond with numerous rivulets leading to and from it (fig. 19). Beginning in 1889, the pond was regularized on all sides and nearly doubled in size through dredging and diking until it became a squarish body of water surrounded by high dikes (fig. 20). Much of what was once called the "east side" of Paradise has been submerged beneath the expanded pond (map 2). Comparing a watercolor executed in 1893 by a local artist from a Middletown family, Louisa C. Sturtevant (1870-1958) (fig. 21), with the same view today (fig. 22) gives some idea of the dramatic changes wrought over the course of the past century. The series of puddingstone boulders and ledges visible in the northwest wall of the pond in the modern photograph are remnants of Ridge VII that once lay far to the northwest side of the pond.

20.
Gardiner's Pond from the North Bank,
Looking Southwest
Photograph by the author
(Oct. 1994)

21.
Louisa C. Sturtevant (1869-1958)
Gardiner's Pond and Paradise Farm, 1893
Watercolor over graphite on paper
Image: 8 x 13 1/2 in.
(20.3 x 34.3 cm.)
The Preservation Society
of Newport County, Newport,
Collection at Kingscote

22.
Gardiner's Pond and Paradise Farm,
Looking North from the Dike
Photograph by the author
(Dec. 1994)

23.
Louisa C. Sturtevant (1869-1958)
The Bridge on Third Beach Road, 1893
Watercolor over graphite
on watercolor paper
Image: 7 3/4 x 13 in.
(19.7 x 33 cm.)
The Preservation Society of Newport
County, Newport, Collection
at Kingscote

RIVERS AND BROOKS

In addition to the ponds, Paradise is crossed by several small rivers or brooks
that, like the ponds, have been changed over the course of time to accommodate the
Newport Water Works. The main river is now called the **Maidford River**, but went by
the name **Paradise Brook** in La Farge's day. Descending from the northern part of
Middletown, the Maidford River follows the west side of Paradise Avenue until turn-
ing to cross under the road about a tenth of a mile before Second Beach. The river
once fed into Nelson's Pond but now runs just outside its southern dike through a
cattail marsh. Then it continues to the Last Valley where it feeds and exits Paradise
Pond before skirting the front of Bishop Berkeley's Rock and crossing under **Hanging Rocks Road**. Now diverted around the south side of Gardiner's Pond, which it
once fed, the river finally exits into the Sakonnet River under a small bridge-like
overpass on Third Beach Road.

In the nineteenth century, this bridge was a picturesque spot frequented by
residents and tourists alike. Mary Clark Sturtevant (1843-1931), mother of the artist Louisa, described the scene as a succession of "desolate sand dunes where sports-
men wandered with their guns and, across which, parties of fashionable people
sometimes found their way to fish for crabs from a bridge back of Third Beach,
under which ran a brook, the waters mingling with the incoming tide."[13] Louisa
painted the bridge in 1893, showing boat houses and other small buildings in the
area beyond the bridge—all framed against a distant vista stretching back to Paradise Avenue (fig. 23). The bridge is now a simple road overpass that overlooks impassable cattail marshes intersected by the dike surrounding Gardiner's Pond (fig.
24). This otherwise dreary vista is punctuated felicitously by the distant spires of
St. George's School.

Another small river, now called Paradise Brook, descends through the woods north of the Norman Bird Sanctuary. This once emptied into Gardiner's Pond but was rerouted into Nelson's Pond sometime after the 1880s. It meanders into the valley alongside the towering cliffs of Ridge IV, bordering the Gray Craig mansion.

FARMS AND FORESTS

The ridges and valleys of Paradise were heavily wooded in pre-colonial days when the Narragansett and Wampanoag Indians came to hunt and fish in Middletown—originally called "Ye Middle Woods" or "Ye Woods" in homage to its dense forests. Before the American Revolution, the British colonists cleared the land for farming, using the timber for housing and firewood.[14] For much of the nineteenth century, rolling farmlands surrounded the ridges on all sides. Green fields, rock walls, farmhouses, and occasional ledges of puddingstone dominated the scene. Grazing sheep, horses, and goats kept the land clear until this century. By World War II, the farms were for the most part converted to single residences, and since have been sub-divided to hold several homes per farm. The east side of Paradise Avenue north of the stone crusher became a golf course for several decades so that expanse has remained somewhat open and clear. By contrast, the pastures east of Peter's Rock where the Gray Craig estate evolved are now a tangle of low brush, trees, and brambles. Patches of dense forest are scattered throughout Paradise, and the hills have resumed a wild appearance, with brambles covering both Flint and Sachuest Points.

Construction of Hanging Rocks Road signaled changes to the topography of Paradise nearly as dramatic as those brought about by the Newport Water Works. Prior to 1883, the route from First Beach to Sachuest Point was convoluted. Visitors coming over Purgatory Avenue had no choice but to proceed down Paradise Avenue, Green End Avenue, and Third Beach Road. This left untrammeled the picturesque expanse of meadows, rivers, ponds, sand dunes, and rocks that once filled the apron of land between Second Beach and the Paradise Hills, shown most clearly in an 1866 view of Bishop Berkeley's Rock by the Boston artist George Quincy Thorndike (1827-1886) (fig. 25).

The idea of a shortcut across the beachfront dawned on Mary Clark Sturtevant's husband, Eugene Sturtevant (1838-1899), in 1872.[15] Having just invested in properties along the present **Indian Avenue**, he realized that his venture was doomed without a direct road connection to Purgatory Avenue, and thus to downtown Newport. Despite approval by the Middletown Town Council in 1876,[16] Sturtevant's road was blocked by **General John Alfred Hazard** (1806-1880), who owned substantial real estate in both Newport and Middletown, and was reputed to be a "lover of litigation for its agreeable excitement."[17] Hazard owned the beachfront properties leading up to Bishop Berkeley's Rock, and two ledges on his land formed a particular impediment to Sturtevant's plan. The latter had one dynamited surreptitiously in order to beat out a court action by Hazard, but it took Hazard's death in 1880 and several years of further litigation to make the road a reality.[18]

25.
George Quincy Thorndike
(1827-1886)
Hanging Rock, 1866
Oil on canvas
33 1/4 x 59 1/4 in.
(84.5 x 150.5 cm.)
The Newport Historical Society,
Newport, Gift of
Mrs. Isabel Thorndike Glenthorn,
1967 (67.1)

The opening of the road in 1883 coincided with the founding of the short-lived Newport Natural History Society, the brainchild of noted writer Raphael Pumpelly (1837-1923) and marine biologist Alexander Agassiz (1835-1910).[19] The next year, T. Nelson Dale—then librarian for the society—included a photograph of the recently-completed road in his study of the geology of Paradise (fig. 26). The road winds over the small river in front of Bishop Berkeley's Rock atop a bed of broken stone. To the right, a corner of Gardiner's Pond appears in its former inconspicuous position, a view blocked today by the dike that runs alongside the road (fig. 27).

26.
Joshua Appleby Williams (1817-1892)
The Hanging Rock, near Newport, R.I., 1884
"Artotype," photograph on paper
Image: 3 3/8 x 5 7/16 in.
(8.3 x 13.6 cm.)
From *Proceedings of The Newport Natural History Society, 1884-5*, no. 3 (May 1885), opp. p. 5

27.
Hanging Rocks Road, Looking Northeast
Photograph by the author
(Jan. 1995)

Another period photograph (fig. 28) shows the road as it winds north through the pastures of the farm also seen in Louisa C. Sturtevant's view from Gardiner's Pond. In the distance, visible above the ridge leading to Bishop Berkeley's Rock, is the crenelated "Gray Crag" mansion that burnt down in 1919. This curve in Hanging Rocks Road now hugs the northern dike of Gardiner's Pond, and the view to the present Gray Craig from this side of the ridge is blocked by trees.

28.
Unidentified Photographer
Hanging Rocks Road, c. 1910
Postcard
3 3/8 x 5 3/8 in. (8.3 x 13.2 cm.)
Middletown Historical Society,
Middletown

BEACHES

Beaches are among the few places at Paradise that remain much as they were in La Farge's day. Only an occasional parking lot mars the dramatic sweep of sand, dunes, and rocky sea walls of **Second Beach** (also called Sachuest Beach), running unencumbered from the Purgatory Rocks to Sachuest Point (fig. 29). The beach opens onto **Sachuest Bay** and the Atlantic Ocean. Second Beach remains a splendid bathing spot, appreciated by beach connoisseurs for its relative seclusion and strong surf.

Also largely unchanged is **Third Beach** (once called Smith Beach), curling down the Sakonnet River to reach Flint Point, the north side of Sachuest Point (fig. 30). Much of this expanse is now a nature preserve covered with thick brambles and other underbrush. Proximity to the ocean and expanding sea marshes have prevented the growth of most high trees, leaving the views open.

29.
Second Beach from Purgatory Rocks,
Looking East
Photograph by the author
(Jan. 1995)

30.
Third Beach and Flint Point from Third Beach Road, Looking South
Photograph by the author
(Jan. 1995)

CHAPTER II

LA FARGE BEFORE PARADISE   1835-1860

Martin Brimmer (1829-1896), the first director of the Museum of Fine Arts in Boston, once labeled La Farge a "half-trained man of genius."[20] His point is well taken. La Farge grew up in New York City wealthy, cultured, and erudite, with values derived from old European culture, French parentage, and the Roman Catholic religion. His father, John Frederick La Farge (1779-1858), considering art an unsuitable profession, sent his son directly from college graduation in 1853 to apprenticeship with a New York law firm. Studying art was simply not allowed to become a priority.

This is not to say that La Farge lacked basic art training. As early as age six, he studied drawing with his maternal grandfather, a miniaturist.[21] After college—which included work in English watercolor techniques—La Farge also studied painting as a sideline with François Régis Gignoux (1816-1882), an artist who had emigrated to New York from France.[22] John Frederick also gave his son a trip to Europe in 1856 as a twenty-first birthday present. Though La Farge studied briefly in the Parisian atelier of Thomas Couture (1815-1879), he benefitted the most from viewing art of both the past and present in European museums and salons. From old masters, the British Pre-Raphaelites, and French artists such as Eugène Delacroix (1798-1863), Jean-Auguste-Dominique Ingres (1780-1867), or Gustave Courbet (1819-1877), he evolved the aesthetic convictions that would govern his life.

These artistic proclivities would have served little purpose had not John Frederick taken ill in the fall of 1857 and died six months later. La Farge, called back from Europe, suddenly found himself independently wealthy—and the master of his own destiny. He quickly tossed aside law in favor of an artistic career, even though he was painfully aware of the deficiencies of his art training. La Farge rented a room in the new Tenth Street Studio Building, just around the corner from his home, in hope of finding artistic direction. As he was making plans to return to Paris for "training in the practice of painting," a chance meeting with the architect Richard Morris Hunt (1828-1895) led La Farge in an unexpected direction. Hunt's brother, William Morris Hunt (1824-1879), was a former pupil of Couture and had just set up a studio to teach painting in Newport. La Farge realized that he did not have to go to Paris after all.

> *I could continue the practical teachings that I had almost begun at Couture's studio, Hunt being, of course, a favorite and brilliant pupil of Couture's. I met thereupon Bill Hunt, saw some piece of his work, and was pleased both with the man and with what he did and said, and with all of that very charming character, so that in the spring of 1859 I came to Newport to try the experiment, and began in a little more serious way than before.[23]*

31.
Unidentified Photographer
John La Farge, c. 1860
Photograph from a lost daguerreotype
7 1/4 x 4 in. (17.9 x 10 cm.)
From Royal Cortissoz, *John La Farge, a Memoir and a Study* (Boston and New York: Houghton Mifflin Company, 1911), frontispiece
This photograph dates from La Farge's first years as a professional artist. La Farge inscribed this photograph to Royal Cortissoz, his biographer, in his characteristic illegible script: "Forgive my bad handwriting. I've been painting hard today. Yrs sincerely, Jno La Farge." The inscription dates from late in La Farge's life, probably 1905 when the artist worked with Cortissoz in preparing his biography.

When he first arrived at Newport during the spring of 1859 (fig. 31), La Farge left few traces, and just where he resided for the next two years is a mystery.[24] His art training took place on the grounds of Hill Top Cottage, where William Morris Hunt had lived since 1856. Hunt's estate overlooking downtown Newport included a large main house on the triangle of land formed by Bellevue Avenue, Touro Street, and Church Street, the site of the present Viking Hotel. In September 1858, he fashioned a studio to use for teaching by adding a second story and skylights to a carriage house fronting on Church Street.[25] His first pupil was a classmate from Harvard, Edward Wheelwright, who hoped to pursue a painting career but went on to become an art editor for the *Atlantic Monthly*. La Farge was only the second pupil to enroll.[26]

Hunt taught Couture's methods for painting the figure in modulated gradations or "values" from posed models. La Farge enthusiastically mastered these oil techniques, producing accomplished figure studies in the contemporary French style. But within several months, though he liked Hunt personally and felt indebted to him, La Farge became frustrated. His reasons were expressed in vague statements such as "My ideas about painting were more general than Hunt's, and in the direction of a scientific study." [27] He spoke of the lack of "air and light and space" in his mentor's paintings, and complained that Hunt had abandoned Couture's methods for those of the Barbizon master, Jean-François Millet (1814-1875).[28] La Farge even claimed that Hunt "despised Couture" and "declined to teach me Couture's *way* of painting," while paradoxically, Hunt taught La Farge just that because "these things stick." [29]

When La Farge decided to find another art instructor, this meant leaving Newport, where Hunt was the only teacher of real stature. Thoughts of returning to Paris that had crossed his mind before coming to Newport now encountered one significant roadblock. At Hunt's studio, he had befriended two summer residents, the future writer Henry James and his older brother William (1842-1910). They introduced him to **Thomas Sergeant Perry** (1845-1928), who later became an important literary critic and Harvard professor. Through Tom, La Farge met his older sister, **Margaret Mason Perry** (1839-1925) (fig. 32).

By the end of the summer of 1859, La Farge and Margaret were taking long romantic strolls through the picturesque Newport countryside. At Spouting Horn, a natural ocean geyser that once was a principal tourist attraction near the present Bailey's Beach on Ocean Drive in Newport, they reportedly declared their love for one another.[30]

Margaret's mother Frances Sergeant Perry (1817-1903) belonged to a distinguished Philadelphia family descended from Benjamin Franklin. Her father, Christopher Grant Perry (1812-1854), was a son of Commodore Oliver Hazard Perry (1785-1819), the hero of the Battle of Lake Erie in the War of 1812. Margaret was born in the Perry Mansion on Touro Street facing Washington Square, a residence purchased by the Commodore not long before his premature death in 1819. She grew up in several different domiciles, including a house now at 28 Catherine Street built by her father around 1850 and where she continued to live with her mother and siblings after his death in 1854. When Hunt opened his studio in 1858, it was just past the end of her street, about two blocks away.

Margaret's involvement with La Farge, a Roman Catholic, created a decided stir in the Episcopalian Perry family. The Commodore's widow, Elizabeth Champlin Mason Perry (1791-1858), had maintained a fanatical "hatred of everything Catholic" while Margaret was growing up, instilling the belief that the Roman Church was the Apocalyptic scarlet woman.[31] After Grandma Perry's death in 1858, Margaret's mother continued the tradition by attempting to thwart the relationship that she saw developing. When Margaret received an invitation from a neighbor to pass the winter of 1859-1860 on a plantation in Louisiana, she knew what lay behind it: "I think my Mother took me away to try to break off the matter, for she was not favourable to my marriage with Mr. La Farge—mainly on the ground of his being a Catholic." [32]

The separation had the opposite effect, however, as rumors reached La Farge that Margaret had attentive suitors pursuing her in Louisiana. In lengthy epistles, he sought to persuade her that their religions could be reconciled, making marriage possible.[33] Finally, after more than four months apart, he finessed his own invitation to the plantation in April 1860. Their courtship intensified and engagement quickly followed; marriage would have taken place immediately had not La Farge come down with malaria. Finally, on October 15, 1860, they exchanged vows before a Roman Catholic priest in Newport.[34] Three weeks later, Margaret converted to Catholicism in New York City.[35]

Throughout this courtship, La Farge remained at Hunt's atelier, taking advantage of the useful studio space, even though his interest in Hunt as a mentor had largely waned. The only practical way to pursue realistic painting was self-instruction: "Hence, I had to develop a method of my own." [36] In this quest, La Farge realized he could apply the principles of Michel-Eugène Chevreul (1786-1889) and other color theorists to the practice of *plein-air* painting.

> *There [in the open air] I wished to apply principles of light and color of which I had learned a little. I wished my studies from nature to indicate something of this, to be free from recipes, as far as possible, and to indicate very carefully, in every part, the exact time of day and circumstances of light. This of course is the most ambitious of all possible ideas, and though attempted to some extent through several centuries from time to time it is only recently that all the problems have been stated, in intention at least, by modern painters.[37]*

33.
John La Farge
Sketch. Blue and White Sky. Rocks and Pond. Newport, 1859
Oil on composition board
7 3/16 x 9 1/4 in. (18.2 x 23.2 cm.)
Private Collection

34.
Inner Wall of The Last Valley from Paradise Pond, Looking Northeast
Photograph by the author
(Oct. 1994)

Beginning in the summer of 1859, La Farge painted outdoors, recording the topography of Newport. His agenda was similar to the slightly later French Impressionists, who also worked from a background in French naturalist art of the 1850s. La Farge kept in mind artists such as Camille Corot (1796-1875) and François Charles Daubigny (1817-1878) as he sketched many of the picturesque tourist spots around the island: the now-destroyed Spouting Horn, the Boat House Beach formerly at the end of Ledge Road, Brenton's Cove near Fort Adams, the Lily Pond, and Long Wharf. Less frequently he ventured far outside of town, for example to The Glen in Portsmouth where he went with William James on a painting expedition.[38]

La Farge also occasionally made the trip of several miles from downtown Newport to Paradise, long a popular place among tourists and artists alike. On one trip, he took along his paint box and positioned himself not far from Bishop Berkeley's Rock (fig. 33). Rather than depict the picturesque Hanging Rocks, he focused on the ridge behind, looking down its long, lumbering inner wall. With characteristic deftness, he sketched the striated sky, the soft scraggly grass, the dark brooding rocks, and a small brackish pool of water. Though this basic topography remains the same as in La Farge's day, many specific features of the site have disappeared beneath brambles and towering reeds (fig. 34).

35.
William Morris Hunt (1824-1879)
Bishop Berkeley's Rock,
1859
Oil on panel
12 1/2 x 8 1/2 in.
(30.3 x 21.3 cm.)
Private Collection

Hunt also painted a view of Bishop Berkeley's Rock in 1859 (fig. 35), looking in a different direction and positioned further in the Last Valley, just beyond Paradise Pond. La Farge and Hunt may even have gone to the Last Valley together to paint at a time when their relationship as mentor and student remained fresh and strong. Their techniques at this point were not dramatically different, with Hunt tending to stylize his brushstrokes more than La Farge. But both employed the popular Barbizon style, using impasted surface effects to apply broad patches of color dominated by green and brown tonalities. Such general similarities would lessen as La Farge began to focus on specialized lighting effects and weather conditions during the next few years.

36.
24 Kay Street, Newport, Looking
Northwest
Photograph by the author
(Dec. 1994)

37.
Maurice Stadtfeld
Grant La Farge and his Nurse,
Mary Pell, c. 1864
Photograph
4 1/2 x 3 in. (11.4 x 7.6 cm.)
Private Collection

Following La Farge's marriage in October 1860, the newlyweds passed time with his mother in New York and at **Glen Cove**, Long Island, where the La Farge family had a country home (see fig. 240). They hoped to relocate to Paris so that La Farge could resume formal training in oil painting, but once again his plan was impeded, this time by the brewing Civil War. With La Farge ineligible to serve in the Union Army because of health problems—reportedly a continuation of his malarial weakness—the couple returned to Newport in March 1861 and purchased an expensive home on fashionable Kay Street (fig. 36).[39] They lived in this large, rambling house, with gardens stretching for a full block down the hill to Mount Vernon Street. Their prosperous lifestyle included maids, grooms, and a nurse to look after their children, the first being **Christopher Grant La Farge** (1862-1938), born on January 5, 1862 (fig. 37).

During these first years of marriage, La Farge fell back again on his own self-tutelage. He expanded his independent program of naturalistic study to the painting of still life (see fig. 41), a genre that allowed him the indulgence of staying close to his wife. The resulting pictures are intimately linked to the couple's daily domestic life.

> *I aimed at making a realistic study of painting, keeping to myself the designs and attempts, serious or slight, which might have a meaning more than that of a strict copy of nature. I painted flowers to get the relation between the softness and brittleness of the flower and the hardness of the bowl or whatever it might be in which the flower might be placed. Instead of arranging my subject, which is the usual studio way, I had it placed for me by chance, with any background and any light, leaving, for instance, the choice of flowers and vase to the servant girl or groom or any one. Or else I copied the corner of the breakfast table as it happened to be. You will see that that is a reasonable method of meeting any difficulties that come up in strict painting.[40]*

These still lifes of flowers on table tops or window sills are among the best pictures of La Farge's career, brimming with light and color, and imbued with organic presence. They reveal his successful adaptation of contemporary French realistic techniques to his personal focus upon delicate effects of light and atmosphere.[41] But his underlying interest in landscape painting remained vital until emerging as a major genre of his work after 1865. Paradise was central to this development.

38.
John La Farge
Hill-Side with House. Paradise Farm, Afternoon Sky, Autumn, 1861
Oil on pine panel
15 1/2 x 11 1/4 in.
(39.4 x 28.6 cm.)
Museum of Fine Arts, Boston,
Bequest of
Mrs. Henry Lee Higginson,
1935

CHAPTER III

LA FARGE AT PARADISE   1861-1864

In June 1863, Thomas Sergeant Perry joked about La Farge sitting "in the fields of his retainer Barker in *il Paradiso*." [42] This is one hint that the La Farges rented a place at Paradise between 1861 and 1864, but seasonal residency lists prior to 1865 contain no formal confirmation of this supposition.[43] Much of what we know of La Farge's early activities at Paradise can only be surmised from paintings and drawings that provide clues as to when and where he worked at Paradise.

39.
Unidentified Photographer
The Hessian House, c. 1895
Photograph
2 1/8 x 3 1/4 in.
(5.3 x 8.2 cm.)
The Newport Historical Society, Newport
The Hessian House was razed after Stephen P. Barker's death in 1898. The rough slate pillars in the foreground of this view from the east still stand at 485 Paradise Avenue. "Bridge House," built in 1930, occupies the ridge behind the spot where the Hessian House formerly stood.

40.
H.W. Rankin and Co.
Stephen Peckham Barker, c. 1885
Photograph
6 1/4 x 3 7/8 in. (15.5 x 9.7 cm.)
Private Collection

In the fall of 1861, La Farge painted *Hill-Side with House. Paradise Farm, Afternoon Sky, Autumn*[44] (fig. 38), depicting an important landmark known as the **Hessian House** that graced the west side of Paradise Avenue until its razing around 1898 (fig. 39). During the American Revolution, this was one of the homes commandeered by the British from Isaac Barker.[45] By 1861, the Hessian House had been in the Barker family for at least four generations and belonged to **Stephen P. Barker** (1815-1898) (fig. 40), who owned considerable land in the area. In 1865, published residency lists prove that Barker rented part of the Hessian House to La Farge for the season.[46] Paintings such as this one, however, suggest that, prior to 1865, La Farge already was lodging at the Hessian House. In this instance, La Farge worked while seated just inside the rough-hewn pillars of the driveway, visible in the old photograph.

One of the key still lifes of La Farge's early career (fig. 41) can be compared to this exterior view of the Hessian House to prove that the La Farges stayed there in 1861 and probably for several years after. A lush floral arrangement, delineated with thick swaths of paint, sits on a wide window ledge before a deep landscape seen through the window. The vista features the same outbuilding and driveway found in the exterior view of the Hessian House. From the relative position of the outbuilding, we can infer that the window from which La Farge painted was in a long, one-story extension tacked onto the west side of the original house, visible in some old photographs (figs. 44, 45). Nothing definitive is known about this edifice, but it seems clear that this is where the La Farges at times boarded before ultimately living there for a year in 1865.

41.
John La Farge
Flowers on a Window Ledge, c. 1861
Oil on canvas
24 x 20 in.
(60.9 x 50.8 cm.)
The Corcoran Gallery of Art,
Washington, D.C., Museum Purchase,
Anna E. Clark Fund, 1949

42.
Baseboard of Window Sill,
Isaac Barker House
Photograph by the author
(Nov. 1994)

43.
Baseboard of Window Sill,
Grayledge Farm
Photograph by the author
(Dec. 1994)

The molding under the sill seen in the still life is a distinctive feature of several houses built along Paradise Avenue around 1860. Such moldings are still found in the house just across the street (fig. 42; see fig. 49), then belonging to **Isaac Barker** (1813-1903), Stephen P. Barker's brother. The same molding also is found in the neighboring residence to the south, **Grayledge Farm** (fig. 43; see fig. 67), then owned by a Barker relative, **E. Truman Peckham** (1831-1903). Both of these houses were built by Peckham, who constructed many other houses along Paradise Avenue as well. It is safe to assume that he built the extension to the Hessian House, explaining how similar moldings might come to be associated with an edifice otherwise dating from many decades before the other houses.

44.
Unidentified Photographer
The Hessian House, c. 1895
Photograph
2 1/8 x 3 1/4 in.
(5.3 x 8.2 cm.)
The Newport Historical Society, Newport
This view of the front taken from the north shows the gabled and much later edifice attached to the west side of the main house that evidently was used for borders

45.
Unidentified Photographer
The Hessian House, c. 1880
Photograph
5 x 7 in. (12.7 x 17.8 cm.)
The Newport Historical Society, Newport
This view of the rear taken from the southwest includes a glimpse of the gabled, one-floor edifice visible also from the front of the house. The figures standing by the door are, on the right, Mrs. Stephen P. Barker (Betsey Gardiner Barker) and her daughter-in-law, Mrs. Alden P. Barker.

29

Though the Hessian House can be readily identified as the subject of *Hill-Side with House. Paradise Farm, Afternoon Sky, Autumn*, La Farge's reference in its title to "Paradise Farm" can readily lead to confusion today. Presently there are two houses called Paradise Farm. One, formerly known as Gardiner's Farm, seen just above Gardiner's Pond in Louisa C. Sturtevant's watercolor (see fig. 21), now serves in part as the headquarters of the Norman Bird Sanctuary.[47] This Paradise Farm had little to do with La Farge's life at Paradise.

The other Paradise Farm is a large hipped-roof farmhouse at 346 Paradise Avenue, three tenths of a mile northeast of the Hessian House and far back from the road at the base of Peter's Rock (fig. 46). Once belonging to the Barker family, La Farge frequently painted in the hills and the meadows around this house. But this does not readily explain why La Farge used the name Paradise Farm to refer to the Hessian House.

This confusion is clarified by land sale records that date from several decades after La Farge began visiting Paradise, when Isaac Barker sold sixty acres of land to O.H.P. Belmont under the name Paradise Farm (see maps 5 and 6).[48] From this, we can infer that a conglomeration of Barker land and farmhouses on both sides of Paradise Avenue (map 4), as well as a large portion of the Paradise Hills, were collectively referred to as Paradise Farm. With this understanding, we can make sense of an otherwise confusing statement by La Farge's son, **Oliver H.P. La Farge** (1869-1936) (see fig. 244):

> we had lived in the summers at Paradise Farm with the Barkers, a place chosen for the family by Mr. William James. I and two of my brothers and sisters were born there.[49]

Indeed, three children were born on Paradise Avenue, each in a different house located several hundred feet apart. **Bancel La Farge** (1865-1938) (see figs. 241-242) was born in the Hessian House; **Margaret Angela La Farge** (1867-1956) (see fig. 243) at Grayledge Farm; and Oliver at the Isaac Barker house two years after her.[50] For Oliver to bundle these houses together as "Paradise Farm" reaffirms the other evidence that this term had a generic rather than specific meaning during the 1860s.

The Barker connection to La Farge nevertheless remains vague—rendered all the more mysterious by Oliver's reference to the role of William James in selecting this place for the La Farge family. The key seems to lie in Stephen P. Barker, who acquired a "comfortable fortune" by farming.[51] In addition to the Hessian House, Barker built another large farmhouse before 1870 just down and across the road, Sea Breeze Farm at 426 Paradise Avenue (fig. 47). This was greatly enlarged as a boarding house in the 1890s (fig. 48), an appearance retained today. Other Barker family houses on Paradise Avenue included the residence of his brother Isaac at 478 Paradise Avenue (fig. 49), facing the Hessian House; and a house once in the Paradise Hills on the site of the present **Orchard Lea**, later moved "over the rocks" to 400 Paradise Avenue (see fig. 158). La Farge lived in or painted alongside each of these houses as the years passed, suggesting that much of his time in Paradise was spent as Barker's guest, tenant, or a combination of the two.

46.
Paradise Farm, 346 Paradise Avenue, Looking East
Photograph by the author (Oct. 1994)
Peter's Rock is directly behind the farmhouse. The gap in the ridge leading to the valley on the other side can still be reached by an old path just behind the farmhouse.

47.
Unidentified Photographer
Sea Breeze Farm, 426 Paradise Avenue, Looking East, c. 1882
Photograph
8 x 10 in. (19.6 x 24.6 cm.)
Private Collection
The only figures that can be identified are the two young granddaughters of Stephen P. Barker, seen in the right foreground. On the left is Adelia Barker (1874-1967); on the right is her sister, Louisa Barker (1878-1965). The woman standing on the porch clutching a hat appears to be a nursemaid.

48.
Unidentified Photographer
Sea Breeze Farm, 426 Paradise Avenue, Looking East, c. 1895
Photograph
8 x 10 in. (19.6 x 24.6 cm.)
Private Collection
The woman in a long dress in the foreground is Adelia Barker; the man in a straw hat at the center of the group in the background is Adelia's father, Lyman H. Barker (1842-1922), a son of Stephen P. Barker. The others cannot be identified. The original photograph was partly out of focus.

49.
Isaac Barker House, 478 Paradise Avenue, Looking East
Photograph by the author
(Apr. 1994)

50.
John La Farge
Nelson's Pond from the Sacred Grove,
c. 1862
Crayon on paper
6 3/4 x 4 1/4 in. (17.1 x 10.8 cm.)
Private Collection
*In the foreground is the Large Basin,
separated from the Small Basin by a line
representing the tip of the peninsula.*

51.
John La Farge
*Boat House beneath the Cliff,
West Side of Nelson's Pond*, 1863
Brown crayon and graphite on smooth
buff paper
3 5/16 x 5 3/4 in. (8.4 x 14.6 cm.)
Addison Gallery of American Art, Phillips
Academy, Andover, Massachusetts,
Addison Purchase Fund

By 1862, the La Farges came to Paradise with great frequency, and probably stayed for protracted periods at the Hessian House. As evidence of La Farge's visits to Paradise in 1862, we have a profusion of pictures and drawings depicting the ridges and shores of Nelson's Pond, the southern boundary of Barker's Paradise Farm.

The topography of Nelson's Pond has survived to some extent as it was in La Farge's day. The artist was most attracted to the western side of the pond where a dramatic puddingstone ledge and cliff emerge from the descending ridge behind Peter's Rock (see fig. 13). Then as now, this cliff was off Paradise Avenue at the end of **Paradise Court**, a small alley running between Grayledge Farm and the Isaac Barker house, and just across from the driveway to the Hessian House. In La Farge's time, the court ended in front of a now-vanished house listed on early maps (map 4) as belonging to an as-yet unidentified J. Nelson, whose name came to be associated with the pond. Passing this, the visitor reached the dramatic puddingstone eruptions of the cliff, rolling in stepped gradations along the side of the pond.

From the puddingstone ledge above the cliff, the view is breathtaking. The pond glistening below gives way to dramatic forested hills on the other side, and opens out onto the dunes lining Second Beach. Easton's Point and Purgatory Rocks frame the right side of the view, with the Cliff Walk of Newport visible in the far distance. Sachuest and Flint Points splay out distinctively on the left, with Little Compton and the Sakonnet River further to the east. The Atlantic coastline of southern Massachusetts, and even the island of Martha's Vineyard, are visible on a clear day. Immediately below the puddingstone ledge, at a drop varying from thirty to sixty feet, is a native oak-hickory forest that extends north until reaching the lawn of the present Gray Craig mansion. La Farge dubbed this the "Sacred Grove" after the glen where the classical poet Virgil (70-19 B.C.) supposedly derived inspiration for writing. La Farge's son, Bancel, later recalled the special significance of the place to the artist:

> There our interests were centred [sic]. The little lichen-covered cliff of pale silvery rocks out of which grew the groups of old hickory trees emerging like spirits from a classic past created for my father an enchanting setting for his compositions. . . . Its classical enchantment came from an indescribable sense of remoteness or abstraction.[52]

The hickory trees of former times are now petrified trunks protruding from the cliff, while a newer oak-hickory forest crowds into a narrow strip of land bordering the water. In La Farge's time, this forest was sparser and relatively open, as shown in a drawing of a hastily-sketched figure standing on the edge of the Sacred Grove, looking across Nelson's Pond toward the ridge on its far east side (fig. 50).

Before dredging of the pond in 1882, the Sacred Grove was wider and more varied, including pasture and pond beach in addition to the forested glens and palisades seen today. A sketch by La Farge shows a boat house in front of the cliff on a wide stretch of land (fig. 51). This area has now been reduced to a mere ribbon of rocks that is usually underwater. Even though much of the Sacred Grove survived the changing water table, Bancel greatly lamented such flooding.

52.
John La Farge
The Lady of Shalott, c. 1862
Oil on panel
9 x 14 3/4 in. (22.9 x 37.5 cm.)
The New Britain Museum of American Art,
New Britain, Connecticut, Harriet Russell
Stanley Memorial Fund

That strange grove is long ago gone, together with all the rest of the Valley, and the actors in the Drama. All its beauties and its mysteries are now but a memory buried beneath the waters of that aimless commercial enterprise.[53]

The cliff beneath the puddingstone ledge and the adjoining Sacred Grove became the background for one of La Farge's first serious figure works, *The Lady of Shalott* (fig. 52), painted in 1862.[54] Like the British Pre-Raphaelites, La Farge admired the popular poetry of Alfred Lord Tennyson (1809-1892) with its legendary Arthurian subject matter. The Lady of Shalott, who expired over unrequited love for Sir Lancelot, was one of the most familiar Tennysonian characters of the time. La Farge depicted her on her final journey to Camelot, floating over dark, placid waters, her lips pursed in half-crazed song. She bears the features of La Farge's wife, recalling a practice of the British Pre-Raphaelites, whose spouses posed in bathtubs as water-borne maidens such as Shakespeare's *Ophelia* or Tennyson's *Elaine*.[55]

The bark bearing the melancholy figure floats on Nelson's Pond before the cliff and hazy trees of the Sacred Grove, with the setting sun in the west casting an eerie glow over the scene. Today, much of the cliff seen in the painting is obscured by trees that have proliferated along the northern bank of the pond (fig. 53). The precise topography in La Farge's day can better be understood by reference to a drawing from the same approximate vantage point as in the painting (fig. 54).

53.
Nelson's Pond, Looking West toward the
cliff and Sacred Grove
Photograph by the author
(Nov. 1994)
*The prow-like end of the peninsula is in the
foreground.*

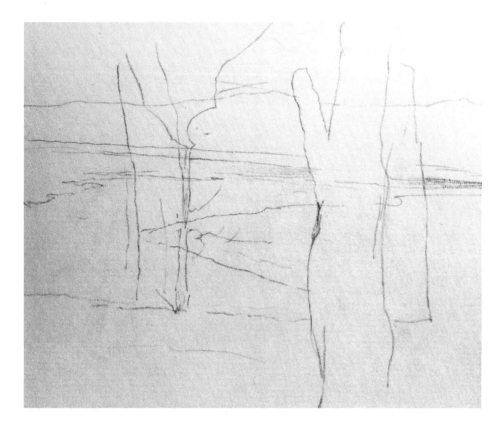

54.
John La Farge
*Nelson's Pond, Looking West toward
Puddingstone Cliff*, c. 1865
Graphite on buff laid paper
7 1/4 x 5 in.
(18.4 x 12.7 cm.)
Private Collection
*The foreground is occupied by the Small
Basin of Nelson's Pond, then the marshy
mouth of an unnamed brook draining into
the pond from the north. The prow-like
peninsula divides this from the Large
Basin. In the distance, rises the cliff seen
in* The Lady of Shalott.

The same cliff appears in *Meadow with Goose* (fig. 55), an 1862 study for the background of a proposed altarpiece commissioned by Father Isaac Thomas Hecker (1819-1888), who founded the Paulist order in 1858. Hecker, a close friend of La Farge's family in New York for years, instructed Margaret in the Catholic faith prior to baptizing her in the fall of 1860. Sometime that same year, he commissioned La Farge for an altarpiece that would have depicted Saint Paul Preaching at Athens. Ultimately, the project fell through, and the painting of Saint Paul that La Farge worked on for over two years has been long-lost and never photographed.[56] *Meadow with Goose* bears an inscription on the back that relates it to this undertaking: "1862/ Landscape Sketch. Painted to try some color for the Saint Paul/ it has a goose in the foreground coming up the bank and 'grubbing'/ painted on Japanese tray/ begun with violets and deep blues in sky/ shadows in foreground gold ochre,

55.
John La Farge
Meadow with Goose; Study of Landscape
for *St. Paul Preaching at Athens*, 1862
Oil on Japanese lacquer tray
6 5/8 x 8 3/4 in. (16.8 x 22.2 cm.)
Private Collection
*The distant profile of the distinctive west
wall of Nelson's Pond, with its
characteristic curving profiles at left and
right, suggests that this was painted
either on the peninsula or else from the
island on the far side of the pond.*

and green reds in mid-distance." The glowing palette of blues, greens, and reds, and the scumbled textures of fleecy clouds floating over the cliff reflect the growing sophistication of La Farge's evolving handling of landscape in oils.

Around this same time, La Farge used a view from the puddingstone ledge atop the cliff as the background for a triptych of *The Crucifixion*, commissioned in 1862 by St. Peter's Roman Catholic Church in New York City.[57] The triptych ultimately did not reach completion, leaving La Farge with only two side panels that would have flanked the central Crucifixion scene. A Mourning Madonna (fig. 56) is the likeness of the artist's wife; she stands on the puddingstone ledge with her back to a view over Nelson's Pond, the east ridge of the Paradise Hills, and the curling shore of Second Beach. The figure of Saint John the Evangelist (fig. 57), bearing the features of the artist's friend William James, stands on the same ledge before a distant view of Second Beach near Purgatory Chasm. The central Crucifixion would have taken place before the remaining stretch of the puddingstone ledge and Second Beach needed to connect the topography of the two backgrounds.

The use of such sites as realistic backgrounds for religious themes was part and parcel of La Farge's desire to impart naturalistic truthfulness to every aspect of his work. Such idealistic or imaginary compositions went hand-in-hand with realistic *plein-air* landscapes painted around Nelson's Pond.

Just across from the Sacred Grove, the marshy side of Nelson's Pond once teemed with water lilies. The artist's son Oliver wrote about the "wonderful pond full of pond lilies, reached only by an ancient leaky boat [from Barker's farm]. The pond always seemed to belong to us, as well as the pond lilies, as we were continually picking them for father to paint." [58] Bancel similarly recalled "Nelson's pond with its wild surroundings, reeds, rushes and swamp—in summer the blooming beds of wa-ter-lilies, destined as models for my father's [pictures]." [59] One of the most descriptive

56.
John La Farge
The Virgin at the Foot of the Cross;
Panel for a Triptych of the Crucifixion,
1862-63
Oil on canvas
Arched format:
97 1/2 x 30 3/4 in.
(247.6 x 78.1 cm.)
Private Collection

57.
John La Farge
*St. John the Evangelist at
the Foot of the Cross*;
Panel for a Triptych of the Crucifixion,
1862-63
Oil on canvas
Arched format:
97 1/2 x 30 3/4 in.
(247.6 x 78.1 cm.)
Private Collection

pictures of the pond is by Hudson River School artist John Frederick Kensett (1816-1872) (fig. 58), who knew La Farge at Paradise. In his aggrandized view of the southeast corner of the pond, the ridge forming a sort of canyon wall along the Gray Craig estate sweeps dramatically across the picture. To the left, marshes and shallow water surround the small island in the southeast corner of the pond. In the foreground near what was then the front of the pond, and is now under the dike, are patches of water lilies.

58.
John Frederick Kensett (1816-1872)
Paradise Rocks, near Newport,
1859
Oil on canvas
14 x 24 in.
(35.5 x 60.9 cm.)
Private Collection

59.
John La Farge
The Last Water Lilies, 1862
Oil on panel
9 5/8 x 7 9/16 in.
(23.8 x 19.3 cm.)
Private Collection

With a strikingly more intimate treatment, La Farge depicted a nearby spot in *The Last Water Lilies* (fig. 59), painted in October 1862. The background shows a rock formation (fig. 60) on the north side of the same small island seen from the other side in Kensett's painting. To paint the picture, La Farge sat at the prow-like point of the peninsula, now found at the end of the lawn of the Gray Craig estate (see fig. 14). In La Farge's day, this was the marshy edge of the pond where it met a small river, often stagnant, depending on the season.

The title *The Last Water Lilies* seems a melancholy premonition of Bancel's lament, but it alludes to the "last water lilies" of the summer about to fade in the cold nights of autumn. The artist may also have wanted to convey the notion that these were "last water lilies" painted before the family left Paradise for the season. La Farge effectively captured the mood of a secluded cove on a dark and melancholy autumn day, and no doubt appreciated the words of an early critic: "This picture, deep in color, low in tone, has the very odor of a spot made for water-lilies and aromatic shrubs." [60]

60.
The Island in Nelson's Pond from the Peninsula, Looking South
Photograph by the author
(Dec. 1994)
The channel in the foreground was the marshy mouth of an unnamed river in La Farge's day. Even when it swelled in wet weather to make the Small Basin, the gentler currents and shallower depths promoted the propagation of water lilies in a way no longer possible.

The site of *A Grey Day—Newport* (fig. 61), also dated 1862, is on the peninsula some fifty feet north from where La Farge sat to paint *The Last Water Lilies*. This finger of land is an eruption of puddingstone and slate that includes several high boulders on its west side. La Farge painted *A Grey Day — Newport* looking southward along the boulders and over the shallow waters of Nelson's Pond (fig. 62). The craggy rocks sprouting wiry bushes in *A Grey Day—Newport* bear superficial similarities to rocks seen in *Twin Lambs* (fig. 63), painted by William Morris Hunt before La Farge arrived in Newport. This resemblance is not coincidental for Hunt's picture was painted from the peninsula, as proven by the position of the cliff on the west side of Nelson's Pond seen at the upper left of his picture (see fig. 13). The prominent rocks in Hunt's picture are no longer visible, buried in a tangle of broken trees, brambles, and low bushes about fifty feet further north on the peninsula from the spot where La Farge painted *A Grey Day—Newport*.

These two paintings, produced in such close proximity, illustrate the artistic gap between Hunt and La Farge that widened as the years passed. *Twin Lambs* is a pastoral idyll of the type found frequently in both English and French art of the 1850s and 1860s. Hunt painted the scene as a quasi-religious exercise, not for the specific attributes of the natural scene. La Farge on the other hand sacrificed the particulars of the site to the brooding mood and somber lighting produced by the dank weather. *A Grey Day—Newport* studies the atmosphere of an overcast day as forms dissolve into the murky air and local color all but disappears. La Farge earlier had criticized Hunt with words that apply to these different approaches.

61.
John La Farge
A Grey Day—Newport,
1862
Oil, gold, and silver gilt on panel
12 1/2 x 9 3/8 in. (31.8 x 23.8 cm.)
Museum of Fine Arts, Boston,
Bequest of Mrs. Henry Lee Higginson,1935

62.
Boulders on the Peninsula,
Nelson's Pond,
Looking South
Photograph by the author
(Nov. 1994)

63.
William Morris Hunt (1824-1879)
Twin Lambs, c. 1857
Oil on canvas
38 1/2 x 32 in.
(97.8 x 81.2 cm.)
Museum of Fine Arts, Boston,
Gift by Subscription
The cliff at the upper left is the west wall of Nelson's Pond. The boulders at the right are now all but buried beneath debris and landfill.

Hunt thought it useless to carry the refinement of tone and color to the extent which I aimed at in my studies, telling me that there would not be one in a hundred or five hundred artists capable of appreciating such differences of accuracy—their eyes and their training would not be sufficient. This objection seemed to me, as I told him, exactly the reason why I should, for certain, aim at these variations from recipe. So much the better, if only one man in a thousand could see it; I should then have exactly what I wanted in the appeal to the man who knew and to the mind like mine.[61]

In 1862, La Farge also executed many drawings of Paradise, most in the small pocket-sized sketchbooks that he carried with him wherever he went. In one drawing, La Farge sat along the edge of the island in the southeast corner of Nelson's Pond, looking towards Easton's Point (fig. 64). The view today is similar, despite the expansive south end of the pond and the dike blocking the view of Second Beach (fig. 65). Another drawing shows a spooky image of hickories in the Sacred Grove, hugging the cliff along the west side of Nelson's Pond (fig. 66).

64.
John La Farge
Newport, Paradise, 1862
(Looking Southwest across Nelson's Pond toward Purgatory Rocks), 1862
Black crayon on mulberry paper
6 3/8 x 4 1/4 in. (16.1 x 10.9 cm.)
Avery Architectural and Fine Arts Library,
Columbia University, New York,
Purchase, 1950

65.
Purgatory Rocks from the Island of Nelson's Pond, Looking Southwest
Photograph by the author
(Nov. 1994)

66.
John La Farge
Study of Trees
(Hickories in the Sacred Grove), c. 1865
Black crayon on smooth white paper
3 7/8 x 4 in. (9.8 x 10 cm.)
Avery Architectural and Fine Arts Library
Columbia University, New York,
Purchase, 1950

67.
Grayledge Farm,
E. Truman Peckham House,
532 Paradise Avenue, Looking East
Photograph by the author
(Nov. 1994)

WITH JOHN BANCROFT AT PARADISE   1863

The contacts that La Farge made in Paradise were few and far between. Even though Paradise Avenue became popular among Newport summer residents late in the nineteenth century, very few chose to stay there around the time of the Civil War. One of the first to do so was **John Neilson** (1837-1903), a socially prominent and independently wealthy New Yorker. The year after his 1861 marriage to Augusta Balch, daughter of a local Newport minister, Neilson leased Grayledge Farm (fig. 67) from E. Truman Peckham.[62] Through Neilson, La Farge met **David Maitland Armstrong** (1836-1918), a lawyer from New York summering in Newport who later became a well-known artist. Armstrong recalled playing croquet with Neilson and La Farge around 1865, a year before he married Neilson's sister Helen.[63]

Whereas Neilson was one of the few New Yorkers who chose Paradise Avenue for a summer residence, La Farge had several close friends who came out with him to visit or stay at Paradise during the Civil War years. The most important was **John Chandler Bancroft** (1835-1901) (fig. 68), who had "been down to try" fighting in the war, but found "that he was not fitted for anything like that, though his health was as good" as La Farge's was bad.[64] In 1862, Bancroft returned to Newport to stay at the Bellevue Avenue mansion of his father, George Bancroft (1800-1891), then a foreign ambassador and later a celebrated historian.

In his recollections, La Farge credited John Bancroft with abetting his explorations of color theory and realistic landscape painting. Just how this took place is unclear. After obtaining a Harvard degree, Bancroft studied art at Düsseldorf and Paris. He shared La Farge's penchant for French realistic methods and theories, but had become so compulsively realistic that he avoided looking at Renaissance pictures for fear that their idealized figures might ruin his perception. In this, La Farge noted that Bancroft was "almost too much a student," thereby explaining Bancroft's failure to become a serious artist. In spite of such differences, the two were "brought very much together for several years," and were in "constant relation" in their studies. Beginning in 1863, they dedicated themselves to joint explorations of specific artistic problems in rendering realistic colors and atmospheric effects.[65] They also began collecting Japanese prints, importing them through another Newport summer resident who headed a leading New York firm engaged in the China trade.[66]

68.
John La Farge
John Chandler Bancroft, 1863
Charcoal on off-white rice paper
8 x 5 5/8 in. (20.3 x 14.3 cm.)
Redwood Library and Athenaeum,
Newport,
Bequest of Frances S. Childs

La Farge's statements provide much of our understanding of this artistic relationship, which evolved in the pastures and hills of Paradise. Their work cannot be readily illustrated by reference to pictures. La Farge and Bancroft became preoccupied with the "great questions of light and color which were beginning to be laid out by scientific men" and engaged in "a great deal of work but of less painting, if I may say so, less picture-making, because of an almost incessant set of observations and comments and inquiries supplemented by actual work in painting."[67] By passing more time discussing Chevreul's theories than painting, Bancroft left behind no works identifiable with this phase of his career. In terms of La Farge, we have only a handful of pictures dating from 1863 that can be examined for some sign of Bancroft's influence.

Clouds over Sea; from Paradise Rocks (fig. 69) is the most unusual picture painted in 1863.[68] The view is looking southeast from the puddingstone ledge above Nelson's Pond (fig. 70), a view similar to that seen in the Crucifixion triptych. In the foreground, the waters of Nelson's Pond reflect the agitated cloud-filled sky. Beyond a strip of land—the meadows and dunes between Nelson's Pond and Second Beach—is the distinctive curve of the beach and, at the left, the tip of Sachuest Point. In the far distance, the ocean surges beneath lowering clouds pierced by shafts of sunlight. The picture conveys the essence of turbulent weather by exploiting color and texture at the expense of precise topography. The problems confronted by the artist are difficult and subtle, requiring extensive forethought and remarkable care in the choice of colors and textures to avoid a muddle of paint. Instead, La Farge gave us the most intriguing, colorful, and daring small picture of his first few years as an artist.

69.
John La Farge
Clouds over Sea; From Paradise Rocks,
1863
Oil on canvas
10 x 14 in.
(25.4 x 35.6 cm.)
Mr. and Mrs. Willard G. Clark

70.
View from the Puddingstone Ledge over Nelson's Pond, Looking Southeast
Photograph by the author
(Jan. 1995)

La Farge gave the title *Mountain Study: Cloud* to another work that he dated to 1863 (fig. 71).[69] Here, the artist contrasted the deep blue shadows in the distant ridges with the brown-orange autumnal tints of the foreground "mountain," a textbook application of complementary color theories. Given his propensity for specifying site names in the titles of his works, just why La Farge chose not to identify the site of *Mountain Study: Cloud* is an enigma. The merging ridges on the east side of Nelson's Pond constitute the "mountain." La Farge painted from the puddingstone ledge on the west side of the pond, at a point today blocked by trees. A sketch executed from further up the puddingstone ledge helps with this identification by showing a more schematic rendering of the ridges and water (fig. 72). A view today from the dike below the puddingstone ledge (fig. 73) approximates the shape of the "mountain" while showing in distorted proportion the background ridges as they appear in the painting and drawing.

71.
John La Farge
Mountain Study: Cloud, 1863
Oil on panel
4 5/8 x 8 5/8 in.
(11.5 x 22.1 cm.)
William Vareika Fine Arts, Newport

72.
John La Farge
From the Puddingstone Ledge over Nelson's Pond, c. 1865
Graphite on buff laid paper
5 x 7 1/4 in. (12.7 x 18.4 cm.)
Private Collection
The puddingstone ledge is in the foreground. Below is Nelson's Pond with the Large Basin in front, a line designating the point of the peninsula, and the Small Basin behind it. The opposite shore shows the merging ridges that now are enclosed by the Norman Bird Sanctuary.

73.
View from the Dike of Nelson's Pond,
Looking Northeast
Photograph by the author
(Oct. 1994)

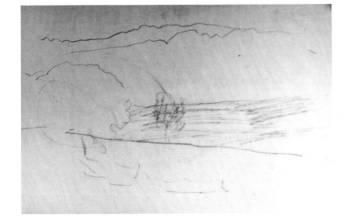

74.
John La Farge
Hollyhocks, 1863
Encaustic on panel
34 x 15 3/4 in.
(86.4 x 40 cm.)
Private Collection, California

In all likelihood, two other now-lost pictures painted this same year were quite similar and involved many of the same artistic issues for La Farge. *Cumulus Cloud. Late Afternoon in Summer* was a less weather-filled version of *Clouds over Sea; from Paradise Rocks*. It represented a single cumulus cloud hovering over Nelson's Pond, viewed from the puddingstone ledge on the west side.[70] In the fall, La Farge painted *Evening. October. Corner of Old Orchard, Paradise Farm*.[71] This unfortunately has been lost since 1879, and never was photographed.

In 1863, La Farge also painted *Hollyhocks* (fig. 74).[72] The flowers occupy the foreground of the deep sloping landscape of the Sacred Grove, looking north along the ridge that leads to Peter's Rock (fig. 75). Hollyhock seeds must have been carried by birds into the woods from gardens of the J. Nelson house on the puddingstone ledge above. The idea for *Hollyhocks* no doubt originated in these real hollyhocks in the Sacred Grove, but it became the arena for experimentation with various artistic styles and materials. The unique glow of the work stems from its medium, a mixture of oil and wax encaustic. La Farge obtained the formula for this paint in 1856 from Henry Styleman Le Strange (1815-1862), the decorator of churches such as Ely Cathedral.[73] The sheeny, smooth surface of the paint contributes to the overall decorative feeling of *Hollyhocks*, and prefigures the interest in decorative art that eventually would take over La Farge's work.

We cannot ignore the obvious influence on this subject of the Japanese prints that La Farge and Bancroft were importing at the time. Japanese floral prints typically included vertical flower arrangements set against a natural background, rendered with decorative abstraction. So too can we detect the influence of the sinuous line and mellow colorations of British Pre-Raphaelite art. Such close-up views of nature filled the salons in England and America at the time, and have much to do with the vital, organic quality of La Farge's spirited rendering.

75.
The Sacred Grove,
Looking North along the Cliff
Photograph by the author (Jan. 1995)
Note the distinctive dip in the horizon and the receding line of the cliff at the left, both seen in Hollyhocks. *Just above this part of the Sacred Grove is the puddingstone ledge that lay behind the house of "J. Nelson."*

La Farge also dated *Figure in Purple Dress. Landscape Background; Afternoon* (fig. 76) to 1863.[74] This portrait of Margaret was painted from atop the same ledge as *Mountain Study: Cloud* and other pictures. Behind the figure, an abrupt drop leads to the bank of Nelson's Pond. La Farge gouged the paint with a palette knife to suggest the rocky and muddy terrain bordering the edge of the pond. The blue band sweeping across the top of the picture like a patch of sky is actually the water of the pond.

These works share few points in common, representing different styles, moods, and levels of resolution. While it is tempting to relate the complicated color contrasts of *Clouds over Sea; From Paradise Rocks* or *Mountain Study: Cloud* to La Farge's work with Bancroft, the artist's failure to produce works with detectable patterns of evolving technique render such analogies tenuous at best. If any general influence of working with Bancroft can be detected, it lies in the growing sophistication of color, light, and texture evident throughout La Farge's work as a whole.

After Bancroft married in 1864 and moved to Milton, Massachusetts, he and La Farge continued to see each other occasionally. A drawing of Margaret's brother Tom Perry dated 1865 is annotated "Talking to Bancroft at Paradise Farm" (fig. 77), and probably was executed in the Hessian House. This proves their continued friendly relations but, as La Farge said, we are still hard-pressed to relate the experience with Bancroft to specific traits in La Farge's art.

La Farge owed at least as great a debt to another acquaintance who came to Paradise on occasion, the photographer **Maurice Stadtfeld** (active c. 1860-1880).[75] Stadtfeld had a shop at 711 Broadway in New York City, just blocks from the Tenth Street Studio Building, where La Farge maintained an atelier throughout his life. From the very start of his career, La Farge had used photographs as artistic aids in producing art works. Several early self-portraits are based on photographs, in at least one case involving elaborate studio staging (fig. 78), perhaps done with the help of Stadtfeld.[76]

From 1864 until 1878, Stadtfeld received payments from La Farge for photography services, suggesting that he was a primary photographer responsible for the photographic aids that had some bearing on the artist's work.[77] In addition, Stadtfeld taught La Farge to use a camera, whimsically proven in a caricature by La Farge's brother, Francis La Farge (1847-1876) (fig. 79). Frank showed his brother taking advantage of the "obliging disposition of Maurice Stadtfeldt [*sic*]" by employing the photographer's back as a substitute platform. La Farge jockeys into position to make an exposure, presumably of a landscape subject. Frank's drawing dates from 1863, the same year that La Farge drew a slight sketch of Stadtfeld in a sketchbook.[78]

78.
Unidentified Photographer
John La Farge
(Posing for a Self-Portrait), c. 1859
Photograph from glass-plate negative
4 x 3 in. (10.2 x 7.6 cm.)
Yale University Art Gallery, New Haven,
Connecticut, Gift of Frances S. Childs
in memory of Henry A. La Farge
The photograph served as the basis for
Portrait of the Painter, *Metropolitan*
Museum of Art. The painting, dated 1859,
shows the artist on a path behind the La
Farge country house at Glen Cove. The
artist leans on a painter's umbrella, used
by landscape painters to shield the sun.

79.
Francis La Farge (1847-1876)
The Obliging Disposition of Maurice
Stadtfeldt [sic], c. 1863
Graphite on paper
3 1/4 x 5 1/2 in. (8.3 x 13.9 cm.)
Yale University Art Gallery,
New Haven, Connecticut,
Gift of Frances S. Childs in memory of
Henry A. La Farge

These lessons led to at least one photographic negative taken by La Farge himself, a view of Second Beach under a turbulent sky (fig. 80).[79] La Farge set up the camera just to the east of a large puddingstone outcropping that erupts near the western end of the beach. The view from this point today is quite similar (fig. 81), including the high dunes that separate the beach from the apron of land leading to Nelson's Pond. Second Beach sweeps dramatically toward the distant Sachuest Point, detectable in La Farge's photograph as a series of hillocks that are white-capped, apparently under a dusting of snow.

80.
John La Farge
Second Beach, Middletown, R.I.,
c. 1863
Platinum print on paper
18 11/16 x 13 5/8 in.
(47.5 x 34.6 cm.)
Bowdoin College Museum of Art,
Brunswick, Maine,
Gift of Mr. and Mrs. William Rand
This photograph may have been taken while La Farge's brother Frank drew his caricature (fig. 79).

81.
Second Beach, Looking East from the Puddingstone Outcropping
Photograph by the author
(Oct. 1994)

Other photographs intended as artistic aids for La Farge's paintings date from late 1863 or early 1864. One glass-plate negative shows Margaret's brother, Tom Perry, seated on a porch in a Japanese kimono (fig. 82). This served as the unlikely model for a figure of Saint Cecilia in a never-published illustration for Tennyson's 1830 poem, *The Palace of Art* (fig. 83).

> Or in a clear-wall'd city on the sea,
> Near gilded organ-pipes, her hair
> Wound with white roses, slept Saint Cecily;
> An angel look'd at her.[80]

In addition to translating the precise form of the figure, La Farge adapted the shape of the window frame to the organ in Saint Cecilia's "clear-wall'd city on the sea." At the left, he added a view of Peter's Rock as seen from around Prospect Avenue.

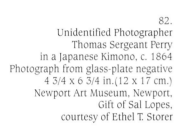
82.
Unidentified Photographer
Thomas Sergeant Perry
in a Japanese Kimono, c. 1864
Photograph from glass-plate negative
4 3/4 x 6 3/4 in.(12 x 17 cm.)
Newport Art Museum, Newport,
Gift of Sal Lopes,
courtesy of Ethel T. Storer

83.
John La Farge
St. Cecilia Asleep at the Organ;
Study for Tennyson's *The Palace of Art*,
c. 1864
Charcoal on paper
9 3/4 x 12 1/8 in.
(24.8 x 30.8 cm.)
Location unknown
Note the profile of Peter's Rock, seen
through the window at the left. Today
about half of the rock up to the central
peak has been devoured by the Peckham
Brothers Quarry.

84.
John La Farge
Early Spring. Sun Struggling Through Clouds, 1864
Oil on wood panel
16 1/8 x 22 in. (40.9 x 55.9 cm.)
Harvard University Art Museums, Fogg Art Museum, Cambridge, Massachusetts, Bequest of Grenville L. Winthrop

It is tempting to connect this intense interest in photography with an ambitious painting executed in the spring of 1864, *Early Spring. Sun Struggling Through Clouds* (fig. 84).[81] This view of the puddingstone ledge from which La Farge so often painted is rendered with geological exactitude that recalls photographic vision. Puddingstone fills the picture, its characteristic fissures and conglomerated masses clearly defined, even as they dissolve into the misty atmosphere. The high horizon line, reminiscent of Japanese prints, also recalls the kind of truncated vision common to photographs taken without a regard for picturesque composition. The perspective blocks the view over the puddingstone ledge to the pond and ridges beyond, forcing the eye to focus on the forlorn tree in the foreground. Upon inspection, we become aware, too, of the large slab of puddingstone lying at the right, its sliced-off end to the viewer.

Time, weathering, and rearrangement have altered the details but not the essential rugged geology of the site (fig. 85). When O.H.P. Belmont purchased this land from the Barkers in 1891, he built a house on the puddingstone ledge, not far from the specific spot depicted in La Farge's picture (map 6). A driveway once ran along the inner lip of the puddingstone ledge, burying the rocks in the foreground, and no doubt leading to removal of a broken-off piece of puddingstone that once lay on the puddingstone ledge. This fragment may be one of many similar fragments now at the bottom of the cliff.

85.
The Puddingstone Ledge
above Nelson's Pond, Looking East
Photograph by the author
(Dec. 1994)

Early Spring. Sun Struggling Through Clouds—twice as large as most of La Farge's other early landscapes—was ambitious and complicated. One sign of the artist's difficulties is found in the color notations now only partly legible under the washy oils laid down in the lower right corner: "mean middle distance plain/ tall tree towards foreground/ and green grass all over/ and, in foreground with a slight slope in foreground/ beyond each green by value." [82] While such annotations often appear on La Farge's watercolors and drawings—including a drawing of the puddingstone ledge viewed from a higher angle and with different weather conditions (fig. 86)—this is the only case in which such color notes appear on an oil painting. That the artist expended time writing out his thoughts about the difficult color and lighting effects—rather than just painting the effects—is a curious anomaly of this work in oil.

A watercolor with a similar subject apparently served as a variation study for the oil painting (fig. 87). Prior to this time, La Farge's use of watercolor had been at best occasional, though by no means lacking in competence. He had mastered English watercolor techniques as a youth, developing a special acquaintance with contemporary English work from a visit in 1857 to the Manchester Art Treasures Exposition, one of the most important exhibitions of the decade.[83] His watercolor study of the puddingstone ledge proficiently exploits the delicate washes of transparent colors common to English watercolors of the period. This is not an exact rendering of the site as seen in the oil—nor did La Farge attempt to depict the smoky effects of haze burning-off. The watercolor served solely as a quick means of learning to sketch the contours of the puddingstone ledge in order to facilitate the later and more serious work in oil.

Early Spring. Sun Struggling Through Clouds must have been executed very early in the spring of 1864—at the very latest before April 14th. It was then that the exorbitant lifestyle of the family—an extravagant house, numerous servants, and a generally pampered existence—caught up with financial reality. La Farge had no real income from painting and, in just over five years, had squandered his considerable inheritance. Thus it came to pass that, hounded by creditors, the family fled their Kay Street domicile amidst financial scandal. A bemused Henry James could only wonder where the "guilty pair" had gone after scurrying away under the cover of night, "none knew whither, leaving prodigious debts behind them, and one silver spoon in the side-board drawer; the servant's wages unpaid, the house dismantled of its richest ornaments. The 'sarcophagus' in the dining-room, the carved chimney piece, the books, the paintings—all the furniture in short had been removed." [84]

86.
John La Farge
Landscape (View of the Puddingstone
Ledge above Nelson's Pond), c. 1864
Charcoal on paper
4 15/16 x 7 3/8 in.
(12.5 x 18.7 cm.)
The Toledo Museum of Art, Toledo,
Gift of Edward Drummond Libbey, 1912

87.
John La Farge
Pastoral Study.—Paradise, Newport, R.I.,
c. 1864
Watercolor and gouache over graphite or
black charcoal on buff fine-wove
watercolor paper
Sheet: 10 x 12 1/4 in. (25.4 x 31.1 cm.);
image: 7 x 9 in. (17.8 x 22.8 cm.)
Yale University Art Gallery,
New Haven, Connecticut,
Bequest of John I.H. Downes '89

CHAPTER IV

A YEAR OF TRANSITION   1864-1865

Roxbury, Massachusetts, then a rural enclave near Boston counting William Morris Hunt among its residents, served as a refuge for the La Farge family during the next year. La Farge made the best of the situation by enrolling in anatomy classes taught by William Rimmer (1816-1879) at the Boston Athenaeum.[85] He also frequented the Studio Building on Summer Street where he revived a friendship with Elihu Vedder (1836-1923), an artist he had met in 1858 at the Tenth Street Studios in New York. In October 1864, Vedder apparently traveled to Newport with La Farge while the latter transacted the sale of the Kay Street house.[86] La Farge received twice what he had paid for the house just three years earlier, a profit that evidently did little more than bail him out of his immediate troubles.

La Farge and Vedder stayed over a month in Newport, probably at the Hessian House. Vedder painted an oil study of a broken-down tree that he dated October 1864 and annotated "Newport,"[87] as Paradise and Middletown often were called at the time. La Farge's 1864 drawing of Bishop Berkeley's Rock with color notes (fig. 88), executed near the end of the ridge bordering the east side of Nelson's Pond, also stems from this stay in the area.

88.
John La Farge
Study at Bishop Berkeley's Rock, Newport,
1864
Graphite on smooth buff paper
3 1/2 x 4 1/8 in. (8.9 x 10.5 cm.)
Museum of Fine Arts, Boston,
Gift of Henry L. Higginson, 1911

In addition to settling the real estate transaction, La Farge and Vedder came to Newport with a specific project in mind. Along with two other artists, they had received a commission to contribute drawings to be made into wood engravings for an edition of *Enoch Arden*, a recent best-selling ballad by Tennyson.[88] The publisher, Ticknor and Fields, was in fierce competition with a rival Boston firm to produce a gift-book edition of *Enoch Arden* for the Christmas season of 1864.[89] The illustrations were due in November, a deadline that Vedder easily met, finishing his work by November 2nd.[90] La Farge, prone to spells of illness and ever the perfectionist, dragged the process out for weeks longer.

To push La Farge along, the wood engraver, Henry Marsh (active 1848-1880), who normally would have received the woodblock drawings by post or courier, came to Paradise to wait for each block to be ready. As soon as La Farge finished a given design, Marsh took the woodblock to cut, pulled a proof, and—once approved by the artist—sent it off to Boston to be published. Word of this unconventional and rather reckless method of working even reached the ears of the Pre-Raphaelite circle in England. Horace Elisha Scudder (1838-1902), an editor for Hurd and Houghton in Boston, wrote to the Pre-Raphaelite art critic William Michael Rossetti (1829-1919) in London: "He [La Farge] did several drawings for *Enoch Arden*—an edition published here by Ticknor and Fields, which was hastily planned and as hastily executed; La Farge, for one, doing some of his work bolstered up in bed, and the blocks put into the press at midnight, fifteen minutes after the engraver had taken his proof."[91]

Both La Farge and Vedder had little actual experience with making illustrations, a failing offset by their extensive knowledge of contemporary European wood engravings. They emulated a style of illustration developed in the 1850s by the Pre-Raphaelites, especially Dante Gabriel Rossetti (1828-1882), brother of William Michael Rossetti, and John Everett Millais (1829-1896), whose illustrations were disseminated widely in 1857 by a vastly popular edition of Tennyson's poems published by Edward Moxon in London.[92] Emphasizing artistically serious compositions, the work of the Pre-Raphaelites formed a stark contrast with the doll-like vignettes of conventional American illustrators.

Enoch Arden tells the tale of a seaman shipwrecked on a desert island. Rescued after many years, he finds his wife happily remarried. Resolving not to make himself known, he dies in silence of a broken heart. La Farge found that Paradise provided an ideal setting for the passages devoted to Enoch's marooning. For *The Island Home* occupied by Enoch and two fellow castaways (fig. 89), La Farge used the Last Valley to illustrate Tennyson's lines.

> There in a seaward-gazing mountain-gorge
> They built, and thatch'd with leaves of palm, a hut,
> Half hut, half native cavern. So the three,
> Set in this Eden plenteousness,
> Dwelt with eternal summer, ill-content.[93]

The illustration reverses the direction of the valley as viewed from along the top of the ridge of Bishop Berkeley's Rock, a mirror image that is a natural outcome of the engraving process. The figures tower over the valley floor, Paradise Pond, and the distant coastline of the Atlantic Ocean. La Farge even included a small building, a peak-roofed edifice that does not logically belong on an uninhabited island, but did exist not far from the mouth of the Last Valley during the 1860s.[94] Subtle linear stylizations and the abrupt, cut-off perspective relate the otherwise realistic rendering to the refined calligraphy of Japanese prints.

Enoch Alone (fig. 90) depicts the protagonist on the brink of madness in the aftermath of the death of his two companions.

> As down the shore he ranged, or all day long
>
> Sat often in the seaward-gazing gorge
>
> A shipwreck'd sailor, waiting for a sail:[95]

The desolate strand occupied by a single cormorant, a spare patch of dune grass, and a solitary protruding rock echoes Enoch's grim plight. La Farge's initial woodblock drawing included a literal representation of Second Beach seen from alongside Purgatory Rocks (fig. 91), much as viewed today (fig. 92). In the final engraving, he eliminated the main mass of rocks—perhaps at the suggestion of the engraver or perhaps by a stroke of inspiration—in favor of a single, isolated rock jutting from the water, a symbol of Enoch's dim prospects.

In *The Solitary* (fig. 93), La Farge returned to the cut-off perspective of a Japanese print to represent Enoch's first encounter with his rescuers, who arrived on the island looking for water.

89.
John La Farge
The Island Home, 1864
Wood engraving on paper
(Engraver: P.F. Annin)
Image: 3 13/16 x 3 1/4 in.
(9.7 x 8.3 cm.)
From Alfred Lord Tennyson, *Enoch Arden*
(Boston: Ticknor and Fields, 1865),
opp. p. 36

90.
John La Farge
Enoch Alone, 1864
Wood engraving on paper
(Engravers: Anthony and Davis)
Image: 3 7/8 x 3 1/4 in.
(9.8 x 8.3 cm.)
From Alfred Lord Tennyson, *Enoch Arden*
(Boston: Ticknor and Fields, 1865),
opp. p. 38

91.
John La Farge
Enoch Alone, 1864
Pen & ink on uncut woodblock
Image: 3 7/8 x 3 1/4 in.
(9.8 x 8.3 cm.)
Destroyed in cutting of the block

92.
Second Beach and Purgatory Rocks,
Looking Southwest
Photograph by the author
(Dec. 1994)

93.
John La Farge
The Solitary, 1864
Wood engraving on paper
(Engravers: Anthony and Davis)
Image: 3 15/16 x 3 3/8 in.
(10 x 8.6 cm.)
From Alfred Lord Tennyson, *Enoch Arden*
(Boston: Ticknor and Fields, 1865),
opp. p. 41

> Downward from his mountain gorge
> Stept the long-hair'd long-bearded solitary,
> Brown, looking hardly human, strangely clad,
> Muttering and mumbling, idiotlike it seem'd.[96]

The figure of Enoch steps out of a path from a ridge of the Paradise Hills. Rather than descend directly onto the ocean beach—something never possible from the hills—Enoch appears to reach the edge of Nelson's Pond, probably at a point once near the small island at the southeast corner of the pond. Meandering paths still lead out of the ridge alongside this part of the pond today, but dredging and diking have obliterated the precise rock formations and banks seen in *The Solitary*.

The ridges of Paradise even served as background for two scenes taking place away from the desert island. For *Philip and Annie in the Wood* (fig. 94), the portrait of Margaret executed in 1863 (see fig. 76) was adapted (reversed by the engraving) to the courtship of Enoch's wife in England after his disappearance.

> Then Philip coming somewhat closer spoke.
> 'Annie, there is one thing upon my mind,
> . . . That he who left you ten long years ago
> Should still be living; well then—let me speak:
> . . . I wish you for my wife.[97]

The background in the earlier painting took a view of part of the shore without woods as seen from the puddingstone ledge above. Here, La Farge showed gnarled trees, rooted in the cliff below, appearing over the ledge. This was the hickory patch of the Sacred Grove, as described by Bancel. Hickories still grow from side of the cliff today, though cloaked in brambles and undergrowth (fig. 95).[98]

94.
John La Farge
Philip and Annie in the Wood, 1864
Wood engraving on paper
(Engravers: Anthony and Davis)
Image: 3 5/16 x 3 15/16 in. (10 x 10 cm.)
From Alfred Lord Tennyson, *Enoch Arden*
(Boston: Ticknor and Fields, 1865),
opp. p. 27

95.
The Sacred Grove and Nelson's Pond,
Looking Down
from the Puddingstone Ledge
Photograph by the author
(Dec. 1994)

Paradise similarly served to inspire a scene occurring after Enoch's rescue from the island. The visionary quality of *Enoch's Supplication* (fig. 96) represents the moment at which Enoch, having returned to his native fishing village in England, makes the wrenching decision to hide his return from his wife.

> Uphold me, Father, in my loneliness
> A little longer! aid me, give me strength
> Not to tell her, never to let her know.[99]

The setting for the scene is the puddingstone ledge above Nelson's Pond, seen from the same angle given in *Early Spring. Sun Struggling Through Clouds.* The dramatic sunbeams coming over the ledge mimic an actual sunrise that might have been seen there.

The *Enoch Arden* wood engravings did much to establish the reputations of both La Farge and Vedder as serious artists. Indeed, the illustrations provided America with its first native application of the serious, artful wood engravings then popular in England and Europe. *Enoch Arden* represented the culmination of La Farge's years of dedicated study of Paradise and its imaginative use in his art, and prefigured his reliance upon Paradise as a source of inspiration for years to come.

96.
John La Farge
Enoch's Supplication, 1864
Wood engraving on paper
(Engravers: Anthony and Davis)
Image: 3 3/16 x 3 11/16 in.
(8.1 x 9.4 cm.)
From Alfred Lord Tennyson, *Enoch Arden*
(Boston: Ticknor and Fields, 1865),
opp. p. 50

Chapter V

LA FARGE IN PARADISE 1865-1871

The La Farges returned to Newport in the spring of 1865 to face the conse-
quences of their precarious finances. Buying another house was out of the question—even renting in downtown Newport at "season" prices was not feasible. Instead, the family began years of frugal living. During the winter, they stayed in
downtown Newport—either with Margaret's mother on Catherine Street or at inex-
pensive rented lodgings.[100] During the "season," they usually moved to Paradise,
but seldom into the same house two years in a row.

A summary of these residences reads like a game of musical chairs. In 1865,
rental lists gave their address as "Stephen Barker's, Paradise road."[101] In 1866,
their address was "Stephen Barker's cottage, near Second Beach"—apparently a
house in the Paradise Hills on the site of the present Orchard Lea.[102] In 1867, they
lived at Grayledge Farm, renting from E. Truman Peckham.[103] In 1869, they were in
the Isaac Barker house.[104] In 1871, they resided at a farm belonging to General John
Alfred Hazard on the west side of Paradise Avenue just above the Maidford River
crossing.[105] In 1868 and 1870, their addresses are less certain. They may have
stayed with Margaret's mother or rented in downtown Newport, but La Farge continued to paint at Paradise, and the family probably spent part of the year there.

"Stephen Barker's, Paradise road"—the first in the succession of temporary
residences—can be identified as the Hessian House (see figs. 39, 44-45). This becomes clear from a later statement by La Farge's daughter, Margaret Angela. In
1938, she noted to her brother Bancel that his birth on September 23, 1865 took
place "on the left" beyond Grayledge Farm in a house "long ago pulled down."[106]
The Hessian House formerly was on the left just past Grayledge Farm and had been
razed in 1898. By contrast, Stephen P. Barker's other house on Paradise Avenue, Sea
Breeze Farm (see figs. 47-48), if built by then, was on the right side of the road and
is still standing.

The move to the Hessian House marked a sort of artistic Renaissance for La
Farge, the start of a golden era of vigorous production in a wide variety of media. By
June 11th, he had already settled into a routine that took him regularly into the
Paradise Hills. On that day, he inscribed a drawing of Bishop Berkeley's Rock viewed
from the west: "Study of Hanging Rock Newport looking like monster" (fig. 97). La
Farge's rendering with the uncanny likeness of a crouching reptile was not as fanciful as it at first appears. From the front of the west ridge of the Last Valley, the
protrusions of the rock merge into this configuration (fig. 98), a phenomenon that
earned it one of its many nicknames, "The Lion's Mouth."

Another drawing dating from June, inscribed simply "line study" (fig. 99), shows
the distant contours of Bishop Berkeley's Rock as seen from what is now the

97.
John La Farge
Study of Hanging Rock, Newport, 1865
Crayon on paper
3 1/4 x 5 1/16 in.
(8.3 x 12.9 cm.)
Private Collection

98.
Bishop Berkeley's Rock, Looking East
Photograph by the author
(Nov. 1994)

99.
John La Farge
*Paradise Rocks, Newport,
from the West*, 1865
Crayon and chalk or charcoal
on smooth buff paper
4 1/4 x 7 1/4 in.
(10.8 x 18.4 cm.)
Museum of Fine Arts, Boston,
Gift of Henry L. Higginson, 1911

100.
Bishop Berkeley's Rock,
Looking East from the
Dike of Nelson's Pond
Photograph by the author
(Nov. 1994)

southwest corner of the dike of Nelson's Pond (fig. 100). La Farge executed a third drawing from the less familiar eastern side of the rock (fig. 101), somewhere along the bank of Gardiner's Pond as seen in works by other artists (see figs. 19, 25), a spot now submerged (fig. 102). He worked in soft crayon or charcoal, emphasizing the massive bulk of the form rather than its linear profile.

101.
John La Farge
*Newport. Bishop Berkeley's Rock.
From the East*, 1865, 1865
Graphite on paper
5 11/16 x 7 15/16 in.
(14.4 x 20.2 cm.)
The Toledo Museum of Art, Toledo,
Gift of Edward Drummond Libbey, 1912

102.
Bishop Berkeley's Rock,
Looking West
from the Puddingstone Ridge
in Gardiner's Pond (Ridge VII)
Photograph by the author
(Nov. 1994)

By contrast to these many studies of the popular Bishop Berkeley's Rock, La Farge virtually ignored Purgatory Chasm, the other site in Paradise that had a similar imaginative appeal to his contemporaries (see fig. 2). Only one unfinished drawing of the chasm (fig. 103) seen from the ledge to its west—now hidden under a small arched bridge—has been located.

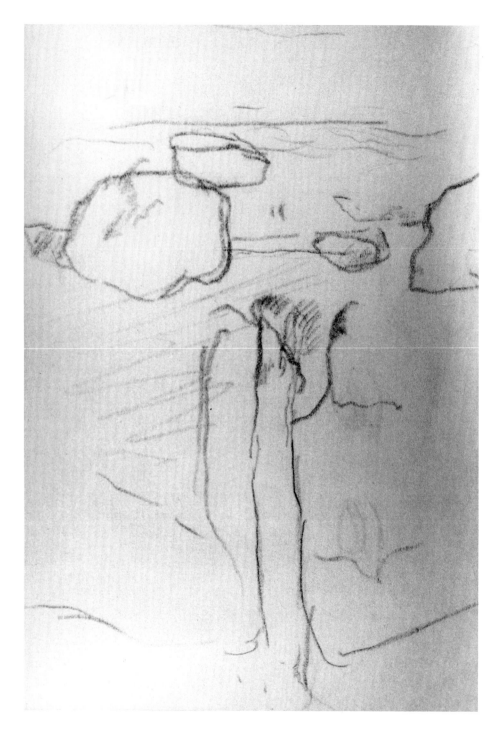

103.
John La Farge
Purgatory Chasm, c. 1865
Graphite on buff laid paper
7 1/4 x 5 in.
(18.4 x 12.7 cm.)
Private Collection
Beneath an arched bridge that today spans Purgatory Chasm is a slate ledge crossed by a tiny rivulet that spills into the depths below. The ledge, easier to reach in La Farge's day than today, was the place from which many of the photographic views of the chasm were made at the time.

OILS AND WATERCOLORS

La Farge's heightened drawing activities after moving to the Hessian House heralded a surge of interest in oil and watercolor painting. Many of the oils are now lost, rendering this part of his work difficult to assess. The most fascinating oil from 1865 that can be located today was painted late in the year as winter commenced, *Snow Storm* (fig. 104).[107]

A forlorn tree, adrift in a white maelstrom, seems more of a mood than the subject of a landscape painting. Henry James lavished praise worth repeating when he saw this picture at the gallery of Doll and Richards in Boston.

> *Another of the landscapes, a small winter-scene, is in some respects one of the most remarkable we have ever seen. It gradually unfolds a nearly endless variety where one would expect, if not monotony, at least closely limited resources. The horizon is placed at about half-way up the picture: all below is a sloping field covered with snow; all above, snowy sky. There is no impossible, conventional multiplication of white specks, to indicate the falling flakes, but the air is nevertheless full of snowiness. It is the spirit of winter which has been seized and depicted, along with all sufficient sensible and visible elements of such a scene. The materials of the picture, however, are almost ludicrously scanty, for description. The only distinct incident in the whole piece is a little tree (a scrub-oak?) in the foreground, with a half dozen or more clusters of brown leaves hanging to it. At some distance behind, is the slightly curving outline of the hill, along which grows a dim, bare wood, blinded with filmy white. The gradations of the blue-gray snowy sky above, and of the field below, are extraordinary. There is discoverable in the snow on the ground an ethereal tinge of pink; so ethereal, that it only appears at instants, in an evanescent way. Between the tree and the wood, there is a tint of green in it. On the left, the snow has been trampled, or else scattered a little by winds, and has become blue. Also a little brook-bed, or other depression in the ground, is faintly marked by blue and violet. It will be seen at once that such a picture as this is not a composition; and yet these little fluctuations in the color of the snow become as important, if we once drop into the mood of the painter, as more striking events in works where the scale of interests is less delicately graduated. Glanced at casually, among other pictures, this small canvas would not attract a moment's attention from the average amateur. Yet, as we let our eyes fall into it, the impression becomes increasingly stronger that there is invention in it, somewhere. That is, we are not altogether sure that Mr. La Farge saw just this, and no more, no less, out of his window, and then sat down to match the different parts, with carefully mixed colors; on the contrary, we get a feeling that he has developed this little reverie of faint tones as a tender fantasy, improvising, as he went on, turns and inflections of hue, as they became necessary to the general harmony.*[108]

The canvas is painted with calligraphic abandon that has been compared to Japanese ink painting. Thick impasted paint, a trademark of the artist's earlier work, here becomes essential in conveying the sensation of weather-filled air. The site is the same puddingstone ledge seen in *Early Spring. Sun Struggling Through Clouds* (see figs. 84-85), viewed here from nearer the edge. The dark jagged shadow entering from the left and crossing to the center of the picture is the distant form of the

105.
The Puddingstone Ledge
above Nelson's Pond,
Looking East
Photograph by the author
(Dec. 1994)

wooded ridge on the other side of Nelson's Pond (fig. 105). This realized, we cannot help but further consider the question that Henry James asked in closing. The ledge was too removed from any known edifice for La Farge to have painted this looking out of a window, and practicality would seem to preclude executing such a picture outdoors during a raging snow storm. We can only ponder to what extent the artist supplemented his observations of the snow storm with imaginative studio work or artistic aids such as photography.

Snow Storm with its bold design and masterful handling appears to represent a new departure in La Farge's work in oil, but it actually stood at the end of an evolution that began the preceding August in a view of *Second Beach and Purgatory Rocks, Newport* (fig. 106).[109] The composition could not be more spare, austere, or lacking in so-called picturesque qualities, consisting solely of a sweep of dark shore, a few waves lapping the beach, and the distant sky and ocean. While quite different from *Snow Storm,* its imaginative, surprising perspective and resourceful handling stem from the same artistic sensibility.

Few people ever see Second Beach in this unusual configuration, with the normally expansive Purgatory Rocks compressed to an insignificant comma shape. But actually only several trees stand in the way today of the same vista from the summit of Peter's Rock (fig. 107). La Farge visited this perch many times, rendering the view from the summit again in an elegant drawing where fanciful clouds dance

104.
John La Farge
Snow Storm, 1865
Oil on panel
16 1/2 x 12 in.
(42 x 30.5 cm.)
Private Collection

106.
John La Farge
*Second Beach and
Purgatory Rocks*,
Newport; 1865
Oil on canvas
12 x 16 in.
(30.5 x 40.6 cm.)
William Vareika Fine Arts,
Newport

107.
Second Beach
and Purgatory Rocks
from Peter's Rock,
Looking South
Photograph by the author
(Nov. 1994)

in sinuous linear precision above the straight lines of the beach below (fig. 108). Several years later, La Farge returned to paint a second version of the subject in oil (see fig. 177).

This site was less difficult for La Farge to reach than might at first be imagined. Peter's Rock was less than half a mile away, as illustrated by a drawing looking north towards Peter's Rock from the vicinity of the Hessian House (fig. 109). The same view today is occluded by trees and bushes growing along the rock walls seen in the drawing.[110] Ascending Peter's Rock also was not as difficult as we might think. Both the north end—now eaten up by the quarry—and a gap just behind the summit have broad, gradual slopes that make climbing a simple matter. La Farge probably ascended through the gap directly behind Paradise Farm, depicted by him in a drawing (fig. 110) that shows its characteristic undulating stone formations (see fig. 10). The climbing roadway shown in La Farge's drawing still exists just behind the present Paradise Farm, though heavily wooded now and providing less ready access to the top of Peter's Rock today than in the past (fig. 111).

Several other oil paintings are known only from descriptions or titles published in early exhibition catalogues. *Girl leaning Against Tree. Study of Blue Sky in Sunlight* was painted sometime during this summer.[111] The late Henry A. La Farge, a grandson of the artist, viewed it around 1934 and penned the only description known of the picture:

108.
John La Farge
Study of Cloud Movement, Newport,
1865
Graphite on smooth off-white paper
6 3/4 x 3 15/16 in. (17.2 x 10 cm.)
Museum of Fine Arts, Boston,
Gift of Major H.L. Higginson, 1911

109.
John La Farge
Landscape (Peter's Rock and
Paradise Farm, Looking Northeast),
1865
Black charcoal or crayon on rice
paper
7 5/8 x 5 3/4 in. (20 x 14.5 cm.)
The Art Museum, Princeton
University, Princeton, New Jersey,
Gift of Frank Jewett Mather, Jr.
In La Farge's day, two farmhouses and a barn stood in front of Peter's Rock, in contrast to the single farmhouse today. At least two of these three edifices can be vaguely made out in this drawing.

110.
John La Farge
The Gap behind Peter's Rock, c. 1865
Black crayon on buff laid paper
5 11/16 x 8 in.
(14.4 x 20.3 cm.)
Yale University Art Gallery,
New Haven, Connecticut,
Gift of Mrs. John Hay Whitney

111.
The Gap behind Peter's Rock,
Looking East
Photograph by the author
(Dec. 1994)

Green pastures, in foreground, and looking out towards sea and rocks. At left, tree, with straight trunk, and dark leaves, strongly accented against sky; below it, is seated a woman in white dress and blue hat. Pond at left, beyond tree; bay and sea in distance, dull greyish-yellow, reflecting cloud. The sky rich in pale blues and greens, with hazy clouds (clearing off after storm).[112]

His words conjure up a clear image of a girl—presumably the artist's wife—seated by Nelson's Pond with Second Beach in the distance. This probably was painted from the pastures just north of the pond, now the lawn of the Gray Craig mansion.

Around 1934, when Henry A. La Farge saw the now-lost *West Wind; Barker's Rocks, Paradise Farm. August*, also painted in 1865,[113] he described it as "Rocky ridge, seen against gray, cloudy sky. Green field in foreground, with cow grazing."[114] Only the title is known of what must have been a similar view painted in 1865: *Evening; Barker's Rocks, Paradise Farm, September.*[115] From these titles, we can infer that both of these pictures represented a dramatic puddingstone formation that surges from the ridge just south of Peter's Rock (fig. 112). The location of this puddingstone directly behind Stephen P. Barker's Sea Breeze Farm explains why La Farge routinely called this part of the ridge "Barker's Rocks." He also depicted the site in a watercolor to which he assigned two different titles: *Paradise Rocks— Study of Orchard and Rocks on the Barker Farm, Paradise, Newport, R.I.*[116] and *Paradise Rocks, Newport, R.I. Faint Sunlight.*[117] This watercolor, known only from a poor photograph that cannot be illustrated here, also shows that an elaborate network of walls, along with a white-fenced paddock and a small, barn-like building, once occupied the land just in front of the ridge. The outline of these structures still remains under the lawn of a modern house just behind Sea Breeze Farm (fig. 113).

112.
The Puddingstone Ridge
behind Sea Breeze Farm,
Looking East
Photograph by the author
(Dec. 1994)

113.
Yard behind Sea Breeze Farm,
Looking East
Photograph by the author
(Dec. 1994)

This part of the ridge behind Peter's Rock abruptly descends underground at the end of a series of stepped gradations, today just behind a new home dubbed "Paradise Ledge," seen in the background of the photograph. La Farge depicted this jagged rock formation in a close-up drawing executed from the east side of the ridge (fig. 114), a site now found next to the point where a private road passes into the Gray Craig estate (fig. 115).

Much of what we know today about La Farge's watercolors dating from the 1860s is recent knowledge, culled since 1989 when a cache of over twenty watercolors turned up unexpectedly in a private collection.[118] Just how one family came to own these works is a mystery given how few other watercolors from the period have come to light. We can only surmise that their ancestors exchanged food or services with La Farge for the watercolors at a time of particular financial need, or that there is some as-yet unknown connection directly to the La Farges through family or social ties.

114.
John La Farge
Puddingstone "Steps" behind Sea Breeze Farm, 1865
Black crayon on mulberry paper
5 11/16 x 7 7/8 in.
(14.4 x 20 cm.)
Private Collection

115.
Puddingstone "Steps" behind Sea Breeze Farm, Looking West
Photograph by the author
(Dec. 1994)

116.
John La Farge
Margaret Mason Perry La Farge,
c. 1865
Watercolor and gouache over graphite
on ivory watercolor paper
18 3/4 x 13 in.
(47.7 x 33 cm.)
Private Collection

The most impressive watercolor shows Margaret during her pregnancy with their third child, Bancel (fig. 116), effectively dating the works as a group to the year around his birth in the fall of 1865. Few watercolorists attain the mastery of line, color, and psychological mood seen in this sensuous portrait. Garbed in a loosely-fitting Japanese robe, Margaret sits against a wall in what must be the Hessian House, where Bancel was born on September 23, 1865. With an open book dropped onto her lap, her gaze is wistful and evocative.

Skillful handling of richly-colored watercolor washes also enlivens La Farge's landscapes painted around 1865. Each paean of light, washy color, and delicate line comes across as a fresh and direct glimpse of Paradise as it existed at the time.

A palette of blue and mauve, punctuated by golden tints of autumn on foliage, dominates a depiction of Peter's Rock seen from the west (fig. 117). The perspective is across the fields from just north of the farmhouse of the present Paradise Farm. Today, only a surfeit of foliage and the blunted northern end of Peter's Rock change the view (fig. 118).

117.
John La Farge
Peter's Rock from Paradise Farm,
c. 1865
Watercolor over graphite
on watercolor paper
9 1/2 x 17 3/4 in.
(24.1 x 45.1 cm.)
Private Collection

118.
Peter's Rock from Paradise Farm,
Looking East
Photograph by the author
(Nov. 1994)
*The original Peckham Brothers Quarry
is on the left, where the rock
terminates abruptly.*

The ridge of Peter's Rock also forms the background for the study of a large apple tree in a field, probably painted in the spring of 1866 along with other views of blooming trees (fig. 119). In the calligraphic handling of the distant low greenery or the shadow cast by the tree, La Farge's love of oriental ink painting can be sensed. He greatly admired the nineteenth-century Japanese artist Hokusai (Katushika Hokusai, 1760-1849), whose deft touch and pronounced realism found a receptive audience in the West after 1860. La Farge saw books of Hokusai's color prints in 1856 when he first visited Paris.[119] By 1860, other prints had come to him through his wife, whose great-uncle Matthew Calbraith Perry (1794-1858) had opened Japan to Western trade in 1854. La Farge's collecting spree with John Chandler Bancroft around 1863 further augmented his access to Japanese prints and contributed to the animated calligraphy and colorful washes used in these watercolors.

The topography shown in another view across the fields with an orchard in bloom (fig. 120) is too unspecific to permit identification of the precise location. The lay of the land suggests the fields along the west side of Peter's Rock. Another watercolor with a profusion of young birch or maple trees, a flowering apple tree, and a fir surrounding a well also does not betray a specific site (fig. 121). Similar trees and a well now grace the yard of Grayledge Farm, but the resemblance may be coincidental.

An animated sketch of rocks spilling onto the forest floor (fig. 122) depicts a rock formation beside an old path that descends to the Sacred Grove from the puddingstone ledge just past the end of Paradise Court (fig. 123). The rocks are now largely buried beneath a fallen tree and other debris deposited by nature in the past century. Such a picture reminds us of how Paradise can take on the aspect of the Forest of Fontainebleau, the favorite haunt of many of the French realist landscape painters that La Farge admired and sought to emulate.

Rock walls, verdant pastures, and expanses of placid blue water make up a view of the Large and Small Basins from atop the puddingstone ledge on the west side of Nelson's Pond (fig. 124). The view today is much the same, especially in dry weather (fig. 125)—but the sense of a well-ordered and hand-hewn rural existence is gone. The foreground pasture in the picture, replete with its rolling meadows and ribbons of stone wall, succumbed to the dredging and flooding of the Newport Water Works after 1882.

This watercolor reminds us that farmlands once extended alongside and past Nelson's Pond, nearly to Second Beach. It is hard today to visualize sheep grazing along what is now Sachuest Point Road, but a summary sketch by La Farge testifies to this typical occurrence in days past (fig. 126). Equally revealing is a view of the same area showing a man plowing, silhouetted against a puddingstone protrusion (fig. 127). All of these features fill a roughly contemporaneous view of Bishop Berkeley's Rock by James A. Suydam (1819-1865) (fig. 128), including the puddingstone protrusion visible at the far left in his picture. Suydam greatly exaggerated the proportions of the ridges[120]—and, one suspects, the vastness of the farms, the rigorous lines of the stone walls, and the profusion of working farmers with grazing cattle.

119.
John La Farge
A Tree at Paradise, near Peter's Rock,
c. 1865
Watercolor over graphite
on watercolor paper
Image: 11 x 15 in.
(27.9 x 38.1 cm.)
William Vareika Fine Arts, Newport

120.
John La Farge
An Orchard in Bloom at Paradise,
c. 1865
Watercolor over graphite
on watercolor paper
7 x 13 3/4 in.
(17.8 x 34.9 cm.)
Private Collection

121.
John La Farge
Flowering Tree and Well at Paradise,
c. 1865
Watercolor over graphite
on watercolor paper
9 1/2 x 15 1/2 in.
(24.1 x 39.4 cm.)
Private Collection

122.
John La Farge
Rocks by the Path in the Sacred Grove at Paradise, c. 1865
Watercolor over graphite
on watercolor paper
16 x 24 in. (40.7 x 61 cm.)
William Vareika Fine Arts, Newport

123.
Rocks by the Path in the Sacred Grove at Paradise, Looking West
Photograph by the author
(Jan. 1995)
The rock formation seen in the watercolor is next to the path that descends from the end of Paradise Court. Today, the rocks are covered with brambles, fallen trees, and other debris, all but hiding the formation.

124.
John La Farge
Nelson's Pond from the Puddingstone
Ledge, at Paradise, c. 1865
Watercolor over graphite
on watercolor paper
10 1/2 x 17 1/2 in. (26.7 x 44.5 cm.)
Charles A. Dana III

125.
Nelson's Pond from the Puddingstone Ledge,
Looking East
Photograph by the author
(Dec. 1994)
This photograph, taken during a dry spell,
shows the Large and Small Basins much as in
La Farge's watercolor. Today, in wet weather,
the pointed end of the peninsula is submerged,
making the distinction between the Large and
Small Basins less definitive.

126.
John La Farge
Second Beach and Bishop Berkeley's Rock, Sheep Grazing, c. 1865
Graphite on buff laid paper
5 x 7 1/4 in. (12.7 x 18.4 cm.)
Private Collection

127.
John La Farge
Landscape, Newport, 1865
(Near Nelson's Pond, Man Plowing), 1865
Black chalk or charcoal on mulberry paper
5 3/4 x 8 1/16 in. (14.6 x 21.9 cm.)
Avery Architectural and Fine Arts Library,
Columbia University, New York,
Purchase, 1950
The once-prominent puddingstone rock formation seen on the left is now buried beneath the southernmost corner of the dike of Nelson's Pond.

128.
James A. Suydam (1819-1865)
Paradise Rocks, 1860 or 1865
Oil on canvas
25 1/8 x 45 1/8 in. (63.9 x 114.7 cm.)
National Academy of Design, New York,
Bequest of the artist to the Suydam
Collection, 1865

La Farge also painted the "east side" of Paradise along Third Beach Road, the area grievously changed by the expansion of Gardiner's Pond after 1889. The former Paradise Brook, now the Maidford River, fed and exited the pond through a meandering river bed that flowed out to the Sakonnet River. This crossed under a bridge on Third Beach Road (see fig. 23) at the same place occupied by a road overpass today. La Farge's view looking north toward the distant ridges past the winding river captures the pastoral qualities of this expansive scene (fig. 129). But the dike along the south side of Gardiner's Pond, combined with the rerouting of the brook and changes to marshlands, have obliterated the spot from which La Farge painted.

The same tall trees in this view appear again, seen from further in the distance, on the left in a drawing (fig. 130) that looks up the river from the old bridge on Third Beach Road (see fig. 23). This study helped to identify the smallest oil sketch known by La Farge, painted from the area seen at the middle of the drawing (fig. 131). This miniature oil is all the more remarkable for suggesting so much of the topography in such a tiny space, and with such great economy of means.

From just above where Third Beach Road now ends in an unpaved parking lot, La Farge painted a view looking north toward what later became Indian Avenue (fig. 132). Third Beach Road then curved gently along the beachfront to meet up with the brook in the distance. Today, this same view along sand dunes encounters a hangar-like building just before the road passes over the river (fig. 133).

Contrasting with these sumptuous, wetly painted watercolors that all seem to date from around 1865 are five watercolors handled quite differently. In each, La Farge painted with a minimalist touch, barely wetting the paper. De-emphasizing dramatic topographical features, the distant horizon dividing the compositions in half becomes a point of special focus in each work. Earth tones of brown, yellow, and green dominate, with the blue of a pond or the ocean serving as the contrasting key in these simple symphonies of muted color.

A view down Third Beach looking south towards Flint Point (fig. 134) was painted from beside Third Beach Road just north of the road overpass. The water to the right is run-off from a storm near a low-lying point where even today the road is submerged for days after heavy rain. This propensity for flooding earned Third Beach Road the nickname "Wet Lane" in the nineteenth century.[121]

From the peninsula jutting into Nelson's Pond, near what is now the end of the lawn of the Gray Craig estate, La Farge painted a view looking southwest along the Large Basin (fig. 135). The distant shore, vaguely defined, embraces the Sacred Grove, the puddingstone cliff on the west side of the pond, and the shadows of ridges leading to the Purgatory Rocks. A few ships and wharf pilings explain the remnants of wharves found today at several locations in the pond, where boating is now prohibited. From rusty red to muted lime green, the washes of color were blurred and blotted while wet to dispel linear contours and evoke the mood of a misty morning, when the sun has not yet burnt a light fog off the water.

The barely-joined land masses that make this picture difficult to fathom contribute to a similar ambiguity in a view painted from the pastures of Barker's Farm, just above and to the east of the peninsula (fig. 136). To the left is the towering ridge that forms a "canyon" along the east side of the Gray Craig mansion.

129.
John La Farge
Tall Trees along Paradise Brook,
near the Bridge on Third Beach Road,
c. 1865
Watercolor over graphite
on watercolor paper
14 x 10 in. (35.6 x 25.4 cm.)
William Vareika Fine Arts, Newport
The view looks towards the north, in part
showing the ridge of Bishop Berkeley's Rock.

130.
John La Farge
Paradise Brook from the Bridge
on Third Beach Road,
c. 1865
Graphite on thin buff wove paper
6 7/16 x 3 7/8 in. (16.4 x 9.8 cm.)
Yale University Art Gallery,
New Haven, Connecticut,
Gift of Mrs. John Hay Whitney
The trees at the left are the same trees seen in the
watercolor of tall trees by the brook. The pool in
the foreground was just before the old bridge on
Third Beach Road, suggesting that La Farge stood
on the bridge to make this drawing.

131.
John La Farge
Paradise Brook near the Bridge
on Third Beach Road, c. 1865
Oil on canvasboard
1 7/8 x 2 3/4 in. (4.5 x 6.6 cm.)
William Vareika Fine Arts,
Newport
In the background, the light purple
ridge is the rise beneath St.
George's School, then a simple
stretch of elevated pasture.

132.
John La Farge
On Third Beach Road at Paradise, c. 1865
Watercolor and gouache
over graphite on paper
11 x 13 1/4 in. (27.9 x 33.6 cm.)
William Vareika Fine Arts, Newport

133.
On Third Beach Road, Looking North
Photograph by the author
(Nov. 1994)

134.
John La Farge
Third Beach and Flint Point at Paradise,
c. 1875
Watercolor over graphite on heavy
off-white Whatman paper
9 1/4 x 13 1/2 in. (23.5 x 34.3 cm.)
William Vareika Fine Arts, Newport
*The view is from near the road by the
present Third Beach Club.*

135.
John La Farge
Nelson's Pond from the Peninsula, Paradise,
c. 1875
Watercolor over graphite on heavy
off-white Whatman paper
Sheet: 9 1/4 x 19 1/2 in.
(23.1 x 49.5 cm.)
William Vareika Fine Arts, Newport

136.
John La Farge
Paradise Farm and Nelson's Pond,
near the "Canyon,"
c. 1875
Watercolor over graphite on heavy
off-white Whatman paper
12 1/4 x 18 15/16 in.
(31.1 x 48.1 cm.)
William Vareika Fine Arts,
Newport

137.
John La Farge
Paradise Farm and Nelson's Pond,
near the Sacred Grove, c. 1865
Oil on sketchbook cover
3 1/2 x 5 1/2 in. (8.9 x 13.9 cm.)
William Vareika Fine Arts, Newport

138.
Nelson's Pond from the Lawn
of Gray Craig,
Looking Southeast
Photograph by the author
(Jan. 1995)

Straight ahead, looking over a stone wall and crotched fence, is the pond, leading the eye back to the distant Sachuest Bay. The colors here are so subdued as to be nearly monochromatic. As a digression, it is interesting to compare a miniature oil on a sketchbook cover, painted from the west side of the same pasture, near the edge of the Sacred Grove (fig. 137). The colors in this case are very intense, and paint is applied thickly, but the ambiguities of merging masses of water and sky are much the same. Were it not for a little rivulet seen in the painting that still zigzags down the lawn of Gray Craig, despite a century of landscaping (fig. 138), we would have no way to comprehend the precise subject.

Two studies of the Sakonnet River viewed from near Flint Point, just behind Third Beach, show the distant shore of Little Compton. Both are painted sparingly, with gray, soft green, and rusty brown washes contrasting with the varied blues of the bodies of water. The first looks over a wooden fence and a small pond (fig. 139), the second through the eaves of a strangely timbered building to a glimpse of the small pond beyond the same wooden fence (fig. 140). The building may have been some sort of ephemeral boat house used for storing equipment and boats, or else a farm structure. The small pond is still there, just east of the unpaved parking lot for Third Beach, but now completely engulfed in a cattail marsh and all but invisible. The pond is near the base of an unusual ridge descending from Flint Point that La Farge studied in a drawing and painting at another time (see figs. 186-188). Today, this area cannot be approached on foot, but the view of the river is still similar from Third Beach, just in front of the cattail marsh (fig. 141).

Dating the five watercolors is difficult, but their distinctive style suggests that they belong to a different period from the more sumptuous watercolors. The only real clue lies in the wooden fence seen in the last two pictures. This appears to be a continuation of a fence seen in several nearly identical views of Second Beach painted by Worthington Whittredge (1820-1910) (fig. 142). The fence was erected sometime between 1865, when Whittredge painted a view without the fence, and 1880, when it appears for the first time in his works.[122] The fence is also missing from all of La Farge's views of the Last Valley or Bishop Berkeley's Rock painted in 1868 or 1869, suggesting that the fence dated from after 1870.

Research has failed to elucidate just when or why the fence was erected, but it cannot be coincidental that the property line of General John Alfred Hazard skirted Bishop Berkeley's Rock to the north and Third Beach to the east, the places that the fence appeared. Beginning in 1872, Hazard's land holdings became the subject of great contention when Eugene Sturtevant sought the right to have Hanging Rocks Road cut across his property. In 1876, the action of the Middletown Town Council to approve the proposed road caused the matter to escalate from a personal dispute to a civil legal matter. The fence seems to have accompanied the growing tension that led to a court battle that lasted for three years beyond Hazard's death in 1880. These watercolors may therefore date from the mid-1870s, and even though the La Farges began living permanently in downtown Newport during the summer of 1873, the artist continued to come to Paradise regularly. Oliver recalled: "For several years, we regularly drove to Barker's on Saturdays and Sundays, in an old fashioned wide embracing phaeton, the rumble of which sometimes contained two or even three children."[123]

139.
John La Farge
*The Sakonnet River near
Flint Point,
View over Fence*, c. 1875
Watercolor over graphite
on heavy off-white
Whatman paper
8 3/8 x 19 in.
(21.4 x 48.3 cm.)
William Vareika Fine Arts,
Newport

140.
John La Farge
*The Sakonnet River
near Flint Point,
View from Hut*, c. 1875
Watercolor over graphite
on heavy off-white
Whatman paper
8 1/2 x 10 3/4 in.
(21.5 x 27.4 cm.)
William Vareika Fine Arts,
Newport
*This strange hut and crotched
fence along Third Beach
probably belonged to General
John Alfred Hazard.*

94

141.
The Sakonnet River from Third Beach
near Flint Point, Looking Northeast
Photograph by the author
(Jan. 1995)

142.
Worthington Whittredge
(1820-1910)
Second Beach, 1900
Oil on canvas
14 3/4 x 21 3/4 in. (37.5 x 55.3 cm.)
Bowdoin College Museum of Art,
Brunswick, Maine

CRONIES AND COLLEAGUES

During his years of living at Paradise, La Farge was relatively isolated. Much of the time he chose to work alone—or restricted his companions to members of the immediate family. But Paradise was hardly cut off from the world, and for decades before La Farge's arrival, it had been a sort of recreational haven for Newporters. Formal and informal expeditions took place all the time. Much of this activity was codified by the "Town and Country Club," the brainchild of Julia Ward Howe (1819-1910), authoress of *The Battle Hymn of the Republic* (fig. 143). She organized "picnics with a purpose" and amateur scientific excursions to Paradise during the early 1870s.[124]

The traffic may have been less distinguished in the 1860s, but artists were among those who made the three-mile trek from downtown Newport to Paradise routinely. La Farge no doubt knew Hudson River School painters like John Frederick Kensett (see fig. 58) and Worthington Whittredge (see fig. 142), both working near Second Beach around 1865. For at least a couple of years, La Farge also was friendly with David Maitland Armstrong (fig. 144), then still practicing law with little thought of an art career. Their interchanges took place in the company of John Neilson, who summered at Paradise, for several seasons at Grayledge Farm. Armstrong, who as an aside aptly observed that "La Farge inherited a good deal of money, but he never could keep money," recalled:

> La Farge was painting in this same neighborhood when I first met him many years ago. This occurred around 1865, while I was staying at my brother-in-law John Neilson's house at Purgatory, and he was boarding at Peckham's near by and working on some of his best landscapes. La Farge used to come over to John Neilson's a good deal that summer to play croquet. John was the best croquet player I've ever seen—it was a scientific game in those days—and La Farge was absolutely the worst. We used to call him "Johnny Croquet."[125]

Armstrong actually meant the summer of 1867 when the La Farges rented Grayledge Farm from E. Truman Peckham. It was also then, and not before, that La Farge could have been found working on "his best landscapes," *Paradise Valley* (see fig. 154) and *The Last Valley* (see fig. 167).

La Farge found time not only to play croquet badly, but also to fish with similar disregard for the success of the venture. Armstrong recounted La Farge's preoccupation with his art when he should have kept his mind on matters at hand.

> Old Peckham, a regular Down East Yankee, long, thin, with an inimitable drawl and a lot of dry humor, used to take La Farge and John Neilson out fishing. John, who liked a good story, said that one day when they were fishing with drop lines and sport was dull, as La Farge's line floated close to Peckham—La Farge all the time intent on some distant effect of atmosphere or light—Peckham gave the line a tremendous pull. Suddenly recalled to mundane things, La Farge pulled in his line in great excitement and could not understand why there was nothing on it. John said that for years after La Farge used to speak of that whale he almost caught.[126]

143.
Alman & Co.
Julia Ward Howe, 1895
Photogravure from a
photograph taken at Newport
on July 25, 1895
4 3/4 x 3/16 in. (11.8 x 7.7 cm.)
From Laura E. Richards and Maud Howe
Elliott, *Julia Ward Howe 1819-1910*
(Boston and New York: Houghton Mifflin
Company, 1916), vol. 2, frontispiece

144.
Gessford Studios
David Maitland Armstrong, c. 1900
Photograph
5 1/2 x 3 7/8 in. (13.9 x 9.8 cm.)
From David Maitland Armstrong,
*Day Before Yesterday: Reminiscences
of a Varied Life* (New York:
Charles Scribner's Sons, 1920),
frontispiece

145.
David Maitland Armstrong
(1836-1918)
Purgatory Chasm, c. 1873
Oil on canvas
16 x 6 1/4 in.
(40.6 x 15.9 cm.)
The Preservation Society
of Newport County, Newport,
Collection at Kingscote

Armstrong never spoke of artistic exchanges with La Farge, and there may not have been any at this time since Armstrong did not become a serious artist until after he went to Rome as a general consul for the Papal States in 1867. But his rendering of Purgatory Chasm dating from around 1873 (fig. 145) is a striking evocation of La Farge's work of the 1860s in scale, support, composition, and handling. On the other hand, Armstrong's view of the Last Valley dated 1877 (fig. 146) differs dramatically from La Farge's version of the same subject (see fig. 167). Whereas La Farge sought great fidelity to the natural view, Armstrong transformed the valley into a hybrid blend of its actual topography and the kind of rolling, orange-hued hills found in the Umbrian countryside.

Many questions surround a painting expedition to the Paradise Hills that La Farge undertook with two other artists around this time, recalled by him late in life while lecturing on art at the Metropolitan Museum of Art in New York. "I remember myself, years ago, sketching with two well-

146.
David Maitland Armstrong
(1836-1918)
The Last Valley—Paradise Rocks,
1877
Oil on canvas
13 1/4 x 28 1/2 in.
(33.3 x 71 cm.)
William Vareika Fine Arts, Newport

known men, artists who were great friends, great cronies, asking each other all the the time how to do this and how to do that."[127] He never identified these "cronies" by name, but logic suggests they must have been Elihu Vedder (fig. 147) and Winslow Homer (fig. 148) (1834-1910). Both men had been La Farge's close friends since they met at the Tenth Street Studio Building in 1858, and the three had spent time together in 1864 while La Farge resided near Boston. During the summer of 1865, Vedder was in Newport prior to several years of study abroad,[128] while Homer was "dividing his summer between Newport and Saratoga."[129] In August, Homer also published an illustration depicting a slice of Newport society life in *Harper's Weekly* (fig. 149).[130]

147.
Benjamin Kimball
Elihu Vedder, c. 1910
Photogravure from a photograph
5 1/2 x 4 3/8 in. (13.6 x 10.9 cm.)
From Elihu Vedder, *The Digressions of V* (Boston and New York: Houghton Mifflin Company, 1910), frontispiece

148.
Unidentified Photographer
An Impromptu Lecture on Art: Winslow Homer and his Man-Servant Lewis, c. 1900
Photogravure from a photograph
2 9/16 x 4 1/16 in. (6.6 x 10.4 cm.)
From William Howe Downes, *The Life and Works of Winslow Homer* (Boston and New York: Houghton Mifflin Company, 1911), ill. opp. p. 20

149.
Winslow Homer
(1834-1910)
Our Watering Places— The Empty Sleeve at Newport, 1865
Wood engraving on paper
(Unidentified Engraver)
9 1/4 x 13 3/4 in. (23.5 x 34.9 cm.)
From *Harper's Weekly*, vol. 9
(26 Aug. 1865), p. 1,
Newport Art Museum, Newport

The expedition evolved into the kind of lesson in perception that became popular among painters in Europe during the nineteenth century. Two or more artists, painting the same scene in each other's company, would arrive at radically different pictorial results. The differences pointed out the vagaries of perception and that all truth to nature is relative. In this case, each artist produced a "twenty-minute sketch" from a high vantage point overlooking hills and water. La Farge's version of the subject (fig. 150) is rapidly blocked-in and handled with great abandon. To appreciate the ambiguous scene that he thus presented, we can turn to a picture signed "W. Homer" that has been assigned at times to La Farge but most likely is by Homer (fig. 151).[131] This gives a readily identifiable view looking southwest towards Easton's Point and Newport, seen from the heights of the western ridge of the Last Valley (fig. 152). With this model in mind, the much sketchier version can be deciphered as the same view.

A corresponding picture by Vedder has yet to be located, but *Paradise Farm, Levity Place, Rhode Island* (fig. 153) is similar in many respects.[132] This view looks in the opposite direction, towards the Sakonnet River, and the vantage point is from an elevation that is now on Gray Craig Trail in the Norman Bird Sanctuary, a long hike from the place where the pictures by La Farge and Homer were painted. While this is not the "twenty-minute sketch" painted in the company of two old cronies, it does treat a similar subject in a style and technique that can be related to the works by the other artists.

Without belaboring the questions of identifying the pictures or their authors, the importance of the expedition lay in its lessons on seeing. La Farge concluded that all art is prejudiced by uncontrollable predilections, and that the artist can never be truly objective. His attempts at realism, however intent and sincere, always start from a subjective and personal basis that cannot be changed. This brought La Farge to a deeper understanding of the impossibility of ever perceiving what is real.

> *Of course there is no absolute nature; as with each slight shifting of the eye, involuntarily we focus more or less distinctly some part to the prejudice of others.*[13]

The artist paints as he sees, through his subjective experience and personal expression. "If you ever know how to paint well, and pass beyond the position of the student who has not yet learned to use his hands as an expression of the memories of his brain, you will always give to nature, that is to say, what is outside you, the character of the lens through which you see it—which is yourself."[134] In the wake of this painting expedition, La Farge embarked on projects that relied upon his ability both to see and to paint. His years of independent and joint study of nature came together in several ambitious large-scale oils of Paradise.

150.
John La Farge
Newport; From Paradise Rocks,
c. 1865
Oil on panel
8 7/8 x 9 3/8 in.
(22.5 x 23.9 cm.)
U.S. Department of the Interior,
National Park Service, Saint-Gaudens
National Historic Site, Cornish,
New Hampshire, Gift of
Mr. & Mrs. Augustus Saint-Gaudens II

151.
Attributed to Winslow Homer
(1834-1910)
*Newport from Paradise Rocks,
Looking West*, c. 1865
Oil on canvas
12 x 20 in.
(30.5 x 50.8 cm.)
Private Collection

152.
From Paradise Rocks, Looking West
Photograph by the author (Nov. 1994)
*The view is from Ridge V, the
west wall of the Last Valley.*

153.
Elihu Vedder
(1836-1923)
*Paradise Farm, Levity Place,
Rhode Island*, c. 1865
Oil on canvas
4 3/4 x 11 7/16 in. (12.1 x 29.1 cm.)
Davison Art Center, Wesleyan
University, Middletown, Connecticut,
Gift of the American Academy of
Arts and Letters, 1955
*The view looks east towards the
Sakonnet River, with the shore of
Little Compton in the far distance.
Third Beach and Flint Point are near
the center of the picture in the middle
distance. The farm buildings at the
left belong to the Paradise Farm now
on Third Beach Road. The picture was
painted from an elevation of slate and
puddingstone now on the Gray Craig
Trail of the Norman Bird Sanctuary.*

Not long after the Bancel's birth in September 1865, La Farge became seriously ill with what generally is believed to have been lead poisoning. Temporary hand paralysis was one symptom of this debilitating episode, which struck suddenly and weakened the artist's health for at least two years.[135] Fortunately, the worst was over by the spring of 1866 when the paralysis lifted enough for the artist to begin to paint again.[136] Around this time, he conceived of a major landscape painting that came to be known as *Paradise Valley* (fig. 154).[137]

La Farge regarded *Paradise Valley* as a means to advance his stalled career. His oil paintings had up to this time enjoyed at best modest success with critics. The *Enoch Arden* illustrations did more to promote his reputation, but not as a painter. La Farge also had tried and failed to make his name as a decorator. For the Eastlake-styled dining room of a prosperous Boston builder, he completed three of six proposed decorative still-life panels before the paralysis stopped his work and cost him the commission.[138] After his recovery, the decision to turn to serious easel painting was a logical resuscitation of such ambitions, channeled in a new direction.

This constructive idea did not lead directly to *Paradise Valley* as we now see it. The large canvas on which it is painted contains an underdrawing, visible only by X-ray (fig. 155), of a *Mother and Child* composition best known from a watercolor produced at a much later time (fig. 156).[139] This abandoned image underscored La Farge's devotion to his wife and newborn son Bancel, the proposed subjects. The theme reflected the secularized Madonnas, using family members as models, that the British Pre-Raphaelites had made into a special genre during the 1850s. Like these other artists, La Farge sought to give the subject personal meaning, not only by including his wife and new child, but also by depicting them in the pasture of Barker's Paradise Farm before a distant vista that included Nelson's Pond and the Purgatory Rocks.[140] La Farge gave up this idea for reasons never stated, but was unwilling to discard a good canvas and simply painted over the figures to make a pasture the central subject.

The title *Paradise Valley*, like the name "Paradise Farm," creates inevitable confusion. There are many valleys in Paradise, none exclusively and universally identified as "Paradise Valley" today. In recent years, the west side of Paradise Avenue just south of Prospect Avenue has been turned into "Paradise Valley Park." In the nineteenth century, even the Last Valley at times was called "Paradise Valley." Perhaps the only correct use of the name is the most generalized: allowing "Paradise Valley" to refer to everything between the ridge of St. George's School and the Sakonnet River. In other words, all of Paradise could be referred to as Paradise Valley. Reportedly, Isaac Barker of Revolutionary fame implied as much when he applied the term "Paradise Valley" to the sweep of land reaching all the way from Four Corners (Turner and Wyatt Roads, a mile north of Green End Avenue) to the ocean.

Paradise Valley was named by Isaac Barker, who figured so conspicuously in the revolution as a spy. This valley begins at or near the Methodist church [at Turner and Wyatt Roads] and runs southward into Purgatory.[141]

Nevertheless, La Farge did have his own definition in mind when deciding to call his large canvas *Paradise Valley*, already noted in Bancel's descriptions of his father's affection for the valley that begins just to the east of Peter's Rock. Bancel identified this area specifically as the "rising Northern slope to the 'Clumps', from where my father painted his famous 'Paradise Valley.'"[142] David Maitland Armstrong luckily clarified that the "Clumps" were "clumps of gnarled cedar-trees" visible in the far distance of *Paradise Valley.*[143] We have O.H.P. Belmont to thank for mapping the valley as "Gray Crag Park" in 1892, showing many of the exact walls and other topographical features seen in La Farge's painting (map 5). Paradise Valley as understood by La Farge thus embraced all of his favorite painting spots: the pastures and banks of Nelson's Pond, the woods of the Sacred Grove, and the puddingstone eruptions and cliffs laying between the ridge of Peter's Rock and the less well-defined ridge to its east.

This "rising Northern slope" now begins with the lawn of the Gray Craig mansion and runs up the valley interrupted by buildings, trees, a road, and finally the Peckham Brothers Quarry. Today the place where La Farge set up his easel lies somewhere in the quarry, at a point no longer accessible by foot. A view from the heights just behind the quarry (fig. 157) gives the characteristic profile of ridges and general lay of the land seen in the painting. Foliage now obscures Nelson's Pond and Purgatory Rocks, as well as the puddingstone formations lying just beyond the bushes that cross the middle distance.

La Farge was proud of his fidelity in rendering what was then a quintessential pastoral scene. "The only artificial or 'art' point introduced was the placing of the lambs and sheep which creatures of the eye were characteristic of the place," the artist noted. "It was a sheep pasture."[144] Despite this contrivance and the occasional tendency of critics to interpret the lambs as religious symbols, La Farge sought to record rather than manipulate this topography.

My programme was to paint from nature a portrait . . . which was both novel and absolutely "everydayish." I therefore had to choose a special moment of the day and a special kind of weather at a special time of year when I could count upon the same effect being repeated. Hence, naturally, I painted just where I lived, within a few hundred yards from my house. I chose a number of difficulties in combination so as to test my acquaintance with them both in theory of color and light and in the practice of painting itself. I chose a time of the day when the shadows falling away from me would not help me to model or draw, or make ready arrangements for me, as in the concoction of pictures usually; and I also took a fairly covered day, which would still increase the absence of shadows. That would be thoroughly commonplace, as we see it all the time, and yet we know it to be beautiful, like most of the "out-of-doors."[145]

Since La Farge painted "a few hundred yards from my house," and since he said that he began *Paradise Valley* during the summer of 1866, the house described in rental lists for that year as "Stephen Barker's cottage, near 2nd Beach" must have

154.
John La Farge
Paradise Valley
(New England Pasture Land),
1866-68
Oil on canvas
33 1/8 x 42 1/2 in. (84.1 x 107.9 cm.)
Private Collection

155.
John La Farge
Underpainting of *Paradise Valley*, c. 1866
X-ray photograph
Conservation Laboratory, Fogg Art
Museum, Harvard University Art
Museums, Cambridge, Massachusetts

156.
John La Farge
Mother and Child, c. 1888
Watercolor and gouache over graphite on
off-white watercolor paper
7 x 7 in. (17.8 x 17.8 cm.)
William Vareika Fine Arts, Newport
*A watercolor of similar design but
different color scheme is in Mount Saint
Mary's College, Emmitsburgh, Maryland.
It was painted by La Farge in 1888 at
the request of an old friend, Charles
Carroll Lee, replicating the design in a
drawing that Lee had purchased in 1884
at auction, also now in Mount Saint
Mary's College. La Farge presumably
made this second colored version at the
same time.*

157.
Valley Behind Peter's Rock, Looking
South from the Peckham Brothers Quarry
Photograph by the author
(Nov. 1994)
*The ridge of Peter's Rock is to the right;
the ridge behind which sits the present
Orchard Lea is to the left.*

158.
Irving Barker House, 400 Paradise Avenue,
Looking Northeast
Photograph by the author (Nov. 1994)
*The foundations under the present Orchard Lea,
built in the 1920s as a gardener's cottage for
Gray Craig estate, incorporate the old brick
foundations that once supported the Irving
Barker house when it was on the same spot in
the Paradise Hills. The house was moved "over
the rocks" or, more correctly, through the gap
behind Peter's Rock, sometime after 1890. The
new site, now 400 Paradise Avenue, was then
part of Stephen P. Barker's Sea Breeze Farm,
which was next door.*

159.
John La Farge
Irving Barker House, Paradise Hills,
c. 1865
Watercolor over graphite on watercolor paper
9 1/2 x 12 1/4 in. (24.1 x 26 cm.)
Private Collection

been nearby. A house now at 400 Paradise Avenue (fig. 158) that was moved after 1890 from the site of the present Orchard Lea has traditionally been called one of La Farge's residences at Paradise. La Farge painted this house at its original site in the hills (fig. 159), perhaps while living there in 1866. His daughter Margaret Angela recalled the other residents of the house, **Irving M. Barker** (1838-1892), a son of Stephen P. Barker, and Irving's wife Elvira (1846-1915).

> *About the Barkers,* Irving *Barker & his wife owned the house that was in Paradise. I remember them both well. He was tall & rather nice looking & I think Mother used to buy eggs from him long after we left going out there.*[146]

This house "in Paradise" occupied an interesting perch on a puddingstone ledge that runs along the west side of a valley that is part of the "canyon" next to the Gray Craig mansion (see fig. 15). The site today is engulfed by trees and hidden amidst the hillocks of the ridge to the left in *Paradise Valley*. That La Farge resided in this house in 1866 not only would match his explanation that he worked "a few hundred yards" from where he lived, but also illuminates the logic of his choice to depict this particular pasture from this precise spot.

La Farge noted that he worked on *Paradise Valley* for over two years, for the most part out-of-doors, but he also stated that later work took place in a studio. In January 1867, George Quincy Thorndike (see fig. 25) reportedly let La Farge use or rent his Newport studio.[147] The Newport Directory for 1867 lists Thorndike as residing in downtown Newport at the corner of Touro and Mill Streets (now Bellevue Avenue and Mill Street), but does not give a separate studio address. Assuming that the studio was in the same building or nearby, it would have been very convenient for La Farge, who probably moved his family for the winter into the house of Margaret's mother, three blocks away on Greenough Place. It seems unlikely that La Farge used this studio for very long since, by the spring of 1867, the family had relocated to Grayledge Farm, renting from E. Truman Peckham. Here, just outside his back door, La Farge set up another studio.

Grayledge Farm has changed little from the days when La Farge lived there—in fact, many trees around the house are believed to date from before the Civil War. A painting dated 1867 (fig. 160) shows this house as viewed from behind at sunset, veiled in golden light that emanates from the western sky. This uncharacteristic work, reminiscent of the later "tonalist" art of painters such as Dwight William Tryon (1849-1925), was executed from the elevated vantage point of a large puddingstone outcropping across the backyard. Aside from overgrowth of weeds that has obscured a tiny stream and a few new outbuildings, the yard and house as viewed from this spot look much the same today (fig. 161). The long, narrow building at the rear of the house (fig. 162), just barely distinguishable in the painting, consists of just one large room. With wide floor-to-ceiling windows on three sides, it appears perfectly suited to an artist's studio.

That this was La Farge's studio is proven by one drawing showing a view through a tall window into the yard behind Grayledge Farm (fig. 163). The drawing includes the distinctive puddingstone outcropping across the yard (fig. 164), as well as interior framework under the window that corresponds to that seen under the window today (fig. 165). The drawing also shows how integral farm life actually was

160.
John La Farge
Grayledge Farm at Sunset, 1867
Oil on canvas
15 x 18 in. (38.1 x 45.7 cm.)
William Vareika Fine Arts, Newport

161.
Grayledge Farm from the Puddingstone
Outcropping in the Backyard,
Looking Northwest
Photograph by the author
(Dec. 1994)

to Grayledge Farm, with a feeding trough perched outside the window and farm animals sketched just beyond.

Other insights into the evolution of this studio are provided by a watercolor (fig. 166) in which the building has the narrow peaked shape detectable today. The edifice then had an entrance on the east side (the left side in the watercolor), a wall that today has a double window opening. The north wall (facing us in the watercolor) then was solid, except for a door-like gap in the foundation. Today the same wall is punctuated by a triple window, centered above the foundation opening.

We can only theorize that the building—perhaps a stable or servant's residence—was adapted to suit specific requirements that emerged after La Farge began working on *Paradise Valley*. This would explain an otherwise enigmatic statement made by La Farge's daughter, Margaret Angela, who was born at Grayledge Farm in 1867: "On the north side of the house is a large window put in by Father to paint by."[148] While all of the north windows in the house proper are original to the initial construction of the edifice, the north window of the studio clearly postdates the execution of the watercolor. The introduction of such a north window to admit what was called the "painter's light" suitable for studio work reflected deliberation, planning, and the cooperation of the owner of Grayledge Farm. Conveniently, this was E. Truman Peckham, a builder by trade, for whom adapting and renting a studio would have posed little difficulty, and would have been a reasonable accommodation to his tenant and friend.

At least two people recalled seeing *Paradise Valley* during its execution, probably in the studio at Grayledge Farm. The Newport author Thomas Wentworth Higginson (1846-1906) took visiting British nobility to see La Farge in 1867, and referred to *Paradise Valley* simply as La Farge's "picture," indicating the modest fame that it garnered during its long execution.

> *The pleasantest things I have done have been with the Amberleys—Lord and Lady. . . . I invited them to drive to Bishop Berkeley's house and haunts at Paradise Rocks (where they seemed anxious to go). Sam Ward added his carriage and daughter, and I drove Lady A. in Sarah Clarke's little phaeton. . . . We stopped at La Farge's and saw his picture. They had never heard of an American painter, though she knows all about the English, and paints in water-colors herself, sketching the Hanging Rocks in that way. We saw beautiful things at La Farge's, especially some drawings from Browning and one to illustrate his 'Protus' which is very remarkable. . . . La Farge went with us to the Hanging Rocks. . . .* [149]

Kate Field (1838-1896), a friend of Elihu Vedder, also recalled coming to "Newport" in September 1868 and seeing *Paradise Valley* on the easel in La Farge's "studio."[150] Even though Paradise often was called Newport, there is a curious note in the *Boston Evening Transcript* for August 1868 that suggests that La Farge had also set up a studio in downtown Newport by the time Field saw the picture: "John La Farge, a master of color, is and long has been a resident of Newport, and is now fitting up a permanent atelier in Thames Street."[151] The year 1868 is a genuinely confusing one in terms of the artist's precise addresses or activities. The residency lists for the period give his address as "Eustis' Kay Street,"[152] presumably somewhere on the part of Kay Street where the La Farges had lived for several years

162.
The Studio at Grayledge Farm, Looking South (Roof Dusted with Snow)
Photograph by the author
(Jan. 1995)

163.
John La Farge
From the Studio at Grayledge Farm, c. 1867
Black crayon on thin buff wove paper
6 1/2 x 3 7/8 in. (16.5 x 9.8 cm.)
Yale University Art Gallery, New Haven, Connecticut, Gift of Mrs. John Hay Whitney

164.
From the Studio at Grayledge Farm,
Looking South at the Puddingstone
Photograph by the author
(Jan. 1995)

165.
The Studio at Grayledge Farm,
Interior Woodwork
Photograph by the author
(Jan. 1995)

112

right after their marriage. But neither this "Eustis" house nor the Thames Street studio can be further identified, nor are these addresses used again after 1868.

Paradise Valley has always received mixed responses from critics. To some, it seemed "simple, almost *naive,* and without trickery or pretence of execution."[153] Others like Henry James recognized that the "picture is apparently simplicity itself, for its complex construction is carefully concealed."[154] La Farge went to lengths to explain this "complex construction," which involved the optical underpinnings that he had explored with Bancroft.

> *I modelled these surfaces of plain and sky upon certain theories of opposition of horizontals and perpendiculars in respect to color and I carried this general programme into as many small points of detail as I could combine. I also took as a problem the question of the actual size of my painting as covering the surface which I really saw at a distance, which would be represented by the first appearance of the picture. A student of optics will understand.[155]*

With its juxtaposition of blue and violet shadows against the predominant gold and green pasture, the picture mirrors Chevreul's complementary color algorithms. Decades later, recognition of this basis led some to compare La Farge to the French Impressionists. La Farge bristled at the analogy, lambasting the Impressionists to prove his point. The "main difficulty was to do all this from nature and to keep steadily at the same time to these theories without having them on the outside stick out of the outside, if I may say so, as some of my intelligent foreign friends managed to do. *In nature nothing sticks out.* They [my foreign friends] also have since worked out similar problems but they have not always insisted upon that main one, that the problems are *not visible* in nature. Nature, meaning in this case the landscape we look at, looks as *if it had done itself* and *not been done by the artist.*"[156]

La Farge's approach actually came closer to the British Pre-Raphaelites.[157] With similar topographical emphasis, their landscapes employed touches of pure color—and even blue and violet shadows—applied with a tightly-knit impasto from which "nothing sticks out." La Farge nonetheless insisted that previous artistic sources did not play a role in what he considered a self-contained theoretical exercise. "I undertook a combination of a large variety of problems which were not in the line of my fellow artists here, nor did I know of any one in Europe who at the time undertook them."[158]

Paradise Valley created a sensation when first exhibited as *New England Pasture Land* at the National Academy of Design in 1876.[159] "The picture is the admiration of a few and the wonder of many," wrote one incredulous critic.[160] In a country where the picturesque, grandiose landscapes of the Hudson River School still dominated, *Paradise Valley* seemed spare and bland. One reviewer mocked: "La Farge has a green map which he has the impudence to call a picture and ask $3000 for it."[161] Another, objecting to the map-like topography, deplored the lack of conventional tonalities: "The colouring is monotonous and cold, and the scene is entirely devoid of those bright touches which give life to a landscape."[162] Such cynics learned their lesson when La Farge sold *Paradise Valley* in late 1876 for the then-shocking $3000 ($150,000 today) that he asked for it.[163] In 1878, he borrowed it back briefly for showing at the Universal Exposition in Paris, the most important French exhibition of the decade.[164] The canvas earned an honorable mention, making La Farge one of only four Americans to be recognized at the exposition.[165]

166.
John La Farge
The Studio at Grayledge Farm, Paradise, c. 1865
Watercolor over graphite on watercolor paper
12 3/4 x 10 1/4 in. (32.4 x 26 cm.)
Private Collection

We have once before quoted Henry James at inordinate length because his familiarity with both La Farge and Paradise gives special resonance to his eloquent words. James had much to say about *Paradise Valley*, so much that he devoted most of his monthly art column in the *Atlantic Monthly* to the picture after seeing it on view in Boston.

> *The picture gives with wonderful fidelity the quiet and softness of the place under the light of a Newport afternoon, so different from the sometimes glaringly noticeable scenery of more famous spots. There are parts of the Hudson River, for instance, that seem designed to justify the paintings on drop-curtains, or, if this sounds harsh, they lack the coy, half-hidden reserve which the damp air of Newport lends to remote objects. Those who have traveled have seen fit to compare this Rhode Island shore with what is to be seen in Greece, and photographs simply confirm their statements. This quality is clear in this picture, which has the gentleness, the repose, the completeness, which the lover of nature finds in a few places which are not necessarily the most obviously picturesque. It is not lugging the highest of the Himalayas into a picture which gives it surely the greatest sublimity; and there is here no straining for effect by display of contrasts, by accumulation of points that cannot fail to catch the eye, but rather the willful rejection of such devices, and a sincere rendering of nature by an artist who has this rare claim to greatness, that he enforces upon us that impression of loveliness in what he has painted, which, when presented us by poet or painter, seems like the easiest simplicity, so high is the art. The evasive, modest beauty of Newport demands of the artist who undertakes to put it on canvas just that sympathy with things delicate and subtle which is shown so often by Mr. La Farge in his paintings. But by subtlety in the present case is meant his power to give what escapes a hasty glance, and rewards only more attentive study. This study, too, it may be said, is not intellectual or literary pondering, which in its time has inspired pictures, but rather that more or less fruitful sensitiveness to emotional impression which some feel in listening to music or in gazing at a sunset. No affectation can acquire this art, which has nothing to do with handiwork, but with the soul with which the painter sets about his work; for after all, the artist shows at the best what is in himself. Mr. La Farge has found here a subject admirably suited for his skill in interpreting gentle, unobtrusive things, and he has performed what he had to do with wonderful success.*[166]

THE LAST VALLEY   1867-1868

In 1867, before he had even finished *Paradise Valley*, La Farge began a second large canvas that he called *The Last Valley—Paradise Rocks* (fig. 167),[167] and that, over time, has become known simply as *The Last Valley*. Featuring a high horizon like that in *Paradise Valley*, this second work logically continues its topography. If the canvases were joined together, the pictures would form a panoramic view of Second Beach from Sachuest Point to Purgatory Rocks.

167.
John La Farge
The Last Valley—Paradise Rocks,
1867
Oil on canvas
32 x 41 1/2 in. (81.3 x 105.4 cm.)
Private Collection

The Last Valley has always been a familiar site to visitors of Paradise. In the nineteenth century, guide books gave the valley different names, including "Happy Valley," "Lost Valley," and at times even "Paradise Valley." With Bishop Berkeley's Rock as a constant lure, visitors came to picnic and frolic on what was then a meadowland.[168] The valley today is impenetrable. The "Valley Trail" of the Norman Bird Sanctuary leads through a mossy forest to the start of the valley floor, only to terminate abruptly in the cattail marsh at some distance from Paradise Pond.

La Farge painted *The Last Valley* from a part of the eastern wall of the valley that bulges out into the valley floor. David Maitland Armstrong's later view of the valley (see fig. 146) shows this jutting plateau from further back and at much greater elevation. The unusual perspective of La Farge's depiction, wherein the left wall soars above the viewer and the right wall seems to fall away, is blocked today from this plateau by a dense forest that has grown up on all sides. From above, the view is still similar, except for the elevation (see fig. 16).

La Farge chose to paint the valley at sunset when its walls displayed stark lighting contrasts. The setting sun shimmers on the east side of the gorge while the deep shadows of dusk engulf the west side. This dramatic effect—antithetical to that in *Paradise Valley*—demanded extra effort to study from nature. *The Last Valley* "was painted from Nature, in the same way as the other, and took a very long time to paint, so as to get the same light as far as possible. By going very frequently,—if necessary, everyday, and watching for a few minutes, I could get occasionally what I wanted."[169]

This regimen required a mechanism for storing the picture at so remote a site as the middle of the Last Valley. La Farge chose the obvious solution: "So that I had to build a little hut among the rocks for my picture," a hut that he sketched in a drawing executed from the plateau looking down towards the valley floor (fig. 168). This permitted him to decide on a moment's notice that the conditions were right for working on the picture. "Then I would take it out if the right light suited; this I did for two years. I regret to say that some fishermen broke into the hut once to injure my picture, and I also had trouble with gipsies,—not so serious. The fishermen having naturally attempted to rob, must have been disappointed, and one can only sympathize with their anger. I should suppose the gipsies to be more accustomed to pry into things without feeling it at all wrong."[170]

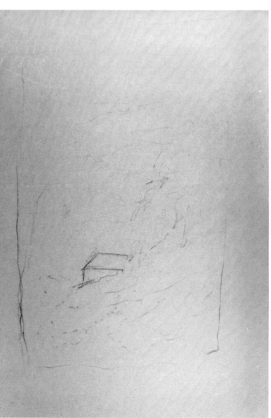

168
John La Farge
Hut in The Last Valley,
c. 1865
Graphite on buff laid paper
7 1/4 x 5 in. (18.4 x 12.7 cm.)
Private Collection

La Farge made several other interesting drawings of the site before undertaking his large picture. A view across to the inner wall of the eastern ridge of the valley (fig. 169) dated "Nov. 1866" suggests that La Farge began to frequent the site not long after beginning to work on *Paradise Valley*. The same view today can be obtained from the western ridge of the valley (fig. 170). Another undated drawing shows a male figure—probably a fellow artist—standing on the plateau gazing out at the view seen in the large painting (fig. 171). Still another drawing served as a study of color and lighting effects (fig. 172). Dated "Nov. 8th '67/ afternoon," this sketch postdated the start of the large painting. It was also executed at a completely different time of day, with the annotations including observations on weather conditions, color, and topography.

In addition, the notes include a tantalizing reference to another painting by La Farge: "sky blue green pinkish toward horizon—clouds very luminous looking somewhat like a S.E. Wind (no *apparent* wind however on land) in general tone & color like the picture Kensett has." The painter John Frederick Kensett, working often at Paradise at this time, owned an oil painting by La Farge about which little is known other than the title: *Morning Study—Newport, R.I.*[171] La Farge's notes on the drawing do little to help elucidate the subject, and since the picture disappeared after Kensett's estate sale in 1873 without being photographed,[172] we may never know why La Farge admired it.

Technically, La Farge considered the execution of *The Last Valley* more conventional than his other large canvas. "The underpainting of the shadows was indeed blue, that of the lights red, and the entire picture was all carefully studied in these balances of tone. Only by such a method could the work go on indefinitely, with continual additions of details, and still remain a simple study of nature."[173] Despite this protracted effort to bring out the subtlest details of geology or foliage, the result is no more picturesque or conventionally sublime than for *Paradise Valley*. *The Last Valley* gives a starkly naturalistic view of a landscape in which, again, "nothing sticks out."

The geological emphasis of *The Last Valley*—reminiscent of such works as *Early Spring. Sun Struggling Through Clouds* (see fig. 84)—related to intense interest in natural science during the 1860s. La Farge had close friends in Boston's scientific community who were instrumental in advancing geological explorations at the time. Clarence King (1842-1901), a member of Newport's large King family, formulated theories of "catastrophism and evolution" that derived in part from his observations of puddingstone rock formations. In 1867, King visited Newport just before becoming head of the United States Geological Survey and embarking for the West.[174] La Farge's old friend Will James went in 1865 on a botanical survey of Brazil with Harvard professor Louis Agassiz (1807-1873).[175] The latter's son, Alexander, purchased *The Last Valley* and eventually hung it at Castle Hill, his combined mansion and laboratory near Ocean Drive in Newport.[176] With Alexander Agassiz as a primary moving force, these interests coalesced during the early 1880s into a professional organization, the Newport Natural History Society, a group that

169.
John La Farge
Newport. The Rocks of the Last Valley, Paradise, 1866
Black chalk or charcoal on mulberry paper
4 1/4 x 6 3/8 in. (10.9 x 16 cm.)
Avery Architectural and Fine Arts Library, Columbia University, New York, Gift of Mrs. Russell Lynes, 1971

170.
Inner Wall of the Last Valley
Photograph by the author
(Nov. 1994)

171.
John La Farge
Man Standing Before a Landscape
(The Last Valley), c. 1867
Black crayon-pencil on tan rice paper
6 1/2 x 4 1/4 in. (16.5 x 10.8 cm.)
The Art Museum, Princeton University,
Princeton, New Jersey,
Gift of Frank Jewett Mather, Jr.

172.
John La Farge
The Last Valley, 1867
Graphite on buff paper
6 1/4 x 8 in. (15.9 x 20.3 cm.)
Yale University Art Gallery, New Haven,
Connecticut, Gift of Frances S. Childs in
memory of Henry A. La Farge

for about two decades intently studied the geology and other scientific phenomena of Aquidneck Island.

Nor should the concept behind the picture be divorced from amateur science that took place in the exclusive social circles to which La Farge belonged. Newport's Town and Country Club, founded in the early 1870s by Julia Ward Howe, grew out of her "blue teas" and other dinner-discussion groups of the late 1860s.[177] With Alexander Agassiz and other local celebrities in the lead, the club embarked on "picnics with a purpose" to Paradise to study botanical and geological oddities, and to discuss current scientific theories. The *Newport Journal* reported in September 1875: "The Town and Country club to the number of about sixty persons had a picnic at Paradise Wednesday afternoon at which Prof. William B. Rogers gave a familiar lecture on the 'Rocks of Our Neighborhood.'"[178] Membership lists prove that La Farge attended such "familiar" lectures during the 1870s, finding himself in the company of many individuals who later became patrons of his decorative work.

The Last Valley garnered critical favor as it traveled the exhibition circuit from New York to Boston between 1869 and 1872. La Farge took particular pride when the Paris dealer, Paul Durand-Ruel (1831-1922), exhibited the picture during the summer of 1873 at his London gallery with works by French artists including Impressionists such as Camille Pissarro (1830-1903), Alfred Sisley (1839-1899), and Claude Monet (1840-1926). Unimpressed by this contingent, La Farge gloated while visiting the show that *The Last Valley* managed to "hold its own against that stern test" when hung between a Théodore Rousseau (1812-1867) and a Delacroix.[179] *The Last Valley* later represented La Farge at the Paris Salon of 1874 and the Philadelphia Centennial Exposition of 1876 where it won a medal for "artistic merit in landscape."[180] In conjunction with the simultaneous success of *Paradise Valley*, this international recognition satisfied La Farge's lifelong ambition to be respected as a salon or easel painter.

A third large canvas dated 1868 shows a view over Bishop Berkeley's Rock from the top of the ridge (fig. 173). Entitled by the artist *Autumn Study. View over Hanging Rock, Newport, R.I.,* the picture was conspicuously absent from La Farge's exhibitions of the 1870s.[181] Unlike his other large canvases, he never discussed the painting and sold it only after his creditors forced him to dispose of the contents of his studio in 1884. Though attractive in its warm coloration and sketchy, spontaneous handling, this should not be mistaken for a finished work. La Farge abandoned it before adding the careful web of detailing that is the primary surface feature of his two other large pictures. The blocked-in colors, sketchy brushstrokes, lack of sharp visual resolution, and absence of "continual additions of details" provide an equivalent of the underpainting that La Farge used for *The Last Valley.*[182]

Further proof of the artist's dissatisfaction with the picture came in a letter written after his death by Grace Edith Barnes, La Farge's executrix. To the Boston dealer Robert C. Vose, she noted that this painting "was not one that Mr. La Farge thought well of . . . "[183] Negative sentiments dogged the picture for years. The first owner was Charles de Kay (1848-1935), an art critic who bought the canvas at the forced sale in 1884. He consigned it to a dealer in New York in 1901, where it garnered the reputation of a work too long unsold. In 1907, one disenchanted collector put it bluntly: "I found in calling at Montross Gallery that the 'La Farge' referred to was the old one that has been knocking around with the big boulder."[184] When de Kay moved the picture to Boston, asking an exorbitant price, Vose reprimanded him: "We have one person interested in the picture, but he would not pay anything like the price asked."[185]

Prior to undertaking the large canvas, La Farge executed many drawings of the landmark rock seen from the ridge. Waves whipping off the ocean on a rainy day, as if to engulf the rock, dominate one sketch (fig. 174). In another (fig. 175), drawn from further back on the ridge, layers of puddingstone rock erupt into rippling masses (fig. 176). La Farge inscribed this drawing "Silent upon a peak of Darien," a reference to a sonnet by John Keats (1795-1821) that reveals the depth of La Farge's admiration for the site. In 1815, Keats read a new translation of writings of the Greek epic poet Homer by George Chapman (1559?-1634), an Elizabethan poet. Keats was so moved that he composed *On First Looking into Chapman's Homer*, a sonnet comparing his emotions to those felt by Cortez upon reaching the Isthmus of Panama, then called Darien.

> Then felt I like some watcher of the skies
> When a new planet swims into his ken;
> Or like stout Cortez when with eagle eyes
> He star'd at the Pacific—and all his men
> Look'd at each other with a wild surmise—
> Silent, upon a peak in Darien.[186]

173.
John La Farge
Autumn Study. View over Hanging Rock, Newport, R.I., 1868
Oil on canvas
30 1/4 x 25 1/4 in. (76.8 x 64.1 cm.)
The Metropolitan Museum of Art,
New York, Gift of Dr. Frank Jewett Mather, Jr., 1949 (49.76)

174.
John La Farge
Bishop's Rock, Newport
(Bishop Berkeley's Rock), c. 1868
Black crayon-pencil on tan rice paper
6 11/16 x 4 1/4 in. (17 x 10.9 cm.)
The Art Museum, Princeton University,
Princeton, New Jersey,
Gift of Frank Jewett Mather, Jr.

175.
John La Farge
Bishop Berkeley's Rock, From the North,
c. 1868
Black crayon on smooth buff paper
Image: 6 3/8 x 4 1/8 in. (16.2 x 10.5 cm.)
Museum of Fine Arts, Boston, Gift of Henry
L. Higginson, 1912

176.
From Bishop Berkeley's Rock,
Looking South
Photograph by the author
(Nov. 1994)

177.
John La Farge
*Second Beach and
Purgatory Rocks;
From Paradise Farm,
Southeast Wind,* 1868
Oil on panel
9 1/2 x 14 1/4 in.
(24.1 x 36.2 cm.)
Private Collection

PARADISE "AT A BLOW" 1868-1871

Only two other views of Paradise date from 1868. In one, La Farge returned to the top of Peter's Rock to reprise his earlier austere view of Second Beach in a work that the artist called *Second Beach and Purgatory Rocks; From Paradise Farm, Southeast Wind* (fig. 177).[187] A few young trees, absent from the earlier view (see fig. 106), remind us that several years have passed. The simple, unassertive composition allows the palette of alternating subdued and bright colors to take on special significance. As in the contemporaneous nocturnes of Whistler, this is an ode to the subtlest interactions of color and light.

In the second work from this year, La Farge combined figure and landscape study (fig. 178) in a picture that he called *A Bather*.[188] Margaret is walking on Second Beach (fig. 179), her gaze downcast as she lifts a long gown above her bare feet. The elegance of the gesture, no less than the classical folds of the gown, recalls a Greek statue. A wave breaking against the craggy shoreline leads the eye back to a view of Purgatory Rocks under a thickly clouded sky. The picture is painted with iridescent touches of red, blue, and green that shimmer through the overall brown and white tonalities. The enchanting figure recalls the words of La Farge's son Bancel: "my mother graceful and pensive melting into the silver-grey rocks in the Valley, or emerging to be silhouetted against the distant sea and sky."[189]

178.
John La Farge
Woman Bathing (A Bather),
c. 1868
Oil on panel
17 15/16 x 12 1/4 in.
(45.6 x 31.1 cm.)
Worcester Art Museum,
Worcester, Massachusetts

179.
Second Beach and
Purgatory Rocks,
Looking South
Photograph by the author
(Dec. 1994)

In 1869, when La Farge returned to the top of Bishop Berkeley's Rock to paint a small view of the crown of the ridge (fig. 180), he sat on an outcropping of flat ground to the left of the spine that is still there today (fig. 181). La Farge had drawn from this spot many times, sketching the gentle slopes leading up to the crown (figs. 182). In one case, he hurriedly outlined a figure, probably a friend but perhaps an imagined Bishop Berkeley (fig. 183). These drawings prepared him to execute his small oil painting in a quick and concise manner, a method that he called working "at a blow."

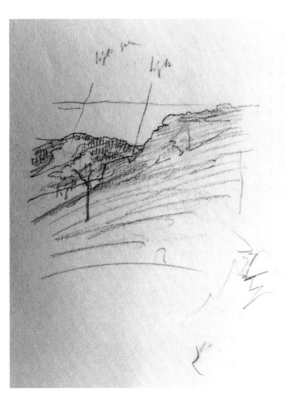

Of the smaller pictures I, as far as possible, painted them at a blow, or with very little extension of time. By making careful and finished preparation— what would be called drawing—beforehand, one could do a great deal in the way of painting. Then, also, the question of using certain principles of light, by pigment, would allow one to prepare the picture in the way it would go.[190]

The great appeal of these small "at a blow" paintings stems from their delicate use of color combined with varied surface textures. This is particularly evident in another picture painted from the south end of the rock at ground level (fig. 184), a view that can be approximated today by standing near Hanging Rocks Road at the border of the cattail marsh surrounding the ridge (fig. 185). The mahogany panel support shows through the sky to give the impression of thick atmosphere surrounding the pensive form of the rock. As in the view of the crown of the rock, the rendering is succinct and economical in the application of paint.

Another now-lost picture dating from 1869, entitled *Afterglow. Evening Study. Newport, R.I,*[191] once belonged to the renowned Boston collector, Mrs. Samuel Dennis Warren (1825-1901). A description published in the 1903 catalogue of her estate sale evokes the image of part of the pasture in *Paradise Valley*:

Afterglow. The foreground of rolling downs, golden green in hue, forms a cleft through which appears a glimpse of the sea, of the color of wine and water. The sky is a faint blue, skeined with wisps of white and pink. A splendid mellowness of color distinguishes the whole composition. Signed at lower left, La Farge, 1869. Height, 13 3/4 inches; width, 12 inches.[192]

The last "at a blow" picture of the 1860s was painted as winter descended on the beaches of Paradise (fig. 186). La Farge traveled past Third Beach to Flint Point, then, as now, not readily accessible by road (fig. 187). A ridge covered by sand and grass crosses this view of Second Beach and the distant Purgatory Rocks. This ridge, perhaps made of underlying puddingstone but inaccessible by foot today, is better shown in a drawing done from just alongside (fig. 188). In the painting, spruce trees like those still growing on Flint and Sachuest Points punctuate the white blanket of the snow. The looming winter sky and opalescent flecks of water merge into this field of white, each barely distinguished by different hues of white, gray, and powder blue. As in *Snow Storm* of 1865 (see fig. 104), the animated sky conveys the crisp energy that fills the air on a snowy day in Newport.

In 1870, residency lists curiously do not mention where the La Farges lived during the "season."[193] Perhaps they stayed at the house of Margaret's mother in downtown Newport, as they often did during the winter. For part of the summer, they visited Shrub Oak near Peekskill, New York, where La Farge's mother had moved in 1868 after remarrying. The only small landscapes that can be securely dated to 1870 show views of the ridges and hills there, handled in the same style used for the "at a blow" paintings painted the previous year at Paradise.

In 1871, the family rented a farmhouse at Paradise belonging to General John Alfred Hazard,[194] then owner of the apron of land between the Paradise Hills and Second Beach, as well as the part of Flint Point where La Farge painted on several

184.
John La Farge
Berkeley's or Hanging Rock,
Paradise.
North Wind. Autumn, 1869
Oil on panel
11 x 9 in.
(27.9 x 22.8 cm.)
William Vareika Fine Arts,
Newport

185.
Bishop Berkeley's Rock,
Looking North
Photograph by the author
(Oct. 1994)

186.
John La Farge
*Snow Weather. Sketch
(Landscape in Snow)*, 1869
Oil on wooden panel
9 1/2 x 9 7/16 in. (23.9 x 24 cm.)
The Art Museum, Princeton University,
Princeton, New Jersey,
Gift of Frank Jewett Mather, Jr.

187.
Second Beach from Flint Point,
Looking West
Photograph by the author
(Dec. 1994)
*Flint and Sachuest Points are overgrown
with brambles today, and the unusual ridge
laying near the end of Sachuest Point Road
cannot be reached on foot.*

188.
John La Farge
Second Beach from Flint Point,
c. 1865
Graphite on buff laid paper
5 x 7 1/4 in. (12.7 x 18.4 cm.)
Private Collection

occasions (see figs. 139-140, 186-188). No edifice remains on the land where this house once stood on the west side of Paradise Avenue, just above the river crossing. One striking "at a blow" picture dated 1871 was painted from this residence (fig. 189). Before a distant view of Bishop Berkeley's Rock, a dirt driveway leads down towards Paradise Avenue, a view that is much the same today (fig. 190).

La Farge painted the oil with great abandon. Reminiscent of Vedder's penchant for depicting contorted trees, he focused on the eerie orchard at the left set against the sweeping green pasture mixed with sand dunes that spreads out before Second Beach and Bishop Berkeley's Rock. The sky is rendered as in the earlier "at a blow" pictures, with patches of cloud freely interspersed with the mahogany of the panel support. Nor did La Farge neglect to make a careful distinction between the sky and the blue strip representing the Sakonnet River along the ribbon of the horizon.

189.
John La Farge
Evening Study.
Newport, R.I.
(From Hazard's
Farm, Paradise),
1871
Oil on panel
12 1/4 x 16 1/2 in.
(31.1 x 41.9 cm.)
William Vareika
Fine Arts, Newport

The artist used the verso of the panel as a palette that, coincidently, resembles abstract expressionist paintings executed over half-a-century later.

190.
Bishop Berkeley's Rock from "Hazard's
Farm," Paradise, Looking East
Photograph by the author
(Nov. 1994)
The land once occupied by Hazard's Farm,
according to an 1870 map, presently is
unoccupied. To obtain the view available to La
Farge in 1871 when he lived there, one today has
to climb the ridge near St. George's School to a
sufficient elevation to clear power lines and trees.

La Farge also painted a lost watercolor of Hazard's farm looking up from Paradise Avenue. When exhibited as *Old Farm-House, and Orchard on Hill-Side*, a critic wrote about the watercolor:

> *Look now at . . . this old farmhouse and its barns on a hill in the cool light*
> *of the early morning. The color is peculiarly delicate even here, but the truth*
> *of detail and effect is more distinct. Note the patient painting of the near*
> *stone wall, the hidden brook in the hollow with the grass grown greener*
> *around it, the low yellow light on the rounded hillside, the hard brown path*
> *leading to the farmhouse, the orchard on the right, the detail of the house*
> *itself, the pale mass—or rather space—of the barn in the morning light.*[195]

We can infer from this description that the view was up the "hard brown path leading to the farmhouse" on which we look down in the 1871 oil painting. The farmhouse evidently was just above the orchard, represented in the oil by the gnarled trees on the left.

A close-up view of irises and a dead tree trunk (fig. 191) also dates from the year of residency at Hazard's Farm. This shows the perspective looking up the ridge now occupied by St. George's School, apparently from the same orchard depicted in the view from Hazard's Farm. The idea of studying flowers at close range in a natural setting is one that La Farge had explored earlier in pictures such as *Hollyhocks* (see fig. 74), but there is an overripe and complicated feeling to the truncated perspective, disorienting composition, and iridescent palette of this and other nature studies executed in 1871. Stark in texture and jewel-like in color, this delightful and startling picture is a fitting coda to La Farge's years of residency at Paradise.

NEXT PAGE: 191.
John La Farge
Flowers. Blue Iris, with Trunk of Dead
Apple-Tree in the Background,
1871   Oil on panel
12 1/4 x 9 5/8 in. (31.1 x 24.4 cm.)
Private Collection

Chapter VI

PARADISE AS ALLEGORY AND MEMORY

In 1870, La Farge painted *Decorative Panel. Seated Figure in Yellow. Study for the Muse of Painting* (fig. 192).[196] In Greek mythology, there are nine muses of the arts and sciences, but not a specific muse for painting. Conventional representations of muses fall into two camps. In the first, the muse is shown in a static pose, with attributes or symbols used to convey the meaning, as when a muse of music is shown holding a lyre. The second tradition uses narrative to convey the muse's functions, often through the interaction of a muse with the person she inspires. This is how La Farge first conceived the Muse of Painting in a preliminary drawing (fig. 193) where the muse is depicted as an art instructor. Seated by a standing artist, the muse gestures to a drawing in her lap while the artist absorbs her lesson. In this initial concept, La Farge set the scene on a marble seat with elaborate Greek detailing, shown in another drawing (fig. 194).

La Farge's final composition departed from any set tradition as he dispensed with the figure of the artist and the classical trappings. The muse sits alone in a landscape, drawing on the palette in her lap. She no longer inspires, nor is she merely a collection of attributes. The muse is now the one being inspired while at work on her art. The landscape that she paints has become the source of her inspiration—Nature has become the true muse of painting.

Appreciating a still more subtle and personal allegorical significance to this painting relies on our identification of the landscape as a specific view at Paradise. The muse sits before the cleft of Bishop Berkeley's Rock, with the ridge behind the rock stretching away in the distance (fig. 195). The symbolism is obvious to anyone familiar with Paradise, since the cleft was the place where Berkeley allegedly set up a writing table to compose his *Alciphron, or The Minute Philosopher.* Just as Hanging Rock and its sublime view inspired Berkeley's writings, so it inspired the muse in La Farge's allegory about the artistic process.

La Farge painted *The Muse of Painting* from nature, as known from an anecdote published by Charles de Kay.

> *He built himself a painter's cot in the beautiful tract beyond the bathing beach, . . . a hut to retire when it rained, a place to store his easel and frames. One day, while this picture was under way, he returned to the hut to find that certain ladies had tracked him to his happy sketching ground and, tearing down the creepers he had carefully suspended to serve as models for one part of his picture, had garlanded therewith the canvas as it stood, partly wrought, on the easel. In their enthusiasm little did they dream that the impulsive act of homage to his skill as an artist had ruined for a time the progress of his work!*
>
> *This was not the only time that intruders took advantage of the absence of the owner. Fishermen landing at Paradise would sometimes maul his canvases about, without the slightest malice, more like inconsiderate children.*[197]

192.
John La Farge
The Muse of Painting
(Decorative Panel. Seated Figure in Yellow. Study for The Muse of Painting), 1870
Oil on canvas   49 1/2 x 38 1/4 in. (125.7 x 97.2 cm.)
The Metropolitan Museum of Art, New York,
Gift of J. Pierpont Morgan and Henry Walters, 1909 (09.176)

193.
John La Farge
The Painter and the Muse;
Study for *The Muse of Painting*, c. 1870
Black chalk or charcoal
on smooth ivory paper
10 3/8 x 7 5/8 in. (26.4 x 19.4 cm.)
Bowdoin College Museum of Art,
Brunswick, Maine,
Gift of Miss Susan Dwight Bliss

194.
John La Farge
Drapery of the Muse;
Study for *The Muse of Painting*, c. 1870
Black chalk or charcoal
on smooth ivory paper
10 3/8 x 7 5/8 in. (26.4 x 19.4 cm.)
Bowdoin College Museum of Art,
Brunswick, Maine,
Gift of Miss Susan Dwight Bliss

195.
Bishop Berkeley's Rock from Dike of
Gardiner's Pond, Looking Northwest
Photograph by the author
(Dec. 1994)

The muse is framed by the hanging vines of five-lobed Virginia creeper, found throughout Paradise then as now. That La Farge "arranged" the creepers to suit his artistic conception is an ironic twist in a reversed allegory about the role of nature in the process of painting. Ironic too is a pervasive blue-green tonality that lends the work a decorative rather than realistic emphasis, in essence altering the character of the natural scene that inspires the muse. Like the landscapes of a contemporary French muralist, Pierre Puvis de Chavannes (1824-1898), this is the Paradise of a dream-state, not of waking vision. We have few clues as to why La Farge interjected this decorative veneer over the composition. Though he called this a "Decorative Panel" and a "Study," apparently for a larger painting, there is little more than the rumor of a proposed domestic decorative scheme by a leading architect of the day, Henry Hobson Richardson (1838-1886), to suggest the impetus for the picture.[198]

Today, it is hard to conceive just how La Farge set up an easel and model to obtain the angle of vision seen in *The Muse of Painting*. Any muse-like qualities of this corner of Paradise have been quashed irreversibly by the double indignities of Hanging Rocks Road and the Newport Water Works. The view of Bishop Berkeley's Rock from the east painted in 1866 by George Quincy Thorndike (see fig. 25) and a later etching from a less elevated perspective (see fig. 19) show a steep hill descending from the rock down to the river emptying into Gardiner's Pond. Just below the cleft of Bishop Berkeley's Rock, a protruding ledge was probably the perch occupied by the model in La Farge's painting—and was one of two ledges blasted away to make Hanging Rocks Road in 1883. A dike nearly as high as the rock now runs just to the east of the stream of water in the foreground of Thorndike's painting. If we did not know the dramatic changes to the area brought about by the grading and filling for both the road and the reservoir that engulfed Gardiner's Pond, we might mistake Thorndike's painting for a fanciful rendition. Actually, it was a true portrayal of the very real site, as experienced in his day.

ALLEGORY AND ILLUSTRATION

The idea of using the topography of Paradise in allegorical compositions had occurred to La Farge when he first began to frequent Paradise Avenue. In 1862, Paradise served as the setting for religious scenes (see figs. 55-57) and a Tennysonian subject (see fig. 52); in 1864, Paradise assumed multiple guises for a complete set of Tennyson illustrations (see figs. 89-96). On several later occasions, Paradise also provided settings for historical or literary depictions that set the stage for serious allegorical adaptations of Paradise during the 1870s.

Horace Elisha Scudder commissioned La Farge in 1866 to produce a series of twelve illustrations for a new children's periodical, *The Riverside Magazine for Young People*.[199] La Farge envisioned a fruitful collaboration, providing Scudder with a proposed list of possible "fantastic themes" that embraced witches, fairies, sea serpents, mermaids, giants, and centaurs. He also suggested "Historical-Novel" or

"Semi-Historical" subjects such as Hadrianic processions, Druidic sacrifices, Argonauts, Amazons, Christian martyrdoms, Nordic myths, or medieval chivalry.[200] Only six of many woodblocks that he prepared for Scudder reached publication before the magazine failed in 1870 but, in the interim, La Farge composed some of the most interesting and artistically serious illustrations of the nineteenth century.

The Wolf Charmer (fig. 196), the first illustration in the series to be published, became one of La Farge's most popular and well-known designs.[201] The illustration accompanied a translation from French writings by George Sand, pseudonym of Amantine Lucile Aurore Dupin (1804-1876). When Sand discovered the hamlet of Gargilesse in the Berry province of France in 1856, she recorded the local peasant lore in *Légendes Rustiques*.[202] Her chapter "Le Meneu' des Loups" (literally "The Wolf Leader") recounts the last vestige of the werewolf saga as it survived from the French Middle Ages. Sand elaborated that there were also at the time many reports about the communing of certain individuals with wolves, usually as a result of musical enchantment.[203]

George Parsons Lathrop noted that one critic "pointed out that the man's figure seems to have been borrowed, and turned from right to left in the removal, from one of Titian's infrequent landscapes. In the latter, it is a shepherd piping to his sheep, who, in Mr. La Farge's hands, becomes a wolf-charmer, playing seductively to a pack of evil-looking brutes."[204] The painting in question is unknown, but the landscape does recall various works by Titian, including *The Martyrdom of Saint Peter Martyr* (1530), a celebrated work destroyed by fire in 1867.[205] Lathrop did not say, however, that the landscape itself was based on Titian and, with the help of the mirror image of the engraving shown in an old studio photograph of the woodblock before cutting (fig. 197), the setting can be identified as the edge of Sacred Grove, leading to the bank of Nelson's Pond.

The precise spot depicted is not easy to make out today because of the combined effects of overgrowth, dredging, and flooding—not to mention certain stylizations and rearrangements interjected by La Farge for dramatic purposes. The Wolf Charmer emerges from between a cleft formed by two puddingstone rocks before a tangled view of the trees of the Sacred Grove, with the cliff visible just beyond. This spot, now usually partially submerged, once gave directly onto a beach, as proven by a preliminary drawing for an alternative composition (fig. 198). In this drawing, the rocks ultimately used to frame the *Wolf Charmer* are seen in the distance, and in positions that they still occupy today (fig. 199). The beach, however, is long gone, and, even in the driest weather, water laps at the rocks, making it impossible to photograph them from the angle seen in The Wolf Charmer. The best one can do is take a photograph from across the pond (fig. 200). When La Farge moved the figures from the beach to within the rock formation, he took also took poetic license. By bringing the rocks much closer together than they actually are, he created a feeling of claustrophobic compression that enhances the fast-flowing movement of the wolf charmer and herd of wolves.

196.
John La Farge
The Wolf Charmer, 1867
Wood engraving on paper
(Engraver: Henry Marsh)
6 15/16 x 5 7/16 in. (17.5 x 13.7 cm.)
From the *Riverside Magazine for Young People*, vol. 1, no. 12 (Dec. 1867), opp. p. 552

197.
John La Farge
The Wolf Charmer, 1867
Brush & ink on uncut woodblock
6 15/16 x 5 7/16 in. (17.5 x 13.7 cm.)
Destroyed in cutting of the block

198.
John La Farge
Study for The Wolf Charmer, c. 1867
Black chalk or charcoal on paper
6 1/4 x 4 5/16 in. (15.9 x 11 cm.)
The Toledo Museum of Art, Toledo,
Gift of Edward Drummond Libbey, 1912

199.
Puddingstone Boulders along West Bank
of Nelson's Pond, Looking South
Photograph by the author
(Jan. 1995)
*The beach seen in La Farge's drawing of
this same spot succumbed to dredging and
flooding.*

200.
Puddingstone Boulders along West Bank
of Nelson's Pond,
Looking West across the Pond
Photograph by the author
(Dec. 1994)
*The Wolf Charmer emerges from between
puddingstone boulders that, in reality, are
not as close as they appear in La Farge's
design. The rock on the right in the original
drawing (on the left in the wood engraving)
is at the end of a puddingstone formation
seen as a whitish outcropping on the right
in this photograph. The rock on the left in
the original drawing (on the right in the
wood engraving) is the same rock seen in*
The Shepherd and the Sea *(see fig. 228),
here on the left, but largely submerged. La
Farge "moved" this rock to the right and
elevated it to make the corridor of rocks
seen in* The Wolf Charmer.

201.
John La Farge
The Wolf Charmer, 1904-07
Oil on canvas
78 x 54 in. (198.1 x 137.2 cm.)
Location unknown

41

143

La Farge also rendered the composition in oil on a monumental scale (fig. 201), reportedly on order from a New York financier and politician who had previously been a patron of his work, William Collins Whitney (1841-1904).[206] This commission came just before Whitney died, leaving the picture on La Farge's hands for several years to come. In 1906, an article in a British periodical featured the painting as one "Selected by the Artist as His Best Picture."[207] Eventually, such promotion led to its sale to a noted Saint Louis collector. Subsequently acquired by Washington University in Saint Louis, the picture disappeared in 1945 after being deaccessioned and sold at auction in New York.[208]

The Fisherman and the Afrite (fig. 202) depicts an episode from a familiar story in the *Arabian Nights Entertainments*.[209] Finding a copper bottle in his net one day, a struggling fisherman dreams of selling it for profit, but recoils when he unleashes a genie locked away for centuries. The genie—punished by God for rebellion—threatens the fisherman with execution, but instead is tricked back into the bottle. The fisherman makes a pact that assures his life and good fortune before releasing the genie again.

Second Beach is the sweeping setting for the scene. Reversed by the process of wood engraving, the curl of the sandy shore complements the fantastic form of the genie, modeled on an ink specter in a print from one of the many published sketchbooks by Hokusai that collectively make up his *Manga*. The fisherman's pose derives from that of Saint Peter Martyr in the altarpiece by Titian destroyed in 1867. La Farge mingled these eastern and western artistic references with the realistic contours of his favorite beach, one that he had photographed from much the same perspective around 1863 (see fig. 80).

La Farge prepared *The Wise Men Out of the East* (fig. 203) for a Christmas issue of the magazine in 1868.[210] He summarized this scene from the Biblical tale of the Three Wise Men guided by a star in their search for the newborn Christ succinctly: "They halt on their journey; two dismount, one with intent to use his astrolabe for reckoning the place of the star in the East. His older companion dissuades him. The scene is at dawn."[211] The group in the foreground—derived from horses and figures found in works by La Farge's artistic heroes, Delacroix and Théodore Chassériau (1819-1856)—stands on the top of Peter's Rock. The illustration served as the basis a decade later for a large oil version entitled *The Three Wise Men* (fig. 204) where this landscape took on the blue-green aura common to Delacroix's work. The surface of the pigment is animated by thick brushwork that seems whipped into a painterly emulation of the great French Romantic painters that La Farge had adulated since 1856.

The background in *The Three Wise Men* gives the vista known at the time as "Paradise Lost." Beyond the Paradise Hills stretch the distinctive hooked profiles of Flint and Sachuest Points, the long line of Second Beach, and the beginnings of the Sakonnet River (fig. 205). The "star of the east" guiding the travelers appears at the point where the sun actually rises. For La Farge, the setting had additional significance since the camels straying below the main group occupy the same valley in which he had painted *Paradise Valley* (see fig. 154), still on his easel as he produced this illustration.

202.
John La Farge
The Fisherman and the Afrite, 1868
Wood engraving on paper
(Engraver: Henry Marsh)
6 3/4 x 5 3/8 in. (17.2 x 14.3 cm.)
From the *Riverside Magazine for Young*
People, vol. 2, no. 19 (Jul. 1868),
opp. p. 289

203.
John La Farge
The Wise Men Out of the East, 1868
Wood engraving on paper
(Engraver: Henry Marsh or W.J. Linton)
5 1/2 x 7 in. (14 x 17.8 cm.)
From the *Riverside Magazine for Young People*, vol. 2, no. 24 (Dec. 1868), opp. p. 528

204.
John La Farge
The Three Wise Men
(Halt of the Wise Men), 1878-79
Oil on canvas
32 3/4 x 42 1/4 in. (82.9 x 107.3 cm.)
Museum of Fine Arts, Boston,
Gift of Edward W. Hooper

205.
"Paradise Lost"—View from Peter's Rock,
Looking East
Photograph by the author
(Nov. 1994)

206.
John La Farge
The Magi; Alternate Study for *The Wise
Men from the East*, c. 1868
Tintype after lost drawing
5 x 8 1/4 in. (12.9 x 20.8 cm.)
(tintype size)
William Vareika Fine Arts, Newport

An alternative design for the illustration is known from a lost drawing that survives only by virtue of a tintype (fig. 206). A procession of figures on camels winds along the puddingstone ledge above the west side of Nelson's Pond. In the distance and far below, we see the pond and the descending ridge along its east side. To the right, the south pond bank with distinctive puddingstone protrusions now covered by the dike merge into vague intimations of marshy meadows leading to Second Beach. The choice of this view seems highly personal given La Farge's long attachment to the ledge in his preceding work at Paradise. Personal, too, is the inclusion of his self-portrait on the central rider, staring out at the viewer. Ultimately, La Farge decided against this design, opting for one with fewer personal references.

207.
John La Farge
The Giant, 1868
Wood engraving on paper
(Engraver: Henry Marsh)
7 x 5 1/2 in. (17.8 x 14 cm.)
From the *Riverside Magazine for Young People*, vol. 3, no. 39 (May 1869), opp. p. 193

208.
John La Farge
The Giant, 1868
Ink brush and Chinese white
on uncut woodblock
6 5/8 x 5 3/16 in. (16.7 x 13.2 cm.)
Destroyed in cutting of the block

The Giant (fig. 207) encountering travelers evidently derives from another *Arabian Nights Entertainment*.[212] Two "wanderers" crossing a vast desert press forward in hope of finding water when a giant materializes out of a hillock in their path. Threatened by death, they resort to flattery until the sun shining on his brow lulls him to sleep. They scamper past, saved by quick thinking and fast talking.

As in *The Fisherman and Afrite*, La Farge merged various artistic and realistic elements to give the illustration both exotic elegance and a sense of credibility. The giant is based on a design from Hokusai's *Manga*; the figures repeat the Orientalist style of French Romantic prototypes seen in *The Three Wise Men*. To these eastern and western models, La Farge added a view of the Last Valley as seen from alongside Bishop Berkeley's Rock. In this case, we again have an old studio photograph of the original drawing on the woodblock, taken before it was cut (fig. 208). With this mirror image, the view of the Last Valley is easier to identify as similar to that seen in an 1884 photograph included in T. Nelson Dale's geological study of Paradise (see fig. 26).

The last illustration by La Farge before the *Riverside Magazine* ceased publication appeared in August 1870 (fig. 209).[213] *Midsummer Eve* depicts the English custom of scouting for St. John's wart or other herbs believed to have the magical power to help a maiden find a husband. The search is conducted on Midsummer Day or June 24th, the church festival known as the Nativity of St. John the Baptist. A maiden at the end of a path bathed in moonlight runs her fingers through the brush, the probable success of her quest suggested by the distant figure of a man hidden under a tree, who hopes to find fern seeds that will render him invisible so that he may follow her home.

209.
John La Farge
Midsummer Eve, 1870
Wood engraving on paper
(Engraver: Henry Marsh)
7 x 5 1/2 in. (17.8 x 14 cm.)
From the *Riverside Magazine for Young People*, vol. 4, no. 44 (Aug. 1870), p. 336

The bucolic scene takes place in the Sacred Grove at the bottom of the hill leading to Nelson's Pond. Above, a puddingstone formation makes a sharp descent to the ground. The figure, based on the artist's wife, sits alongside another puddingstone outcropping alongside the pond near the path coming from above. The characteristics of these rocks and the lay of the land behind the figure can be identified readily as part of the same formation seen in the *Wolf Charmer* and several later mythological paintings (see figs. 223, 227). But changes to this part of Nelson's Pond to make the Newport Water Works have obscured the precise spot depicted, most likely putting it underwater.

EASEL PAINTINGS AND DECORATIVE WORK

The decade of the 1870s was an unsettling one for La Farge. Around the time he executed *The Muse of Painting*, he decided that the family's need for income could no longer be satisfied if he continued his isolated existence in Paradise. In the fall of 1871, La Farge became an art instructor for the academic year at Harvard College.[214] Renewed contacts with the Boston social and business community became the basis for many lucrative commissions that would later come his way. The time was ripe for decorative work. In the era of Reconstruction following the Civil War, great fortunes sprang from industry and commerce, and plans for civic monuments, ecclesiastical buildings, and private mansions abounded. Henry Hobson Richardson had already promised La Farge the "first decorative work at his disposal."[215] This eventually led to La Farge's commission in 1876 to mastermind the interior decoration of Trinity Church in Boston—a venture whose success made La Farge one of the most sought-after decorative artists of the early 1880s.

La Farge's transition to decorative art required a gradual divorce from what his youngest son called the "Paradise Valley period."[216] This began in 1872 when the La Farges moved to a popular boarding house in downtown Newport, on the northwest corner of Kay Street and Mann Avenue, where the artist reportedly also rented a studio.[217] Here, he prepared four woodblocks for Abby Sage Richardson's anthology of poetry, *Songs from the Old Dramatists*, published in 1873 by Hurd and Houghton. The plate heading the section devoted to *Songs of Feeling & Songs of Thought* (fig. 210) combined a likeness of Margaret based upon a photograph (fig. 211), the puddingstone ledge overlooking Nelson's Pond (fig. 212), a portrait of Bancel, and lettering similar to that found in William Blake's illustrated books *Songs of Innocence and of Experience* (1789 and 1794). The odd fusion of varied sources creates a striking if anachronistic illustration that suits the curious amalgam of disparate poems making up the anthology.

Though no longer living at Paradise, La Farge continued to go there occasionally on artistic expeditions, usually to introduce other artists to his painting lairs. On several occasions in the spring of 1872, he took the young art students Helena de Kay (1848-1916) and Maria Oakey (1845-1927) to Paradise for lessons.[218] During the

210.
John La Farge
Songs of Feeling & Songs of Thought, 1872
Wood engraving on paper
(Engraver: Henry Marsh)
5 1/4 x 3 1/2 in. (13.3 x 8.9 cm.)
From Abby Sage Richardson, *Songs from the Old Dramatists* (New York: Hurd and Houghton, 1873), opp. p. 94

211.
Unidentified Photographer
Margaret Mason Perry La Farge, c. 1864
Photograph from glass-plate negative
3 5/8 x 4 7/8 in. (9.4 x 11.7 cm.)
Newport Art Museum, Newport,
Gift of Sal Lopes,
courtesy of Ethel T. Storer

212.
The Puddingstone Ledge above Nelson's Pond, Looking East
Photograph by the author
(Dec. 1994)

fall, he also "initiated" Robert Swain Gifford (1840-1905) "into the beauties of Paradise."[219]

In the spring of 1873, Margaret used an earlier inheritance from Grandma Perry to buy a house at 10 Sunnyside Place in downtown Newport (fig. 213), where the family moved around August 10th.[220] Unlike their first home on Kay Street over a decade earlier, this was a modest residence with few pretensions. Originally called "Swallow's Nest," the edifice dated from around 1845 and had once opened to the south. By the time Margaret bought the house, the entrance had been moved to the west, where it remains today. The interior, while roomy, was simple and intimate, and the La Farges filled the house with the kind of Victorian clutter that might be expected of an eclectic artist and his wife descended from the distinguished Perry family: Japanese hanging scrolls, religious icons, paintings by La Farge, photographs and miniatures, Newport furniture, and imported French furniture inherited from La Farge's father (figs. 214, 215).

213.
Unidentified Photographer
10 Sunnyside Place, Exterior View
Looking Southeast, c. 1880
Photograph
8 x 10 in. (19.6 x 24.6 cm.)
Private Collection

214.
Unidentified Photographer
10 Sunnyside Place,
Front Parlor, South Wall,
c. 1880
Photograph
8 x 10 in. (19.6 x 24.6 cm.)
Private Collection

215.
Unidentified Photographer
10 Sunnyside Place, Front Parlor,
Northwest Corner,
c. 1880
Photograph
8 x 10 in. (19.6 x 24.6 cm.)
Private Collection

216.
John La Farge
Blue Iris. Study, 1879
Watercolor and gouache on
off-white thick-wove paper
10 5/8 x 8 5/8 in. (27 x 22 cm.)
Jordan-Volpe Gallery Inc., New York

The purchase of Sunnyside Place ended any chance that the family would ever live again at Paradise—even though they continued to frequent Paradise on weekends throughout the 1870s. As late as 1879, La Farge still painted some of his floral studies from nature near the places that he had frequented a decade earlier. A watercolor of blue irises set against a sensuously painted background of sand dunes lining Second Beach (fig. 216) both recalls his oil study painted at Hazard's Farm in 1871 (see fig. 189) and predicts a surge of studio still-life painting in the early 1880s. Meanwhile, Paradise became less and less a place of daily artistic activity for La Farge as his focus on *plein-air* painting gave way to the exploration of allegory in themes drawn from religion or mythology.

Bancel identified the Sacred Grove as the place where "my mother posed sometimes for the figures in these religious paintings in classical draperies, flecked by the sunlight and shadows of the overhanging hickories."[221] He spoke primarily of the landscape backgrounds of two mural panels in an altarpiece for the Church of St. Thomas in New York, executed in 1877 and destroyed by fire in 1905 (fig. 217).[222] Representing scenes of Christ's Resurrection, the compositions taken together form a panorama of the Sacred Grove.

The Three Maries (all three with features of Margaret La Farge) encounter two angels of the Resurrection at the base of a dramatic rocky cliff that soars above the figures and into the distance (fig. 218). This is the cliff lining the west side of the Sacred Grove, depicted just north of the spot seen in the earlier painting of *Hollyhocks* (see figs. 74-75). The exact point in the cliff can be pinpointed by the rock on the ground just behind the angels, today buried beneath a fallen tree and other debris (fig. 219). The cliff at this point consists of sheets of sheer slate, yielding the jagged, craggy, yet sleek look seen in the background of the painting (fig. 220). While steep, the angle of the cliff was too slight for the spatial arrangement of the panel, so La Farge depicted the cliff more upright, enhancing its irregular profile.

Directly to the east from this point in the cliff, a narrow brook flowing from the north sets off a wide strip of heavily-wooded land that contains a monumental puddingstone outcropping (fig. 221). These rocks became the setting for the panel showing an angel at the open tomb (fig. 222) and a *Noli me tangere*, enacted by Mary Magdalene and the Resurrected Christ (fig. 223). Many familiar spots around

217.
John La Farge
The Resurrection; Altarpiece formerly in
Church of St. Thomas, New York, 1877
Encaustic on canvas
Each lancet, approx. 120 x 180 in.
(304.8 x 457.2 cm.)
Destroyed by fire in 1905

218. John La Farge
The Three Maries; right lancet of
The Resurrection Altarpiece, 1877
Encaustic on canvas
Approx. 120 x 180 in. (304.8 x 457.2 cm.)
From Charles H. Caffin, "The Beginning
and Growth of Mural Painting in
America," *The Bookman*, vol. 28 (Oct.
1908), p. 129

Nelson's Pond are included in the landscape composition. Across the water through the gap in the puddingstone formation is the north side of the island depicted in *The Last Water Lilies* (see figs. 59-60). A boulder seen just beyond the trees on this side of the pond is the same boulder found in *The Shepherd and the Sea* (see figs. 227-228), as well as at the left in *The Wolf Charmer* (see figs. 197 and 201, or the right side of the wood engraving, fig. 196).

La Farge wanted to position these scenes with the panel of *The Three Maries* on the left and the *Noli me tangere* panel on the right. Arranged this way, the panels would have formed a landscape giving an actual view of the Sacred Grove looking both north up the cliff and east towards the misty waters. The viewer in the congregation would thereby experience the Sacred Grove much as if actually standing in it. "All this allowed me to have a look of peace and quiet in the scene," La Farge noted," and to try to make it look as natural as if we saw it happening."[223] The rector meddled with this concept when he realized that the figure of Christ in the *Noli me tangere* had been relegated to the far right corner. He had La Farge switch the panels, placing Christ more centrally, just to the left of the altar.[224]

219.
Rock at Base of Cliff in the Sacred
Grove, Looking West
Photograph by the author
(Jan. 1995)
Beneath the rippling slate and pudding-stone protrusions of the cliff in the Sacred Grove is the distinctive pedestal-like rock seen behind the angels in The Three Maries *and other works. Although readily identifiable by its specific crags and cracks, this large rock is almost lost beneath fallen trees and rocky debris.*

220.
The Cliff in the Sacred Grove,
Looking Up
Photograph by the author
(Jan. 1995)
The steep, almost perpendicular, rise of cliffs seen in the background of The Three Maries *does not correspond to the actual rise of the cliff in the Sacred Grove. The rippling slate and puddingstone projections, however, were repeated in La Farge's rendering.*

221.
The Puddingstone Outcropping near
Nelson's Pond, Looking East
Photograph by the author (Jan. 1995)
*The heavily wooded and brambled rock
formation is difficult to photograph from
the perspective seen in the St. Thomas
altarpiece.*

222.
John La Farge
Angel at the Tomb; left lancet, left wing of
The Resurrection Altarpiece, 1877
Encaustic on canvas
Approx. 120 x 90 in. (304.8 x 228.6 cm.)
Destroyed by fire in 1905

158

223.
John La Farge
Noli me tangere; right lancet, left wing of
The Resurrection Altarpiece, 1877
Encaustic on canvas
Approx. 120 x 90 in. (304.8 x 228.6 cm.)
Destroyed by fire in 1905

La Farge not surprisingly was upset by the change, finding it arbitrary at best: "I do not think it has mattered much but I feel that it would have been much better the other way, and so much more within the meaning of the work and the meaning of the picture that I think it is worth mentioning. It is also certainly worth mentioning as an example of what the artist in monumental work has to contend with. And you can see how fallible any criticism must be of the past when we have no chance of knowing the enormous complications which have influenced the entire work of the past."[225] Still, La Farge felt overall that the sense of naturalistic space and convincing atmosphere that led him to use the Sacred Grove as a setting was not impaired. He was especially pleased that the landscape captured a "successful representation of the time of day intended."[226] Contemporary critics seconded his high estimation, appreciating how the realistic, dawn-like lighting heightened the sense of the sublime.

> *How fine that rolling gloom of darkly mingled tints, in the falling land of the background! Both, viewed from the places of the congregation, seem to float off into an atmosphere of the visionary and unapproachable, tinged with some ray of divination, going beyond the real, yet arresting the real aspect, also, and fixing it in a dimly luminous beauty.[227]*

Even Clarence Cook (1828-1900), usually an unfavorable critic of La Farge's work, found the landscape "charming in its suggestion of early dawn" while attaining at the same time "the effect of tapestry; it unites with great skill this decorative charm with the pleasure that belongs only to a painting."[228] Another critic compared the commingled decorative and realistic qualities of the scene to "a piece of tapestry colored by a Venetian master."[229]

The combination of realistic and decorative principles that found their most appropriate expression in such murals also became the primary feature of La Farge's mythological easel paintings executed during the 1870s. Most of these pictures also employed the Sacred Grove as their setting.

Virgil (fig. 224) is among the works that Bancel situated in the Sacred Grove, making it a sort of *double-entendre* for La Farge. Virgil's writings gave birth to the notion of a "Sacred Grove" as a place identified with artistic inspiration. That Virgil sits in La Farge's actual Sacred Grove makes it clear that he is a surrogate for the artist. Like the muse in *The Muse of Painting*, Virgil derives his inspiration from Paradise. La Farge's caption when he exhibited the picture echoes this meaning, quoting from the French nineteenth-century critic and writer Charles-Augustin Sainte-Beuve (1804-1869), who published his own 1857 lectures on Virgil: "His pleasures consisted in creating beautiful things in silence and shadow and without ceasing to live among the nymphs of the forests and fountains, among the hidden gods."[230]

224.
John La Farge
Virgil, 1874; retouched 1883
Oil on canvas
41 1/2 x 32 in. (105.4 x 81.3 cm.)
Harvard University Art Museums, Fogg
Art Museum, Cambridge, Massachusetts,
Gift of Hon. and Mrs. Robert Woods Bliss

The background in the painting is difficult to correlate with a specific spot in Paradise until we look at a drawing inscribed "For Virgil" that shows the linear contours of the rock upon which Virgil sits (fig. 225). This is the same rock seen at the base of the cliff behind the two angels in *The Three Maries* portion of the right wing of the St. Thomas Church altarpiece (see fig. 219).

The same rock was used as the posing stand for the enigmatically titled *The Golden Age* (fig. 226), also called *Eve* at times by La Farge[231] and *Woodland Nymph* at other times by Bancel.[232] The nude figure is engulfed in a rich tapestry of apple blossoms and foliage flecked with realistic lighting and texture. Still, as in *Virgil* and *The Muse of Painting*, the pervasive decorative glow cannot be called naturalistic, and betrays La Farge's admiration for artists such as Delacroix, Titian, or Rubens.

225.
John La Farge
Oak Leaves and Branches, c. 1874
Black chalk or charcoal
on smooth ivory paper
10 3/8 x 7 5/8 in. (26.4 x 19.4 cm.)
Bowdoin College Museum of Art,
Brunswick, Maine,
Gift of Miss Susan Dwight Bliss

226.
John La Farge
The Golden Age, 1878-79; retouched 1884
Oil on canvas
35 5/8 x 16 1/2 in. (90.5 x 41.9 cm.)
National Museum of American Art,
Smithsonian Institution,
Washington, D.C., Bequest of John Gellatly

227.
John La Farge
The Shepherd and the Sea. Aesop Fable,
1875; retouched 1879-83
Oil on canvas
30 x 25 in. (76.2 x 63.5 cm.)
William Vareika Fine Arts, Newport

Bancel did not similarly situate *The Shepherd and the Sea* (fig. 227) in the Sacred Grove, but the prominent rock behind which the shepherd crouches is a major feature of the west bank of Nelson's Pond (fig. 228). La Farge had visited this site frequently since first coming to Paradise, as shown in early drawings looking out over adjacent puddingstone outcroppings towards the distant Purgatory Rocks (fig. 229). This same rock appears in other works of this period as seen from different angles—for example, through the trees behind the *Noli me tangere* panel of the St. Thomas Altarpiece (see fig. 223) or, moved from its actual location a bit north, in *The Wolf Charmer* (see fig. 197). The artist subtitled *The Shepherd and the Sea* "Les conseils de la mer et de l'ambition" ("the advice of the sea and of ambition ") when he exhibited it.[233] The quote is taken from a La Fontaine fable called *Le Berger et La Mer*, which relates the temptations of the mermaid to the follies of ambition and greed.

164

228.
On the West Bank of Nelson's Pond,
Looking South
Photograph by the author
(Dec. 1994)
*In the dry season, the rock looks much
as it did in La Farge's day. In the wet
season, it is completely submerged.*

The picture has a lively palette reminiscent of contemporaneous French Impressionist painting. Laid down in loose touches of pastel colors, the foreground dances with bright swaths of pigment that flicker like sunlight. The main rock formation—actually composed of several rocks—also is handled with light-filled striations of multi-colored pigment. The animated surface drew particular admiration at the time.

> *The delicate sky and summer sea are given with exquisite sense of tone and rare appreciation of color. The flesh is pure and rich and the greens harmonious and well-lighted. Altogether, it is a picture dignified in general aspect, full of feeling and beautiful in color.*[234]

The image evolved from La Farge's 1872 illustration in Abby Sage Richardson's *Song from the Old Dramatists* (fig. 230) in which the site is not readily distinguishable and the features of the mermaid are generalized. In the easel painting, however, we not only can identify the site but also the female. The mermaid's features are those of **Mary Whitney** (1855-1940), a model and studio assistant who joined the decorative arts atelier that La Farge established in New York in 1880. Though the artist dated *The Shepherd and the Sea* to 1875 when he first exhibited it, he reworked the painting several times between 1879 and 1883. One revision turned the mermaid into a likeness of Mary Whitney, who in 1882 became romantically involved with the artist.[235] With this knowledge, we can read between the suggestive lines of a critique published in 1883 by another studio assistant, Roger Riordan (1848-1904), who wrote about the "decidedly fishy mermaid" with a "slightly-swaggering air" engaged in singing and:

*trolling a rollicking fol-de-rol caught up from some jolly tar half-seas-over
in more senses than one. Crisp little wavelets are leaping up around her. In
the foreground, glued to the rocks like a barnacle, is the nude figure of a
man. His dog standing beside him is almost as intent as he in watching the
strange phenomenon. It is a humorous though somewhat salty satire on
the creation for even the dog and the waves appear to be by no means
impeccable.*[236]

Once recognized, the face of Mary Whitney becomes a familiar presence in La
Farge's stained glass and murals, as well as in easel paintings created or reworked
in the early 1880s. In the case of *The Golden Age,* the irony seems colossal. La Farge
derived the pose and idea for the figure from the half of Titian's *Sacred and Profane
Love* meant to represent Chastity. He evidently added the features of Mary Whitney
in early 1883 when repainting the picture in order to send it to Munich for an
important international exposition that July.[237]

Mary's rise to prominence as the focus of La Farge's artistic and romantic attention marked the final stage of a growing estrangement between La Farge and his
wife, who had refused to relocate to New York in 1879 so that the family could stay
together while La Farge worked.[238] From that time on, La Farge made only occasional visits to Newport for the rest of his life, generally staying only a total of five
or six weeks over the course of the year.

229.
John La Farge
On the West Bank of Nelson's Pond,
c. 1865
Graphite on buff laid paper
5 x 7 1/4 in. (12.7 x 18.4 cm.)
Private Collection
*These rocks lay just alongside the
distinctive rock seen in* The Shepherd
and the Sea. *This drawing is one of
two similar drawings of the site in
the same sketchbook*

230.
John La Farge
The Song of the Siren, 1872
Wood engraving on paper
(Engraver: Henry Marsh)
5 3/4 x 3 9/16 in. (14.6 x 9.0 cm.)
From Abby Sage Richardson, *Songs from the Old Dramatists* (New York Hurd and Houghton, 1873), opp. p. 1

STUDIO MEMORIES

On May 19, 1885, La Farge received a summons at the Tenth Street Studio Building, ordering him to face charges of grand larceny. Before a judge at the Jefferson Market Court later that day, his business partners in the La Farge Decorative Art Company accused him of stealing drawings and studio photographs. "What we say, Judge, is that Mr. La Farge has concealed or given away our property and all we wish is to get it back," the lawyer for the company complained. La Farge replied, rather feebly: "I have delivered up all the property I had belonging to the company. The Sheriff came in and took all there was."[239]

This climax to years of business troubles marked the nadir of La Farge's career. His rise to prominence in the field of decorative arts had been a stunning victory for an artist who, for many years, was unable to find a buyer for his paintings. Universal acclaim for his murals and opalescent glass windows had brought him fame and fortune beyond his wildest expectations. But with the glory came a host of problems, ranging from the strain on his marriage to a surfeit of commissions that taxed his constitution and befuddled his business capabilities.

In the two years leading up to his arrest, La Farge already had been subjected to grievous indignities. On the brink of bankruptcy, he entered into partnership with businessmen who were as greedy and ruthless as they were incompetent. Promising to rescue him from his financial troubles, instead they sought to enslave La Farge to petty schemes that would commercialize his glass and other decorations.[240] One part of their takeover involved legal tactics that gave assignees control over his assets and art works. This led to several forced sales in which La Farge sought to bail himself out of debt by emptying the contents of his studio and producing new works to sell.[241]

Under intense pressure to boost his output, La Farge realized that by using his older compositions as stepping stones to new ones, he could quickly double or triple the number of works available for sale. A watercolor version of *Snow Storm* (fig. 231), for example, may at first appear to be a study for the painting of the puddingstone ledge above Nelson's Pond covered by snow executed in 1865 (see fig. 104), but like many pictures executed between 1883 and 1885, this is a repetition of the earlier work in different media. La Farge painted over a photomechanical reproduction of the earlier painting, using the memories of Paradise as embodied in his own previous works and preserved in photographs to create a new picture.

As this demonstrates, La Farge realized that one advantage to his working methods was that he had many photographic records to assist in making new works from old ones. This was particularly true in the case of his woodblock illustrations. It had become routine during the 1860s to photograph woodblock drawings before sending them to the wood engraver for cutting. This assured the artist that he could compare, correct, and critique the proofs pulled by the engraver after the woodblocks were cut. These left-over photographic images later became a commercial entity for La Farge and, as early as 1873, he used them to produce editions of prints that he published in different colored inks like wood engravings.[242] These reproductions then became the basis for "new" watercolors beginning in 1883. In the case of *Enoch Alone* (fig. 232), it is more than obvious that this was painted over a photomechanical reproduction of the original woodblock drawing (see fig. 91). The watercolor restores the detailed topography of Purgatory Rocks that had been removed from the illustration (see fig. 90).

Similar copies of most of the artist's woodblock drawings—including his series for the *Riverside Magazine*—were produced during this period, most using heavy gouache to help cover the underlying photomechanical image. But we should not be disdainful or overly judgmental of this episode of La Farge's career. Pressure and trauma brought out the best in the artist, and the furious pace of production coupled with the unusual circumstances surrounding it ultimately led to felicitous results. La Farge produced some of the best watercolors of his career during this

231.
John La Farge
Study of Snow, c. 1884
Watercolor and gouache
on mechanical reproduction
7 x 5 1/2 in. (17.8 x 14 cm.)
Private Collection

232.
John La Farge
Enoch Alone, c. 1883
Watercolor and gouache on mechanical
 reproduction of woodblock drawing
8 x 6 in. (20.3 x 15.2 cm.)
Location unknown

crisis, including an inspired series of water lily paintings, sumptuous figure studies
in elaborate interior settings, and a number of landscape compositions that reveal
great mastery of the difficult wet and dry techniques of watercolor painting.

Among the latter are two views of Paradise, both based upon—but not painted
over—photographic images. To create a view of the ridge lining the east side of
Nelson's Pond and the adjoining spine that forms the west wall of the Last Valley
(fig. 233), La Farge referred to a stereograph that he owned (fig. 234). Here thick
gouache and loosely applied watercolor animate the simple composition, emanat-
ing rich blue and green tonalities. The handling prefigures the liberation of technique that emerged during La Farge's trip to the South Pacific in 1890-1891.[243] explaining the misidentification of this picture at one time as a view of the South
Seas.[244]

A watercolor of Bishop Berkeley's Rock viewed from the south (fig. 235) has its
basis in a photograph by a Newport photographer, Joshua Appleby Williams (1817-
1892) (fig. 236). La Farge probably did not receive this photograph directly from
Williams, who had a studio in downtown Newport as early as 1854.[245] Rather he
very likely obtained the image through its publication by T. Nelson Dale as the frontispiece to an 1884 study of the geology of Paradise (see fig. 26). In the watercolor,
the washes of color are handled with a light and tightly controlled touch, matching
the geological precision of the photograph. But La Farge tellingly eliminated the
new Hanging Rocks Road that occupies the front of the photograph, unwilling to
allow modern realities intrude upon his studio memories of Paradise.

233.
John La Farge
Paradise Rocks.—Study at Paradise.
Newport, R.I., c. 1884
Watercolor and gouache
on white wove paper
8 x 9 7/16 in. (20.3 x 24 cm.)
The Metropolitan Museum of Art, New
York, Bequest of Susan Dwight Bliss, 1966
(67.55.171)

234.
Unidentified Photographer
Paradise Rocks, Looking East, c. 1884
Stereograph
Each frame, 4 1/2 x 4 1/2 in.
(11.4 x 11.4 cm.)
Private Collection

235.
John La Farge
*Study at Berkeley Ridge or Hanging Rock
(Rocks at Newport)*, c. 1883
Watercolor and gouache
on off-white watercolor paper
10 1/2 x 13 in. (26.7 x 33 cm.)
Museum of Fine Arts, Boston, Bequest of
Mrs. Henry Lee Higginson, 1935

236.
Joshua Appleby Williams
(1817-1892)
Bishop Berkeley's Rock, c. 1884
Photograph
4 x 5 in. (10.2 x 12.7 cm.)
Middletown Historical Society, Middletown
*The roadbed of Hanging Rocks Road,
consisting of tightly-packed stones (no doubt
from Peckham Brothers Quarry), is in the
middle ground. This photograph was taken
sometime between the completion of Hanging
Rocks Road in May 1883 and the publication
of this photograph in the Newport Natural
History Society's* Proceedings *in May 1885.*

POSTLUDE

John La Farge, c. 1895
Photograph
6 1/2 x 4 1/2 in. (16.5 x 11.4 cm.)
Private Collection

On June 27, 1899, La Farge suffered an attack of sciatica while on a visit to Boston and, unable to make it back to New York, ended up at Sunnyside Place in Newport to recover. "I thought myself freed" from such back troubles, he wrote to the New York architect Russell Sturgis (1836-1909), then about to publish an article on the artist in *Scribner's Magazine*. "Still I am being treated & in great hope of being better very soon."[246] By July 8th, La Farge could only write "I am still suffering greatly, but hope that this will pass over and that I may get down in a few days to New York."[247] When he next wrote to Sturgis on August 9th, the artist had reached New York and was working again at his studio.

This forced stay in Newport may at first sound like a trifling and unpleasant episode which hardly merits mention, but it became the occasion for what may have been La Farge's last visit to Paradise to paint from nature (fig. 237). Despite his "suffering," he found his way to the corner of Nelson's Pond just south of the cliff and Sacred Grove. From a spot now buried under the corner of the dike alongside the present pumping station (fig. 238), La Farge painted a sumptuous watercolor sketch looking out over the pond to the ridge on the far east side. Our eyes are especially drawn to the grove of three windswept black pine trees, with twisted trunks that seem to strain to stay in the ground. They are silhouetted against rolling, emerald green and royal blue hillocks beneath a delicately washed sky, pink at the right with the glow of morning light from the east. With an assortment of wet and dry techniques that resemble those used for his South Sea watercolors, La Farge created a vivid rendering of the verdant trees, lumbering hills, and placid blue waters so familiar to him for so many years.

This final image seems a fitting conclusion to the story of John La Farge in Paradise. Better than words, it reminds us of the relationship between the painter and his muse that prospered throughout his career. Much of the place has changed—much remains the same—but La Farge's special vision of Paradise lives on in his pictures.

La Farge used a personalized stamp, with his name in Japanese, to authenticate works during the last decade of his life.

237.
John La Farge
*Pine Trees near Nelson's Pond
at Paradise*, 1899
Watercolor, gouache, and pastel over
graphite on watercolor paper
8 3/4 x 11 15/16 in. (21.9 x 29.9 cm.)
William Vareika Fine Arts, Newport

238.
Nelson's Pond from the Southwest
Corner of the Dike, Looking East from
the Pumping Station
Photograph by the author
(Jan. 1995)
*The dike seen in the foreground covers the
hillocks seen in the watercolor of pine trees
by the pond bank.*

NOTES

1. Significant writings related to the topics of La Farge's early landscape painting or of Paradise, listed chronologically, are: Cecilia Waern, *John La Farge: Artist and Writer* (London: Seeley and Co. and New York: Macmillan and Co., 1896); Royal Cortissoz, *John La Farge: A Memoir and a Study* (Boston and New York: Houghton Mifflin Company, 1911); Henry Adams, "John La Farge, 1830-1870: From Amateur to Artist" (Ph.D. dissertation, Yale University, 1980), pp. 225-43; James L. Yarnall, "The Role of Landscape in the Art of John La Farge" (Ph.D. dissertation, University of Chicago, 1981); James L. Yarnall, "John La Farge's 'New England Pasture Land,'" *Bulletin of the Newport Historical Society*, vol. 55, pt. 3, no. 187 (Summer 1982), pp. 79-91; James L. Yarnall, "John La Farge's 'Paradise Valley Period,'" *Bulletin of the Newport Historical Society*, vol. 55, pt. 1, no. 182 (Winter 1982), pp. 1-25; James L. Yarnall, "John La Farge's 'The Last Valley,'" *Bulletin of the Newport Historical Society*, vol. 55, pt. 4, no. 188 (Fall 1982), pp. 130-42; Henry A. La Farge, "John La Farge and the 1878 Auction of His Works," *American Art Journal*, vol. 15, no. 3 (Summer 1983), pp. 4-34; James L. Yarnall, "Nature and Art in the Painting of John La Farge" in *John La Farge* (New York: Abbeville Press, 1987), pp. 79-122. No attempt has been made to cross-reference this essay to all references to specific pictures made in each of these texts. Information from conversations in December 1994 and January 1995 with a Newport horticulturist, Ralph Sabetta, provided many insights into the flora of Paradise, and I am most grateful to him for his time and expertise. Most manuscript references are from the two major repositories of La Farge letters and catalogue drafts: the La Farge Family Papers, Department of Manuscripts and Archives, Sterling Memorial Library, Yale University, New Haven, Connecticut (hereafter LFFP); and the Henry A. La Farge Papers, La Farge Catalogue Raisonné Inc., New Canaan, Connecticut (hereafter HLFP).

2. Middletown Historical Society, *Middletown, Rhode Island: Houses, History, Heritage* (Middletown, Rhode Island: Middletown Historical Society, 1990), p. 1.

3. For example, "Newport" [by W.E.A.], *The Family Magazine*, vol. 6 (1838-1839), p. 386; T. Addison Richards, "Newport," *The Knickerbocker*, vol. 54 (Oct. 1859), p. 339; and Oramel S. Senter, "Scenic and Civic New England—Newport 1877," *Potter's American Monthly*, vol. 9 (Jul. 1877), p. 7. Nor is it irrelevant that Aquidneck Island means "Isle of Peace" in native American and "Rhode Island" came from the fancied resemblance of the state to the Isle of Rhodes in Greece.

4. The dimensions of Purgatory were given by J.N. Stanley in a letter to the editor of the *Newport Mercury* (14 Feb. 1852), p. [3]; and repeated in "Dimensions of Purgatory," *Newport Daily News* (12 Aug. 1893), p. [1].

5. L.H. Foster, *Newport Guide, 1876* (Newport: J.P. Sanborn, 1876), pp. 28-29; "The Purgatory," *Appleton's Journal*, vol. 3 (22 Jan. 1870), pp. 100-02; *Harris 1879 Guide to Newport* (Newport: Harris and Co., 1879), pp. 34-36; J.R. Cole, "Town of Middletown," in Richard M. Bayles, *History of Newport County, Rhode Island* (New York: L.E. Preston & Co., 1888), p. 754; Mrs. John King Van Rensselaer, *Newport: Our Social Capital* (Philadelphia and London: J.B. Lippincott Company, 1905), pp. 68-70; "The Grist Mill [Purgatory Legends by E.E.E.]," *Newport Mercury* (1 Jun. 1934), p. [3].

6. T. Nelson Dale, "The Geology of the Tract Known as 'Paradise,' Near Newport," *Proceedings of the Newport Natural History Society*, no. 2 (Jul. 1884), pp. 3-5; "Remarks on Some of the Evidences of Geological Disturbances in the Vicinity of Newport," same journal and issue, pp. 5-8; and "The Geology of the Mouth of Narragansett Bay," same journal, no. 3 (Jul. 1885), pp. 5-14.

7. Charles T. Jackson, *Report on the Geological and Agricultural Survey of the State of Rhode Island made under a resolve of Legislature in the Year 1839* (Providence: B. Cranston and Co., 1840), pp. 92-93.

8. "Seasonal Notes," *Newport Daily News* (15 Sept. 1894), p. [3].

9. Phillip Michael O'shea, *Peckham Bros. Quarry, Middletown, R.I.* (Middletown, R.I.: Middletown Historical Society, 1986), pp. [1-20].

10. Edward Field, "Isaac Barker's Signal," *Newport Mercury* (28 Nov. 1903), p. 7. Similarly in Cole, "Town of Middletown," pp. 764-65.

11. Henry James, "Art," *Atlantic Monthly*, vol. 38 (Aug. 1876), p. 251.

12. Clipping from unidentified Newport newspaper, date unknown, Newport History card file under heading "Ponds," Newport Historical Society. The article also derides the pond as a "mud hole."

13. Mary C. Sturtevant, "The East Shore of Middletown, R.I.," *Bulletin of the Newport Historical Society*, no. 54 (Jul. 1925), p. 13.

14. Middletown Historical Society, *The Story of Our Town, Middletown, Rhode Island* (Middletown: Middletown Historical Society, 1993), pp. 1-2, 13.

15. Sturtevant, "East Shore of Middletown," p. 13. Mary Clark Sturtevant, daughter of the Episcopal Bishop of Rhode Island, Rt. Reverend Thomas M. Clark, became the driving force in the early 1880s behind the building of St. Columba's Chapel just off Indian Avenue. Eugene Sturtevant donated the land for the chapel to the Episcopal diocese. The Sturtevants and their four children are buried in the churchyard just behind the chancel of the chapel.

16. "Middletown," *Newport Mercury* (26 Aug. 1876), p. [2], noting approval on 21 Aug. 1876.

17. Clarke, "East Shore of Middletown," p. 16.

18. "A New Road in Middletown," *Newport Daily News* (15 May 1883), p. [2]. The lawsuits are noted in Hazard's obituary appearing in the *Newport Mercury* (29 May 1880), p. [2].

19. *The Newport Natural History Society 1883* (Newport: Davis and Pitman, 1883). This document contains the by-laws and founding principles of the society.

20. Martin Brimmer to Sarah Wyman Whitman, 10 Nov. 1881, Archives of American Art, Smithsonian Institution, Martin Brimmer Letters for Years 1880-1895, Roll D-32, frame 156. Whitman was a stained-glass designer who followed La Farge's example in working with opalescent glass.

21. Cortissoz, *John La Farge*, p. 66.

22. Léonce Bénédite, "La Peinture Française et Les États-Unis," in É. Boutroux et al., *Les États-Unis et la France, leurs rapports historiques, artistiques et sociaux* (Paris: Librairie Félix Alcan, 1914), p. 78. Cf. H. Barbara Weinberg, *The Decorative Work of John La Farge* (New York: Garland Press, 1977; Ph.D. dissertation, Columbia University, 1972), p. 23. In Gignoux's studio, the principles of French Barbizon art reigned, especially after the young George Inness (1824-1894) returned from studies in Paris sometime in 1855. In his company, and reportedly that of Homer Dodge Martin (1836-1897), La Farge painted his first oils under the influence of current French realistic styles.

23. Cortissoz, *John La Farge*, p. 110; cf. Waern, *John La Farge*, p. 15.

24. La Farge's name is absent from the rental lists published in the local newspapers both in 1859 (*Newport Daily News*: 29 Apr., p. [2]; 19 May, p. [2]; 26 May, p. [2]) and 1860 (*Newport Daily News*: 23 Jun., p. [2]). He may have resided in a boarding house, where his presence would not have merited publication. He may also have stayed somewhere on William Morris Hunt's estate, whose house was "roomy" according to Van Rensselaer, *Newport: Our Social Capital*, p. 46. Hunt also had a separate cottage that he offered for summer rental in 1862 (*Newport Daily News*: 14 Jul., p. [2]; 15 Jul., p. [1]).

25. Bruce Howe, "Early Days of the Art Association," *Newport Historical Society Bulletin*, no. 110 (Apr. 1963), p. 12 (reproducing photographs taken before razing in 1951). The date of the renovation to make the studio is given in the local news column of the *Newport Mercury* (11 Sept. 1858), p. [2]. Cf. Gibson Danes, "William Morris Hunt and His Newport Circle," *Magazine of Art* 43 (Apr. 1950), p. 144; Sally Webster, *William Morris Hunt 1824-1879* (Cambridge, England: Cambridge University Press, 1991), pp. 54-55; and Paul Baker, *Richard Morris Hunt* (Cambridge, Massachusetts and London, England: The MIT Press, 1980), pp. 122-23.

26. Webster, *William Morris Hunt*, p. 55.

27. J. Walker McSpadden, *Famous Painters of America* (New York: Thomas W. Crowell and Company, 1907), pp. 203-04.

28. Cortissoz, *John La Farge*, pp. 111-13.

29. John La Farge to Russell Sturgis, 11 Oct. 1899, LFFP.

30. John La Farge S.J., *The Manner is Ordinary* (New York: Harcourt, Brace and Company, 1954), p. 17.

31. La Farge, *Manner is Ordinary*, p. 18.

32. Oliver H.P. La Farge, [Notes on a Conversation with Margaret Mason Perry La Farge], 4 Jan. 1923 (Private Archives, Princeton, New Jersey). This was not the first trip south that Margaret took with Mary Porter, a widow who owned a large stone house now at 25 Greenough Place, not far from the Catherine Street residence of Margaret and her family. In 1856-1857, Margaret also wintered at the Porter plantation near Franklin, Louisiana.

33. The letters dating from December 1859 through April 1860 are in the La Farge Family Papers, The New-York Historical Society. They are quoted in part in La Farge, *Manner is Ordinary*.

34. *Newport Marriage Records*, vol. 1, p. 45, Newport City Hall; and "Married," *Newport Mercury* (27 Oct. 1860), p. [3]. The couple was married by a Roman Catholic priest in the rectory of St. Mary's Church, Newport.

35. Weinberg, *Decorative Work*, pp. 43-44.

36. McSpadden, *Famous Painters*, p. 207.

37. Cortissoz, *John La Farge*, pp. 112-13.

38. Cortissoz, *John La Farge*, pp. 118-19. The places that La Farge painted can be surmised from the titles of works dated to 1859 in two key auction catalogues authored by the artist: Peirce and Company, Boston, *Catalogue. The Paintings of Mr. John La Farge. To Be Sold at Auction*, 19-20 November [1878] (hereafter Peirce 1878); and Leonard's Gallery, Boston, *The Drawings, Water-Colors, and Oil-Paintings by John La Farge*, 18-19 Dec. [1879] (hereafter Leonard's 1879).

39. Newport City Hall, *Land Evidence Books*, vol. 35, p. 652. The transaction for $9,000 occurred on March 23, 1861. The house is now at 24 Kay Street.

40. Cortissoz, *John La Farge*, p. 116.

41. For a detailed discussion of La Farge's still lifes, including all pictures mentioned in this book, see James L. Yarnall, *Nature Vivante: The Still Lifes of John La Farge* (New York: Jordan-Volpe Gallery Inc., 1995).

42. Thomas Sergeant Perry to John La Farge, 4 Jun. 1863, Thomas Sergeant Perry Papers, Colby College, Waterville, Maine.

43. See the residency lists noted in chronological order in the bibliography. Despite intensive research, no residency list has been located for the year 1863. The Civil War may have prevented the compilation or publication of the list that year.

44. Title and date from Peirce 1878, 1st day, lot 2. Two paintings that cannot be readily identified as either Paradise or Newport proper date from the spring of 1861. The first, unknown by any visual record, was entitled "1861. Study of Spring. Orchard-Trees, with Horse Browsing." in Leonard's 1879, lot 15 (oils). The second, now privately owned, is too unspecific to suggest a site, and was entitled "Study of Appletree. Spring. Signed and dated 1861" when sold at Ortgies and Co., New York, *Important Collection of Oil and Water Color Paintings, by John La Farge of This City. To Be Sold at Auction*, 14-17 Apr. [1884] (hereafter Ortgies 1884), cat. no. 5.

45. Cole, "Town of Middletown," p. 764.

46. See detailed discussion in chapter 5.

47. According to *Norman Bird Sanctuary History*, an undated but recent brochure published by the Norman Bird Sanctuary, Benjamin Gardiner purchased the land in 1783 from Isaac Smith, who in turn had purchased it in 1871 from William Taggart. The name Paradise Farm, replacing the earlier appellation Gardiner's Farm, probably dates from when George H. Norman purchased the farm around 1900.

48. In August 1891, Isaac Barker sold sixty acres of "Paradise Farm" to O.H.P. Belmont, for $12,500 according to the *Newport Observer* (28 Aug. 1891), p. 8. Belmont also purchased Nelson's Pond, the house belonging to "J. Nelson," and part of Paradise Hills for $11,000, according to the *Newport Observer* (31 Oct. 1891), p. 8. This information is courtesy of Natalie N. Nicholson.

49. Margaret La Farge Hamill, comp. for Oliver H.P. La Farge, *The Gold Rush of 1898 and Other Reminiscences* (Princeton, New Jersey: Privately Published, 1990), p. 88 (republished in part in Appendix III).

50. Margaret Angela La Farge to Bancel La Farge, 14 Jul. 1938, HLFP (published for the first time in Appendix II).

51. "Middletown," *Newport Daily News* (4 Mar. 1898), p. [5]. This article was brought to my attention by Natalie N. Nicholson.

52. Bancel La Farge, "Paradise Valley" (manuscript, HLFP, Jul. 1938) (published for the first time in Appendix I).

53. La Farge, "Paradise Valley" (see Appendix I).

54. The artist dated the picture to 1862 in an exhibition catalogue for the Boston gallery of Doll and Richards: *Exhibition and Private Sale of Paintings in Water Color Chiefly from South Sea Islands and Japan*, 18-30 Mar. 1898, cat. no. 41. The picture was first listed as for sale in an inventory from an 1864 sketchbook (Yale University Art Gallery, acc. no. 1984.71.23). The earliest studies for the painting are found in a sketchbook dated 1861 on the cover (Yale University Art Gallery, acc. no. 1984.71.18).

55. A listing of works depicting similar dead or dying water-borne maidens would be extensive. Among the most famous examples are Delacroix's *Ophelia* (1842; Louvre Museum, Paris); Henry Wallis's *Elaine* (1861; location unknown); John Everett Millais's *Ophelia* (1851-1852; Tate Gallery, London); and Dante Gabriel Rossetti's *Elaine* in an important illustrated edition of Tennyson's poems published in 1857 by Edward Moxon in London.

56. Weinberg, *Decorative Work*, pp. 43-47.

57. Weinberg, *Decorative Work*, pp. 48-49.

58. Hamill, *Gold Rush*, p. 88 (see Appendix III).

59. La Farge, "Paradise Valley" (see Appendix I).

60. "New Pictures at Williams & Everett's," *Boston Evening Transcript* (9 Feb. 1864), p. 1.

61. Cortissoz, *John La Farge*, pp. 114-15.

62. "Summer Cottages and Villas Rented for the Season of 1862," *Newport Daily News* (14 Jul. 1862), p. [2]; repeated next day, p. [1].

63. David Maitland Armstrong, *Day Before Yesterday: Reminiscences of a Varied Life* (New York: Charles Scribner's Sons, 1920), pp. 304-06.

64. Cortissoz, *John La Farge*, p. 121. According to Elizabeth de Sabato Swinton, "John Chandler Bancroft: Portrait of a Collector," *Journal of the Worcester Art Museum*, vol. 6 (1982-83), p. 54, chronic ill health led to Bancroft's rejection from service and prevented his taking a first commission obtained for him by his father. Later, he decided to turn down another commission for an unknown reason.

65. John La Farge, "The Son of Bancroft," letter to the editor, *New York Times Saturday Review of Books and Art* (17 Aug. 1901), p. 581.

66. Swinton, "John Chandler Bancroft," pp. 56-58.

67. Cortissoz, *John La Farge*, pp. 121-22.

68. Title and date from Peirce 1878, 1st day, lot 9.

69. Title and date from Leonard's 1879, lot 6 (oils). The panel, originally 4 3/8 x 12 inches according to the 1879 catalogue, was cut down at an unknown date to a length of 8 5/8 inches.

70. Title and date from Leonard's 1879, lot 9 (oils). The appearance of this picture is known from a small photograph taken in late 1910 when it was loaned to the Boston Museum of Fine Arts by the owner at the time, Mrs. Andrew Cunningham Wheelwright of Boston. See a loan file in the Paintings Department, card no. 1829.10 (also numbered 67.40). The painting disappeared after the death in 1958 of Mrs. Wheelwright's unmarried daughter, Mary Cabot Wheelwright.

71. Title and date from Leonard's 1879, lot 8 (oils).

72. Title and date from Peirce 1878, 2nd day, lot 10.

73. Cortissoz, *John La Farge*, p. 89.

74. Title and date from Leonard's 1879, lot 42 (oils).

75. In the course of intensive research, Francine Corcione was able to find out very little about Stadtfeld. Two photographs of the Metropolitan Fair in New York taken in 1867 are in the New York Public Library. A collection of photographs of John Rogers sculpture is in the New-York Historical Society. A book by Peter B. Wight published in conjunction with the opening of the new National Academy of Design in 1866 contains twenty photographs by Stadtfeld. A photograph by Stadtfeld taken out of the window of his studio at 711 Broadway at Tilman's Flower Shop across the street is reproduced in Mary Black, *Old New York in Early Photographs* (New York: Dover Publications, 1976), p. 98. In addition, Stadtfeld published ten photographs after paintings by American Pre-Raphaelite artists in *The New Path* in 1864, according to William H. Gerdts and Russell Burke, *American Still-Life Painting* (New York: Praeger Publishers, 1971), p. 120.

76. James L. Yarnall, "John La Farge's *Portrait of the Painter* and the Use of Photography in His Work," *American Art Journal*, vol. 18, no. 1 (1986), pp. 4-9.

77. The payments are recorded in sketchbooks in the Yale University Art Gallery (acc. no. 1984.71.22, dating from around 1864; and acc. no. 1984.71.33, a payment dated April 26, 1878).

78. Yale University Art Gallery, acc. no. 1984.71.20.

79. The photograph is a platinum print on paper made by Eric E. Soderholtz, a landscape architect and self-taught photographer from Gouldsboro, Maine. His print is annotated: "Negative by La Farge/ Print by E.E.S." It is unknown how he came into possession of the negative by La Farge.

80. *The Palace of Art* is included in every standard anthology of Tennyson's work, for example, *The Poetic and Dramatic Works of Alfred Lord Tennyson* (Boston and New York: Houghton, Mifflin and Company, 1899), pp. 54-61.

81. Title and date from Leonard's 1879, lot 46 (oils).

82. The inscriptions are difficult to decipher because they lie under a surface layer of thin oil paint. Infrared viewing of the canvas in 1982 by the curatorial and registrar's staff of the Fogg Art Museum, coupled with a recent viewing by the author, have allowed the proposal of the inscription that is presented here.

83. La Farge stopped in Manchester on his way to Liverpool, where he caught a steamer to New York in late November or early December 1857. The *Catalogue of the Art Treasures of the United Kingdom collected at Manchester in 1857* (Manchester, England: Bradbury and Evans, 1857), drawn from British private collections and the Royal Collections, included 1123 old-master paintings, 639 paintings by contemporary British artists, 386 British portraits, 160 modern sculptures, a large selection of decorative art, 969 watercolors and drawings, and 59 miniatures. The watercolors spanned two centuries of English watercolor art, including many works by the Pre-Raphaelites and key English watercolorists like Joseph Mallord Turner.

84. Henry James to Thomas S. Perry, 18 Apr. 1864, cited in Leon Edel, *Henry James Letters*, (Cambridge, Massachusetts: The Belknap Press of Harvard University Press, 1974), vol. 1, p. 52.

85. Baker, *Richard Morris Hunt*, pp. 139-41. La Farge's pictures executed in Roxbury include a snow scene (Art Institute of Chicago) and a *Centaur* (William Vareika Fine Arts). The figure in the latter is based on Rimmer's famous statue of a dying centaur, while the landscape is a variation of the Roxbury hillside that appears in the snow scene.

86. *Land Evidence Book*, vol. 39, p. 99, Newport City Hall (deeded on 10 Oct. 1864 to Ann M. Wood for $18,000 [$800,000 today]); and "Real Estate Sales," *Newport Mercury* (10 Oct. 1864), p. [2].

87. Oil on wood, 7 3/8 x 9 1/2 inches, Davison Art Center, Wesleyan University, Middletown, Connecticut.

88. Alfred Lord Tennyson, *Enoch Arden* (Boston: Ticknor and Fields, 1865). The other artists were Octavius Carr Darley (1822-1888) and William John Hennessey (1839-1917), part of an older generation of established illustrators working in a more conservative, conventional style. Darley provided only one illustration, Hennessey four, and Vedder four. La Farge provided nine illustrations, of which eight appeared in all editions of the book, and one appeared only in editions published after Christmas 1864. Critical reception of the volume was not always appreciative of the mingling of styles and artists. In "Art. La Farge and Vedder," *Aldine*, vol. 6 (Aug. 1873), p. 167, they were termed "the queerest four-in hand ever harnessed together," with La Farge's plates "the strangest of all."

89. Charles F. Richardson, "A Book of Beginnings," *The Nation*, vol. 91 (1 Dec. 1910), p. 520. In this letter to the editor, Richardson discusses the illustrations of La Farge and Vedder at length and notes the competition with another publisher (J.E. Tilton and Company) to produce an edition before the Christmas book season of 1864.

90. Elihu Vedder to Kate Field, cited by Regina Soria, *Elihu Vedder* (Rutherford, N.J.: Farleigh Dickinson Press, 1970), p. 42. According to this letter, Vedder had finished by November 2.

91. Horace Scudder to William Rossetti, 27 Mar. 1868, cited in William Rossetti, comp., *Rossetti Papers 1862 to 1870* (London: Sands & Co., 1903), p. 349; cf. Cortissoz, *John La Farge*, p. 137.

92. David Bland, *A History of Book Illustration; The Illustrated Manuscript and the Printed Book* (Berkeley and Los Angeles: University of California Press, 1969), pp. 257-60; and Forrest Reid, *Book Illustrators of the Sixties* (London: Archibald Constable and Co., Ltd., 1897), pp. 36-43. The Moxon Tennyson was readily available in America through an 1862 edition published by the New York firm of George Routledge and Sons. For further discussion of contrasting styles of illustration in Boston during this period, see James L. Yarnall, "Tennyson Illustration in Boston, 1864-1872," *Imprint: Journal of the American Historical Print Collectors Society*, vol. 7 (Autumn 1982), pp. 10-16.

93. Tennyson, *Enoch Arden*, pp. 36-37. The illustration faces p. 36.

94. Anthony F. Janson, *Worthington Whittredge* (Cambridge, England: Cambridge University Press, 1989), p. 95, fig. 68.

95. Tennyson, *Enoch Arden*, p. 38. The illustration faces p. 38.

96. Tennyson, *Enoch Arden*, p. 41. The illustration faces p. 41.

97. Tennyson, *Enoch Arden*, pp. 27-28. The illustration faces p. 27.

98. A similar background had been used earlier in the poem for the illustration of Enoch's courtship of Annie entitled *The Lovers*; see Tennyson, *Enoch Arden*, facing p. 7.

99. Tennyson, *Enoch Arden*, p. 50. The illustration faces p. 50.

100. La Farge, *Manner is Ordinary*, p. 28.

101. "Newport Cottages and Villas Rented for the Season of 1865 [reported by Alfred Smith]," *Newport Daily News* (18 Jul. 1865), p. [2]; *New York Times* (18 Jul. 1865), p. 2; and *Newport Daily News* (5 Aug. 1865), p. [2].

102. "Our Watering Places," *New York Times* (22 Aug. 1866), p. 5; similarly as "Stephen Barker's near 2nd beach Middletown" in "Summer Cottages and Villas Rented for the Season of 1866," *Newport Daily News* (17 Aug. 1866), p. [2]

103. The address "Peckham's Paradise Road" appears in a circular published by Hazard, Ford & Co., *List of Families Residing in Newport, R.I.,* 1867; the address "E. Truman Peckham, Swamp road, Middletown" appears in "Cottages and Villas Rented for the Season of 1867," *Newport Daily News* (5 Jul. 1867), p. [2].

104. The listing "Barker's, Paradise Road, Middletown" appears in *Newport and How to See It* (Newport: Davis & Pitman, 1869), p. 72. That this was the Isaac Barker house is noted in the letter from Margaret Angela La Farge to Bancel La Farge, 14 Jul. 1938, HLFP (see Appendix II). In "Summer Residents," *Newport Daily News* (12 Jul. 1869), p. [2], his address is given as "Kay Street," suggesting just how haphazard and dated the rental reporting could be.

105. "List of Cottages. Season of 1871," *Newport Daily News* (8 Jun. 1871), p. [2]. Hazard owned the land running parallel to Second Beach as well as the land along the west side of Paradise Avenue south of Easton Farm. The only house on the land indicated on the 1870 map of the area (map 4) is just south of the Easton Farm above the turn in the Maidford River. That this was the house where the family resided is proven by the picture of Bishop Berkeley's Rock dated 1871 (see fig. 189), painted from the front yard.

106. Margaret Angela La Farge to Bancel La Farge, 14 Jul. 1938, HLFP (see Appendix II).

107. Title from Peirce 1878, 1st day, lot 7, with the note "Newport. 1865."

108. Henry James, "Art," *Atlantic Monthly*, vol. 34 (Sept. 1874), p. 377. La Farge mounted an exhibition of eight pictures at Doll and Richards during the summer of 1874. No catalogue of the show was published. All of the pictures had been rejected the previous spring by the exhibition committee of the National Academy of Design.

109. The title is a traditional one without clear documentary basis. See Metropolitan Museum of Art, *An Exhibition of the Work of John La Farge* (New York: Metropolitan Museum of Art, 1936), cat. no. 15. The inscription "Wind S. East/ Aug. 1865," visible in this photograph, is difficult to read today.

110. In La Farge's day, the buildings alongside Peter's Rock were more numerous. A plat map in the Middletown Town Hall, "surveyed by S.B. Cushing & Co. Feb. 11 1880" shows "Dwelling House A" and "Dwelling House B" in positions corresponding to the two houses in the drawing, along with a barn to the north that is just barely suggested in the drawing. Natalie N. Nicholson brought this map to my attention; she in turn was given a copy of the map by the present owner of Paradise Farm.

111. Title and date from Ortgies 1884, lot 17.

112. Quote from Henry A. La Farge's first catalogue raisonné (1933-34), card 33 (oils), LFFP.

113. Title and date from Peirce 1878, 1st day, lot 12.

114. Henry A. La Farge, first catalogue raisonné, card 26 (oils), LFFP. Martin Brimmer purchased the picture at auction and it descended to his wife's niece, Mary Ann Timmins. It was last known in the possession of the latter's husband, Charles H. Parker, who died in 1958.

115. Title and date from Peirce 1878, 1st day, lot 20.

116. Moore's Art Gallery, New York, *Catalogue of a Collection of Oil and Water Color Paintings by John La Farge*, 26-27 Mar. [1885] (hereafter Moore's 1885), cat. no. 41.

117. Doll and Richards, Boston, *Catalogue of Drawings, Watercolors, and Paintings by Mr. John La Farge on Exhibition and Sale*, 25 Jan.-6 Feb. 1890, cat. no. 10.

118. The owners, Gorham and Beatrice Cross, were postal workers from Hingham, Massachusetts. Nothing further can be learned of their identity.

119. John La Farge, *Hokusai: A Talk about Hokusai, the Japanese Painter at The Century Club March 28, 1896* (New York: Wm. C. Martin Printing House, 1897), pp. 5-6; reprinted in John La Farge, *Great Masters* (New York: McClure, Phillips and Co., 1903), pp. 221-22. Cf. Henry Adams, "John La Farge's Discovery of Japanese Art," *Art Bulletin*, vol. 67 (Sept. 1985), pp. 449-85.

120. Robert G. Workman, *The Eden of America: Rhode Island Landscapes, 1820-1920* (Providence: Museum of Art, Rhode Island School of Design, 1986), p. 40.

121. Sturtevant, "East Shore of Middletown," p. 13.

122. Janson, *Worthington Whittredge*, col. plate XV and figs. 68, 123, 165, and 166.

123. Hamill, *Gold Rush*, p. 88.

124. The records of the Newport Town and Country Club in the Newport Historical Society include information on the full range of activities and membership. These records formed the basis of a study by Virginia Galvin Covell, "A Critical Examination of the Town and Country Club of Newport, Rhode Island" (Master's Thesis, University of Rhode Island, 1964). See additional references in Yarnall, "John La Farge's 'The Last Valley,'" p. 132.

125. Armstrong, *Day Before Yesterday*, p. 304.

126. Armstrong, *Day Before Yesterday*, p. 304.

127. John La Farge, *Considerations on Painting* (New York: Macmillan and Company, 1895), p. 71. The book consisted of five lectures delivered at the Metropolitan Museum of Art in New York from 11 Nov.-15 Dec. 1893. This expedition was studied at greater length in Yarnall, "John La Farge's 'Paradise Valley Period,'" pp. 15-20.

128. Lilian Whiting, *Kate Field: A Record* (Boston: Little, Brown and Company, 1899), p. 167, citing a letter from Kate Field written in the summer of 1865. Field also noted that the artist Charles Caryl Coleman (1840-1928) was in Newport at this time, and that, with Vedder, they made excursions to Paradise to walk in the hills. La Farge is not known to have had any special friendship with Coleman that would suggest he was one of the "cronies." Vedder went abroad for several years to further his art studies beginning in 1866.

129. "Art. Art Notes," *Round Table* (9 Sept. 1865), p. 7. Much like Vedder, Homer went abroad to study for several years beginning in 1867.

130. "Our Watering Places—The Empty Sleeve at Newport," *Harper's Weekly*, vol. 9 (26 Aug. 1865), p. 1.

131. Summarized in Henry Adams, "Winslow Homer's 'Impressionism' and Its Relation to His Trip to France," in *Winslow Homer: A Symposium, National Gallery of Art Studies in the History of Art*, vol. 26 (1990), p. 80.

132. In Yarnall, "John La Farge's 'Paradise Valley Period,'" p. 17, the site of this picture was incorrectly postulated as the same as in the two other pictures under discussion here.

133. La Farge, *Considerations*, p. 73.

134. La Farge, *Considerations*, p. 75.

135. Waern, *John La Farge*, p. 21.

136. Rumors that La Farge's ill health was a graver matter, stopping him from working altogether for years, first appeared in "Art. American Art and Artists," *Round Table* (23 Sept. 1865), p. 36, ironically dated the day of Bancel's birth. A claim made here that La Farge had been ill for much of the preceding year and unable to work seems immediately contradicted by the watercolor portrait of Margaret pregnant with Bancel, and the surfeit of other works that can be dated in various ways to the summer of 1865. In "Art. Art Notes," *Round Table* (14 Jul. 1866), p. 7, it was presumably the same writer who wrote that La Farge had done little work for the past two years but would resume work shortly. He based this claim on La Farge's failure to exhibit at the National Academy of Design in 1865 and 1866, but does not seem to have been genuinely informed about La Farge's health or the scope of his activities. Again in "Pictures at the National Academy," *Round Table* (18 May 1867), p. 310, the claim was made that La Farge had not worked for "three or four" years due to ill health, and again it was based on La Farge's poor contributions to the National Academy of Design. I thank Colonel Merl M. Moore Jr., Falls Church, Virginia, for bringing these citations to my attention.

137. See also Yarnall, "John La Farge's 'New England Pasture Land,'" pp. 79-91. When this article was written, the precise residences of La Farge in Paradise had not yet been researched; nor had the specific valley seen in *Paradise Valley* been correctly identified.

138. Henry Adams, "A Fish by John La Farge," *Art Bulletin*, vol. 62 (Jun. 1980), pp. 269-80.

139. The X-ray taken around 1933 at the Fogg Art Museum Conservation Lab revealed the underdrawing of this composition on the canvas. Henry A. La Farge further identified the subject from a drawing (Mount St. Mary's College, Emmitsburgh, Maryland) and two watercolors (Mount St. Mary's College and William Vareika Fine Arts). The three versions are discussed and illustrated in James L. Yarnall, "New Insights on John La Farge and Photography," *American Art Journal*, vol. 19, no. 2 (1987), pp. 73-76.

140. A drawing in a sketchbook dating from 1866 (Yale University Art Gallery, acc. no. 1984.71.26) shows the mother and child in a landscape with the view down the valley to the Purgatory Rocks. This is one of many hundreds of drawings that have not yet been systematically catalogued or photographed.

141. Cole, "Town of Middletown," p. 753.

142. La Farge, "Paradise Valley" (see Appendix I).

143. Armstrong, *Day Before Yesterday*, p. 304.

144. John La Farge to Russell Sturgis, 1 Dec. 1904, LFFP.

145. John La Farge, "Autobiographical Notes, Memoranda, and Other Material by and about John La Farge: Recorded to Aid in Writing His Biography [1905]" (hereafter "Autobiographical Memorandum"), Royal Cortissoz Correspondence, Beinicke Manuscript Library, Yale University, items 113-14. The item numbers are those assigned by the Beinicke Library. Cf. Cortissoz, *John La Farge*, pp. 129-30. Cortissoz compiled this material in preparation for writing his biography, but in the case of La Farge's large landscape paintings, the original source material is more useful than the biography. This stems from omissions and changes, as well as from actual errors in using the material.

146. Margaret Angela La Farge to Bancel La Farge, 14 Jul. 1938, HLFP (see Appendix II).

147. "Fine Arts. What the Artists are Doing," *New York Evening Post* (14 Jan. 1867), p. 1.

148. Margaret Angela La Farge to Bancel La Farge, 14 Jul. 1938, HLFP (see Appendix II).

149. Mary Thacher Higginson, ed., *Letters and Journals of Thomas Wentworth Higginson 1846-1906* (Boston and New York: Houghton Mifflin Company and The Riverside Press, 1921), pp. 225-27. *Protus* was a now-lost drawing on glass illustrating an allegorical figure of a child from Robert Browning's *Men and Women*. The design is known from an impression (Private Collection) made from the glass drawing by a photographic process called *cliché verre*.

150. Whiting, *Kate Field*, p. 185.

151. "Fine Arts in Newport," *Boston Evening Transcript* (11 Aug. 1868), p. 1.

152. "Summer Residents," *Newport Daily News* (11 Jul. 1868), p. [2]. Similarly as "the Eustis House, Kay Street" in "Cottages and Villas Rented for the Season of 1868," *Newport Mercury* (18 Jul. 1868), p. [2].

153. William W. Story, *Reports of the United States Commissioners to the Paris Universal Exposition, 1878* (Washington, D.C., 1880), vol. 2, p. 112. Similarly in William J. Stillman, "The Paris Exposition—XI," *Nation*, vol. 27 (3 Oct. 1878), p. 211.

154. Henry James, "Art," *Atlantic Monthly*, vol. 37 (Jun. 1876), p. 760.

155. La Farge, "Autobiographical Memorandum," item 114. Cf. Cortissoz, *John La Farge*, p. 130.

156. La Farge, "Autobiographical Memorandum," item 114. Cf. Cortissoz, *John La Farge*, p. 131.

157. Discussed at greater length with comparative illustrations in Yarnall, "New England Pasture-Land," pp. 82-83.

158. Cortissoz, *John La Farge*, p. 129.

159. National Academy of Design, New York, *Catalogue of the Fifty-First Annual Exhibition*, 1876, cat. no. 188.

160. "The National Academy of Design. (Second Notice)," *Art Journal* [New York], vol. 2 (1876), p. 190.

161. "The Fine Arts. Exhibition of the National Academy," *New York Times* (8 Apr. 1876), p. 7.

162. "The National Academy of Design. (Second Notice)," *Art Journal* [New York], vol. 2 (Jun. 1876), p. 190.

163. According to "List of Pictures by Mr. John La Farge sold by Doll & Richards, Inc., Boston" (Typescript, Vose Gallery Papers, Boston), p. 1, the picture was sold at Doll and Richards, Boston, on 7 Sept. 1876 to Miss Alice Sturgis Hooper (1841-1879). Upon her death, her sister inherited the picture and it remains among her direct descendants.

164. Exposition Universelle Internationale, Paris, *Catalogue Officiel* (Paris: Imprimerie Nationale, 1878), vol. 1, p. 205, cat. no. 73, as "Vallée du Paradis à Newport."

165. Richard C. McCormick, "Our Success at Paris in 1878," *North American Review*, vol. 129 (Jul. 1879), p. 3.

166. Henry James, "Art," *Atlantic Monthly*, vol. 38 (Aug. 1876), pp. 251-52.

167. Pierce 1878, cat. no. 18 (2nd day): "The Last Valley. Paradise, Newport, R.I. A Sunset Study, with the line of the Hanging Rocks, or Bishop Berkeley's Rocks. This picture has been painted entirely from nature and out of doors, except where an accident has necessitated repairs." The picture is discussed at greater length in Yarnall, "John La Farge's 'The Last Valley,'" pp. 130-42.

168. Susan Coolidge, *A Little Country Girl* (Boston: Little, Brown and Company, 1885), pp. 191-93; and Sarah S. Cahoone, *Visit to Grandpapa; or, A Week at Newport* (New York: Taylor and Dodd, 1840), pp. 114-19.

169. La Farge, "Autobiographical Memoir," item 106. This passage does not appear in Cortissoz, *John La Farge*.

170. La Farge, "Autobiographical Memorandum," item 106. This passage does not appear in Cortissoz, *John La Farge*.

171. The title appeared in the Forty-Second annual exhibition of the National Academy of Design in 1867, cat. no. 352. In 1871, when again exhibited at the Academy during the Second Summer Exhibition, cat. no. 353, the picture was entitled *Sea Side Study*. Reviews of both shows make very meager mention of the picture.

172. The picture was entitled "The Seashore" and given the dimensions 15 x 11 inches when sold at Somerville Auctioneers, New York, *The Collection of over Five Hundred Paintings and Studies by the Late John F. Kensett*, 24-29 Mar. 1873, lot no. 462. Photographs of the paintings hanging in this auction, taken a wall at a time, do exist in the archives of the National Academy of Design. If La Farge's picture is among the works thus recorded, it cannot be readily picked out from these photographs.

173. Waern, *John La Farge*, p. 27.

174. Thurman Wilkins, *Clarence King: A Biography* (New York: Macmillan Company, 1958), pp. 120, 194.

175. Prof. and Mrs. Louis Agassiz, *A Journey in Brazil* (London: Trubner & Co., 1868), p. 112.

176. Agassiz purchased the picture for $900 at Peirce 1878, 2nd day, lot 18. This was a relatively low price compared to the $3000 paid for *Paradise Valley* in 1876.

177. John Torrey Morse, *Thomas Sergeant Perry: A Memoir* (Boston: Houghton Mifflin Company, 1929), p. 62.

178. "Local Affairs," *Newport Journal* (16 Sept. 1875), p. 2.

179. Cortissoz, *John La Farge*, p. 186. Cf. London Society of French Artists, *Seventh Exhibition of the Society of French Artists*, [Summer] 1873, cat. no. 18, as "The Last Valley, Newport, U.S.A., The Scene of Bishop Berkeley's Meditations." Delacroix's contribution to the show was cat. no. 20, *The Entombment*. Rousseau was represented by cat. no. 45, *A Farm on the Banks of the Oise*.

180. Francis A. Walker, ed., *United States Centennial Commission, International Exhibition, 1876: Reports and Awards Group XXVII* (Philadelphia, 1877), p. 113; Philadelphia, Centennial Exposition, *Official Catalogue, Art Gallery, Annexes and Out-Door Works of Art*, 1876, cat. no. 5.

181. Title from Ortgies 1884, cat. no. 23. An erroneous association of this picture with the Philadelphia Centennial Exposition of 1876 and the Society of American Artists exhibition of 1878 was made in Natalie Spassky et al., *American Paintings in the Metropolitan Museum of Art, Volume II, A Catalogue of Works by Artists Born Between 1816 and 1845* (New York: Metropolitan Museum of Art, 1985), pp. 403-05. The picture shown on both of these occasions was *The Last Valley*, as known from reviews and other sources.

182. The underpainting of *The Last Valley* was described in Waern, *John La Farge*, p. 27.

183. Grace Edith Barnes to Robert C. Vose, 8 Mar. 1913, Macbeth Papers, Archives of American Art, Reel 2605, frame 1298,

184. Joseph Shepherd to William Macbeth, 27 May 1907, Macbeth Papers, Archives of American Art, Reel NMc20, frame 392.

185. Robert C. Vose to Charles de Kay, 18 Nov. 1911, Vose Gallery Papers, Boston. De Kay still owned the picture when he died in 1935; his widow sold it in 1949 to Frank Jewett Mather Jr., a Professor of Art History at Princeton. When given the option of accepting it as part of a large gift from Mather, the University Art Museum declined in favor of a small oil by La Farge depicting the Old Boat House Beach. Mather then gave this picture to the Metropolitan Museum of Art, and it is continually on display in the American Wing galleries.

186. John Keats, *The Complete Poetical Works of Keats* (Boston: Houghton Mifflin Company, 1899), p. 9. Cf. Henry A. La Farge, "The Early Drawings of John La Farge," *American Art Journal*, vol. 16, no. 2 (Spring 1984), p. 27.

187. Title from Peirce 1878, 1st day, lot 6, with the note "Newport. 1868."

188. National Academy of Design, New York, *Catalogue of the Fifty-Third Annual Exhibition*, 1878, cat. no. 555.

189. La Farge, "Paradise Valley" (see Appendix I).

190. La Farge, "Autobiographical Memorandum," item 106. This passage does not appear in Cortissoz, *John La Farge*.

191. Title and date from Leonard's 1879, lot 31 (oils). This was painted on canvas, according to the catalogue.

192. American Art Association (at Mendelssohn Hall), New York, *A Descriptive Catalogue of Paintings, Pastels, and Water Colors collected by the late Mrs. S. D. Warren of Boston*, 8-9 Jan. 1903, lot 68.

193. Only one residency list for the season of 1870 has been located, but it does not contain La Farge's name: "Cottages and Villas Rented for the Season of 1870," *Newport Mercury* (9 Jul. 1870), p. [2]. The reason that there is no listing in the *Newport Daily News* in 1870 may have to do with a small book entitled *Newport and How to See It* that the newspaper published from 1869-1873. Editions of this book that have been located contain a complete listing of Newport summer residents. The volume for 1870 has not been located, however, even though its pending publication was noted in "Newport and How to See It," *Newport Daily News* (20 Jun. 1870), p. [2].

194. *Newport and How to See It* (Newport: Davis & Pitman, 1871), p. 54; and "List of Cottages, Season of 1871," *Newport Daily News* (8 Jun. 1871), p. [2].

195. "Art Notes," *Boston Evening Transcript* (20 Feb. 1885), p. 2.

196. Title from Ortgies 1884, cat. no. 18.

197. Charles de Kay, "A Notable Gift to the Metropolitan Museum: La Farge's 'Muse of Painting,'" *Harper's Weekly*, vol. 54 (12 Mar. 1910), p. 7.

198. The intimation of a decorative scheme of mythological paintings for Richardson is made regarding La Farge's *Centaur* (William Vareika Fine Arts) in "Mr. La Farge's Pictures," *The American Architect and Building News*, vol. 4 (30 Nov. 1878), pp. 182-83. Richardson is also believed to have owned *Cupid and Psyche* (Scripps College, Claremont, California). Taken together, these paintings combined with other mythologies like *The Muse of Painting* might potentially make a coherent mythological decorative ensemble.

199. Ellen B. Ballou, "Horace Elisha Scudder and the *Riverside Magazine*," *Harvard Library Bulletin*, vol. 14 (Winter 1960), p. 436.

200. John La Farge to Horace Elisha Scudder, 21 or 22 Oct. 1868, Horace Elisha Scudder Papers, Houghton Library, Harvard University (hereafter Scudder Papers).

201. *Riverside Magazine for Young People*, vol. 1, no. 12 (Dec. 1867), ill. opp. p. 552. The text of the story is on pp. 552-53. The first design that La Farge prepared in the series, *Bishop Hatto and the Rats*, did not get published in the magazine but is known from proofs pulled from the cut block. Apparently, the horrific subject matter of this illustration led to its rejection by Scudder (James L. Yarnall, "John La Farge's *Bishop Hatto and the Rats* and *The Pied Piper of Hamelin*

Town in the Chicago Sketchbook," *Master Drawings*, vol. 29, no. 2 [Summer 1991], pp. 115-44). For *The Wolf Charmer*, La Farge was very displeased with the cutting of the block by Henry Marsh. In addition to proofs of the block that he annotated with vigorous suggestions (copies in Metropolitan Museum of Art, New York, and Horace Elisha Scudder Papers, Houghton Library, Harvard University), he also complained to Scudder in a letter on 30 Oct. 1867 (Scudder Papers).

202. Curtis Cate, *George Sand* (Boston: Houghton Mifflin Company, 1975), pp. 646-52.

203. George Sand, *Légendes Rustiques* (Paris: Calmann Lévy, 1877), chapter 8, pp. 95-105.

204. Lathrop, "John La Farge," p. 507.

205. Though destroyed in 1867, the altarpiece by Titian was widely known by engravings. La Farge may have intended his use of the image as a sort of homage to the destroyed work.

206. Cortissoz, *John La Farge*, p. 143.

207. Adrian Margaux, "My Best Picture. No. VII.—The Choice of Eminent American Painters," *Strand Magazine*, vol. 32 (Dec. 1906), pp. 497-504. The article included a lengthy explanation by the artist of the subject.

208. William Kenney Bixby, who commissioned La Farge in 1904 to make a memorial window for a church in Saint Louis, purchased the picture for Washington University in 1907. When sold at auction at Kende Galleries at Gimbel Brothers, New York (*Representative Paintings by Famous XIX Century Artists*, 4 May 1945, lot 170), the purchaser was Patrick O'Connor of O'Connor Galleries in New York. Attempts to trace its subsequent whereabouts have failed.

209. Frontispiece, *Riverside Magazine for Young People*, vol. 2, no. 19 (Jul. 1868), ill. opp. p. 289. The text of the story is on pp. 289-91. La Farge delivered the uncut woodblock to Scudder on 7 Apr. 1868, according to a letter of that date between the parties in the Scudder Papers.

210. Frontispiece, *Riverside Magazine for Young People*, vol. 2, no. 24 (Dec. 1868), ill. opp. p. 528. There is no corresponding text, but Scudder wrote a brief explanation of the illustration on p. 576, in order to inform the young readers about the subject.

211. This description by La Farge refers to the later oil version of the subject, as published in Peirce 1878, 2nd day, lot 22.

212. Frontispiece, *Riverside Magazine for Young People*, vol. 3, no. 39 (May 1869), ill. opp. p. 193. The text is on pp. 193-94.

213. Frontispiece, *Riverside Magazine for Young People*, vol. 4, no. 44 (Aug. 1870), ill. opp. p. 336. The text is on pp. 380-81. Uncut woodblocks left over from the project are in the Carnegie Museum of Art, the Preservation Society of Newport County, and various private collections.

214. Linnea Homer Wren, "The Animated Prism: A Study of La Farge as Author, Critic, and Aesthetician," (Ph.D. dissertation, University of Minnesota, 1979), pp. 66-67, citing *Records of the Board of Overseers of Harvard College*, vol. 11 (1871-1882), Harvard University Archives.

215. George Parsons Lathrop, "John La Farge," *Scribner's Monthly*, vol. 21 (Feb. 1881), p. 513.

216. La Farge, *Manner is Ordinary*, p. 28.

217. Andrew Boyd, comp., *Boyd's Newport City Directory for 1871-72* (Newport: A.T. Ward, 1871), p. 158. La Farge is listed as an "artist" with the address 34 Mann Avenue and a house at the same address. This edifice, still standing on the northwest corner of Kay Street and Mann Avenue, was run by a widow named Mrs. Lovie as a boarding house at the time.

218. Helena de Kay to Mary Hallock, letters dated simply "Aug. 1872" and "Fall 1872," in a collection of letters owned by a descendant of Richard Watson and Helena de Kay Gilder.

219. Margaret La Farge to Helena de Kay, 16 Sept. [1872], in a collection of letters owned by a descendant of Richard Watson and Helena de Kay Gilder.

220. *Land Evidence Book*, vol. 44, p. 287, Newport City Hall. Family tradition maintains that Margaret inherited this money in 1858 upon the death of her grandmother, the widow of Commodore Oliver Hazard Perry. She gave the date August 10th as that when the family would move in a letter to Helena de Kay, 29 Jul. 1873, in a collection of letters owned by a descendant of Richard Watson and Helena de Kay Gilder.

221. La Farge, "Paradise Valley" (see Appendix I).

222. Weinberg, *Decorative Work*, pp. 146-67.

223. Quoted in W.B. Van Ingen, "Notes on a Masterpiece of American Art," August F. Jaccaci Papers, Archives of American Art, Smithsonian Institution, Reel D-120, frame 1494; also found in the La Farge Family Papers, Yale LFFP, reel 2, frames 909-10.

224. Weinberg, *Decorative Work*, pp. 150-51; and Van Ingen, "Notes on a Masterpiece," frame 1496.

225. Van Ingen, "Notes on a Masterpiece," frame 1496.

226. John La Farge to Russell Sturgis, 23 Aug. 1895, LFFP.

227. Lathrop, "John La Farge," p. 514.

228. Clarence Cook, "Recent Church Decoration," *Scribner's Monthly*, vol. 15 (Feb. 1878), p. 574.

229. Wyatt Eaton to Augustus Saint-Gaudens, n.d., cited in Homer Saint-Gaudens, ed., *The Autobiography of Augustus Saint-Gaudens* (New York: The Century Co., 1913), vol. 1, p. 210.

230. Translation by the author of the French verses in Leonard's 1879, lot 50 (oils). The catalogue also gives the date 1874 for the work, but the picture was retouched or finished much later than this. It was described on La Farge's easel and "almost finished" by Roger Riordan, "A Pilgrimage Down East," *Lippincott's Magazine*, vol. 31 (Apr. 1883), p. 347. Sainte-Beuve's lectures were published in numerous editions, including Charles-Augustin Sainte-Beuve, *Étude sur Virgile* (Paris: Michel Lévy Frères, 1870). The passage that La Farge excerpted, with necessary changes for his context, is on p. 48 of this edition.

231. La Farge entitled the picture *Eve, or The Golden Age* when he sold it at Ortgies 1884, cat. no. 45, with the note: "Study of partly nude figure, half in shade, half in sunshine, with apple tree blossoms over head. Exhibited at Munich, 1883, and damaged in return transportation." At the Munich exhibition, the title that La Farge used was *Das goldene alter*, which in translation means "The Golden Age." See Royal Palace, Munich, *Illustrirter Katalog der Internationalen Künstaustellung*, 1 Jul.-15 Oct. 1883, cat. no. 1131.

232. Bancel annotated a photograph of this painting with the title "Woodland Nymph" (original photograph in the Yale University Art Gallery). Bancel identified this picture with the Sacred Grove in "Paradise Valley" (see Appendix I).

233. Leonard's 1879, lot 39 (oils). La Farge noted in this catalogue that the source of the imagery is an Aesop fable, but no corresponding fable can be located.

234. "The Fine Arts: Mr. La Farge's Pictures," *Boston Daily Advertiser* (18 Dec. 1879), p. 2.

235. Letters in the La Farge Family Papers, The New-York Historical Society, reveal this relationship. For further information, see the entry on Mary Whitney in the *Dictionary of People and Places*.

236. Riordan, "Pilgrimage Down East," p. 347.

237. "Sale of the La Farge Collection," *New York Times* (18 Apr. 1884), p. 5. Titian's *Sacred and Profane Love* is in the Borghese Gallery in Rome.

238. La Farge, *Manner is Ordinary*, p. 32.

239. "Artist La Farge Arrested," *New York World* (20 May 1885), p. 2.

240. James L. Yarnall, *John La Farge: Watercolors and Drawings* (Yonkers, New York: Hudson River Museum, 1990), pp. 39-42, citing documents in the New York City Municipal Archives and contemporary newspaper articles. See also Julie L. Sloan and James L. Yarnall, "Art of an Opaline Mind: The Stained Glass of John La Farge," *American Art Journal*, vol. 24, nos. 1-2 (1992), pp. 17-18.

241. There were four catalogues of forced sales, including two already mentioned: Ortgies 1884 and Moore's 1885. In addition, a supplemental catalogue of watercolors was published for the Ortgies exhibition: *Supplementary Catalogue of Water Colors, by John La Farge. To Be Sold at Auction*, 14-17 Apr. [1884]; and a later sale of stained glass, books, embroidery, and bric-a-brac was held at Ortgies also: *Catalogue of Stained Glass, Classic and Illustrated Art Books, Stuffs and Bric-a-Brac*, 23 May 1884.

242. Discussed at length in Yarnall, "New Insights on John La Farge and Photography," pp. 52-79.

243. For a full discussion of the trip, with illustrations, see James L. Yarnall, "John La Farge and Henry Adams in the South Seas," *American Art Journal*, vol. 20, no. 1 (1988), pp. 51-109.

244. Metropolitan Museum of Art, *An Exhibition of the Work of John La Farge*, cat. no. 56.

245. A letter to the editor written by Joshua Appleby Williams from his "Daguerreotype Rooms" appeared in the *Newport Daily News* (8 May 1854), p. [2]. An advertisement for making ambrotype portraits appeared frequently in the *Newport Daily News* (for example, 13 Apr. 1859, p. [4]). Williams had a studio at the foot of the Parade (Washington Square and Thames Street), and was in business with a Providence artist named P.T. Griffith, who evidently touched up the photographs.

246. John La Farge to Russell Sturgis, 29 Jun. [1899], LFFP. Sturgis wrote "John La Farge," *Scribner's Magazine*, vol. 26 (Jul. 1899), pp. 3-19.

247. John La Farge to Russell Sturgis, 8 Jul. [1899], LFFP.

MAPS

1   (a) Map of Narragansett Bay with Aquidneck Island, inserted in Edgar
    Mayhew Bacon, *Narragansett Bay: Its Historic and Romantic Associa-
    tions and Picturesque Setting* (New York and London: G.P. Putnam's Sons,
    1904);
    (b) Map of Paradise (detail), inserted in Mrs. John King van Rensselaer,
    Newport: Our Social Capital (Philadelphia and London: J.B. Lippincott
    Company, 1905).

2   Paradise, showing the places that John La Farge lived and worked (see key).
    Map by Nancy Thomas and Micrographix.

3   "Geology of Rhode Island;" map of Paradise showing the seven puddingstone
    ridges from T. Nelson Dale, "The Geology of the Tract Known as 'Paradise,'
    near Newport," *Proceedings of the Newport Natural History Society 1883-
    4*, no. 2 (Jul. 1884), plate 1.

4   *Map of Newport & Vicinity or Rhode Island*, published by M. Dripps, New
    York, 1860. Revised & Published by Wm. Dane, Civil Engineer & A.J. Ward,
    Bookseller, Newport, R.I. 1870.

5   Surveyed by William H. Lawton, *Map of Gray Crag Park, (Paradise Valley)
    Middletown, R.I.—Scale [1:100 feet]*, 1892, Diazo print. Courtesy of the
    Rhode Island Historical Society.

6   1895 Atlas of Middletown, *New Topographical Atlas of Surveys, Southern
    Rhode Island* (Philadelphia: Everts & Richards, 1895), plate 59 (detail).

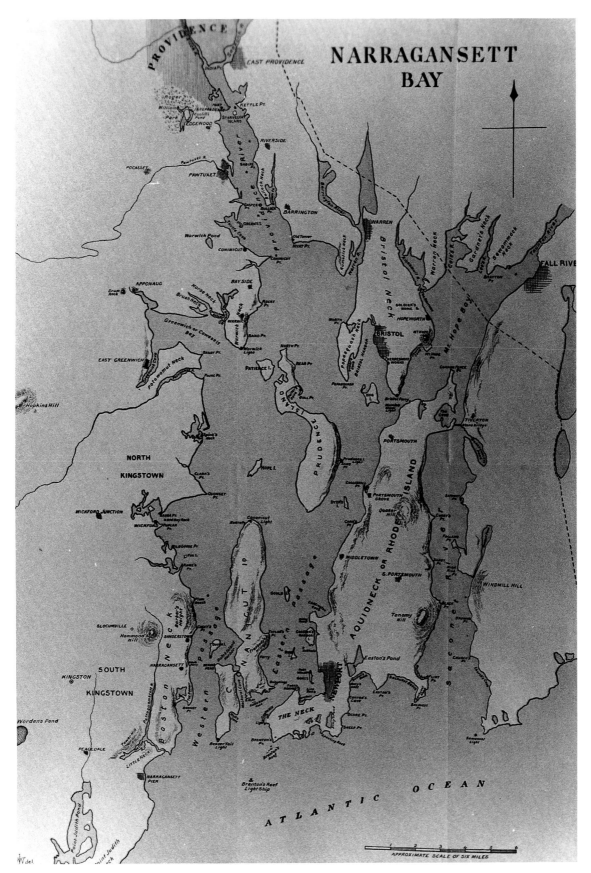

(a) Map of Narragansett Bay with Aquidneck Island (1904)

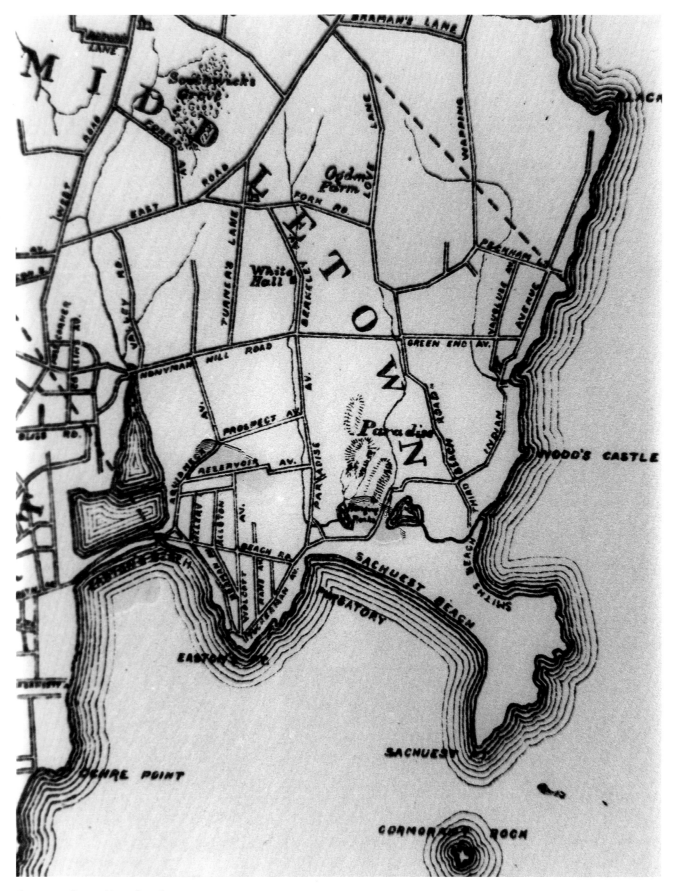

(b) Map of Paradise (detail) (1905)

The map combines topographical features of Paradise in La Farge's day and today. For ponds, solid outlines show the banks before 1880; broken lines indicate later expansion by the Newport Water Works to the present size and shape. Hanging Rocks Road, Sachuest Point Road, and Indian Avenue are shown by broken lines because they did not exist in La Farge's day. Third Beach Road is shown as it existed at the time; today the road no longer extends onto Flint and Sachuest Points and ends in a parking lot behind Third Beach. The road names shown are modern. Paradise Avenue was called Swamp Road until around 1865 and then became Paradise Road until this century. Green End Avenue similarly was known as Green End Road until recent years.

SITES

1. Purgatory Rocks and Purgatory Chasm
   figs. 2-3, 103, 145
2. Southwest Corner or South Side of Nelson's Pond
   figs. 73, 99, 100, 126-28, 233-34, 237-38
3. Peter's Rock
   from summit: figs. 8-9, 106-08, 177, 203-05;
   gap: 10, 110, 111
4. Pasture North of Paradise Farm
   figs. 6, 83, 109, 117-19
5. The Sacred Grove
   bank of pond: figs. 196-201, 209, 227-30;
   looking from grove: figs. 50, 74-75;
   near cliff: figs. 66, 122-23, 218-20, 224-26;
   puddingstone formation: 217, 221-23
6. The Puddingstone Ledge and Cliff
   looking at cliff from below: figs. 13, 51-55;
   looking at top of ledge: figs. 84-87, 94-96, 104-05, 210, 212, 231;
   looking from top of ledge: figs. 56-57, 69-72, 76, 124-25, 206
7. Second Beach near Puddingstone Outcropping
   looking at beach: figs. 29, 216; on beach: figs. 80-81, 90-92, 142, 178-79, 202, 232
8. Pasture East of Peter's Rock ("Paradise Valley" or Peckham Brothers Quarry)
   figs. 154, 157
9. Pasture to North of Peninsula (Lawn of Gray Craig)
   figs. 14, 136-38
10. Ledge in Paradise Hills (Gray Craig Trail)
    fig. 153

11. Barker's Rocks behind Sea Breeze Farm
    figs. 112-15
12. The Island in Nelson's Pond
    looking at: figs. 58-60;
    looking from: figs. 64-6513.
The Peninsula in Nelson's Pond
    looking at: fig. 135;
    looking from: figs. 61-63
14. "Canyon" (Ridge IV near Gray Craig estate)
    fig. 15
15. Front of West Wall of the Last Valley
    figs. 18, 33-35, 88, 97-98
16. Center of West Wall of the Last Valley
    figs. 150-52
17. Back of West Wall of the Last Valley
    figs. 169-70
18. Crown of Bishop Berkeley's Rock (Ridge VI)
    figs. 173-76, 180-83
19. The Last Valley, in Front of Bishop Berkeley's Rock
    figs. 1, 17, 26-27, 184-85, 207-08, 235-36
20. Plateau in the Last Valley (West Side of Ridge VI)
    from above: figs. 16, 89;
    from plateau: figs. 146, 167-68, 171-72
21. Gardiner's Pond, West Side
    figs. 25, 101, 102
22. Gardiner's Pond, North Side
    figs. 19-22, 28
23. Gardiner's Pond, Southwest Corner
    figs. 4, 192, 195
24. River near Third Beach Road
    looking at: figs. 130-31;
    looking from: fig. 129
25. Bridge on Third Beach Road (Now an Overpass)
    looking at: fig. 23;
    looking from: fig. 24
26. Third Beach, North End
    figs. 30, 134

27. Third Beach Road
    figs. 132-33
28. Pond behind Third Beach, near Flint Point
    figs. 139-41
29. Ridge on Flint Point
    figs. 186-88

HOUSES

A. The Hessian House (Stephen P. Barker House) (razed c. 1898)
   figs. 38-39, 44-45;
   interior: fig. 41
B. Isaac Barker House (478 Paradise Avenue):
   fig. 49; interior: fig. 42
C. Grayledge Farm, 532 Paradise Avenue
   facade: fig. 67;
   from backyard: figs. 160-161; interior: fig. 43;
   studio: figs. 162-66
D. Hazard's Farm (razed c. 1880)
   from grounds of:
   figs. 189-91
E. J. Nelson House
F. Paradise Farm, 346 Paradise Avenue
   fig. 46
G. Gray Craig Mansion (formerly "Gray Crag")
   fig. 12;
   former house: fig. 11
H. Sea Breeze Farm, 426 Paradise Avenue
   figs. 47-48
I. Irving Barker House, 400 Paradise Avenue
   fig. 158
J. Irving Barker House (Former Site in Paradise Hills)
   fig. 159
K. Paradise Farm on Third Beach Road (formerly Gardiner's Farm)
   figs. 21-22, 28

MAP 2

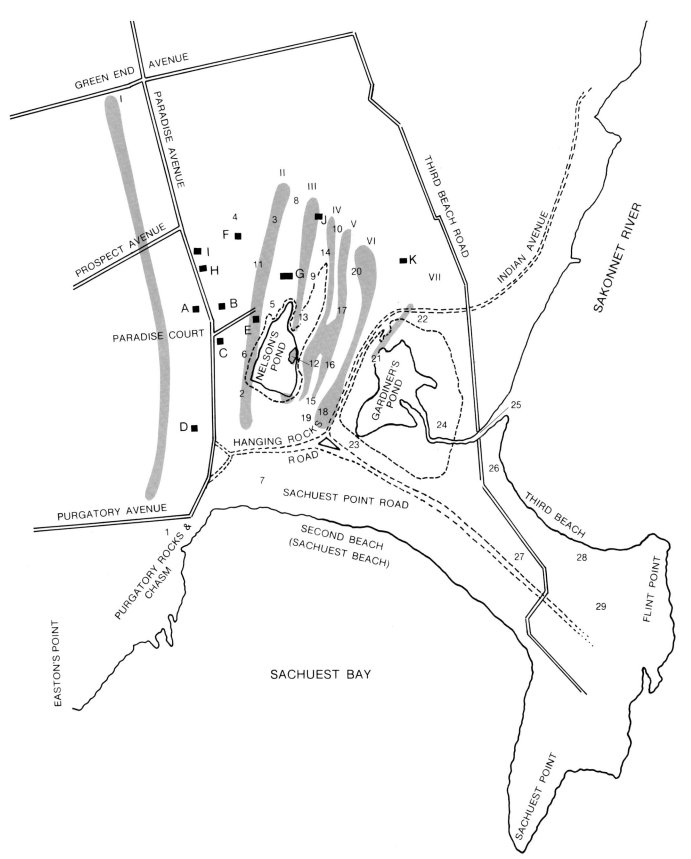

Paradise: the Places Where La Farge Lived and Worked (1995)

MAP 3

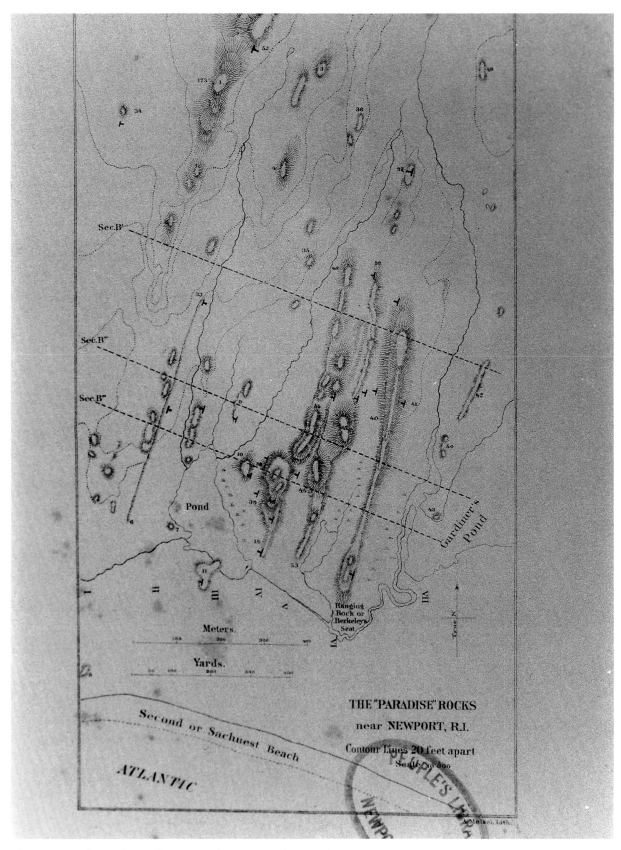

The Seven Ridges of Paradise, According to T. Nelson Dale (1884)

MAP 4

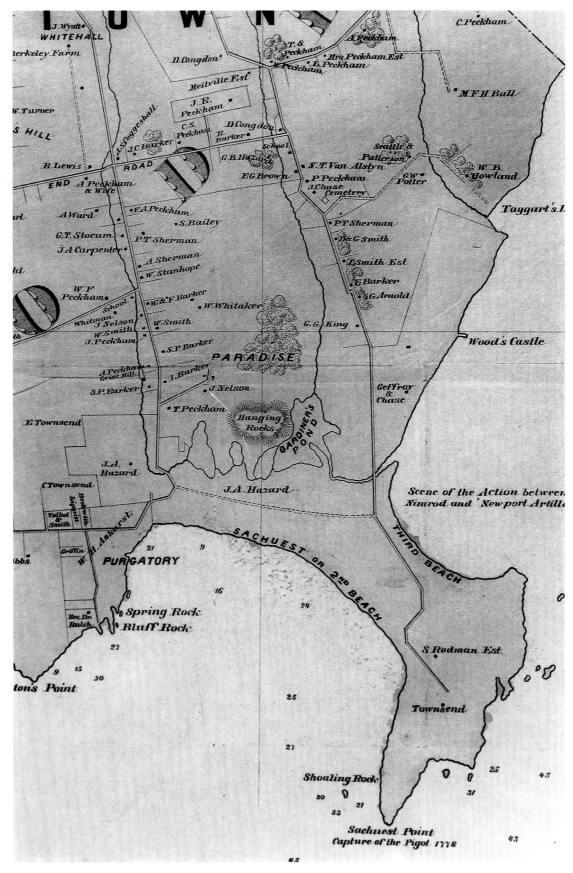

Paradise, Showing the Names of Property Owners (1870)

MAP 5

Wm. F. Peckham

David King   Pasture
Swamp

Wm. F. Peckham   Elevation 120

Pasture

Isaac Barker

Sheep Pen

Elevation 130

Rocky Pasture (3)

Pasture (2)

Pond

Stephen P. Barker

Meadow

Cultivated Field

Rocky Pasture

Isaac Barker

Farm Buildings

Swamp

Highway

Isaac Manchester   Farm Buildings

Nelson's Pond

Wooded Island

Newport Hospital

Newport Water Works
Pumping Station

Newport Water Works

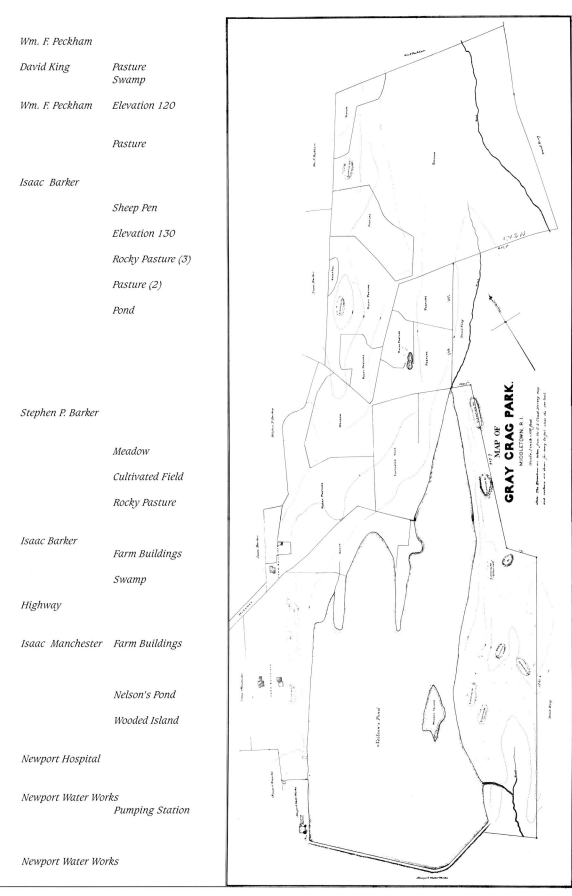

Map of "Gray Crag Park" (1892).   *To assist the reader the original lettering has been repeated on the left.*

MAP 6

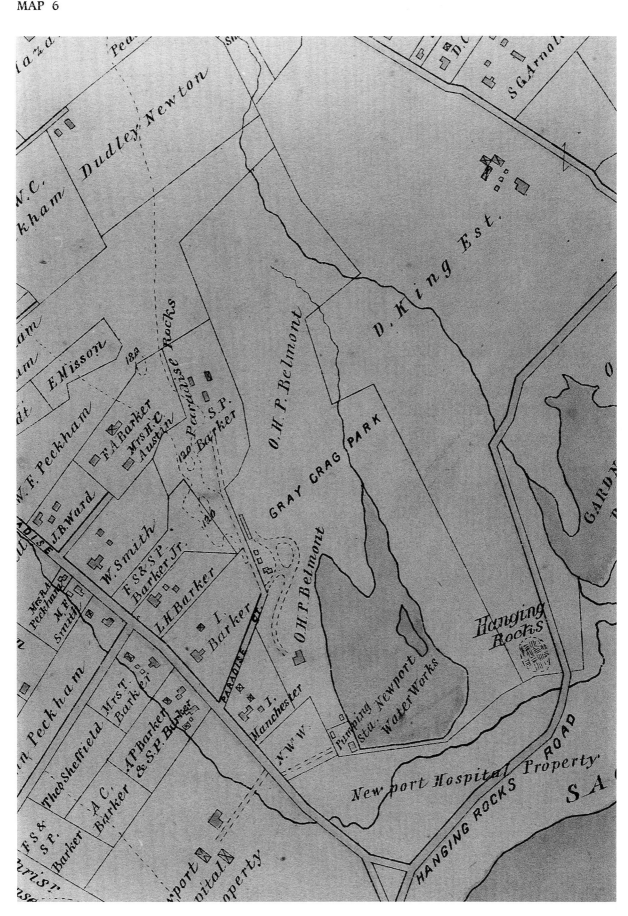

Atlas of Middletown showing O.H.P. Belmont's "Gray Crag Park" (1895)

CHRONOLOGY

This is an abbreviated version of the chronology compiled by James L. Yarnall with Mary A. La Farge in John La Farge *(New York: Abbeville Press, 1987), pp. 239-45. Many factual emendations relevant to La Farge's life at Paradise, based upon recent research, have been added.*

1835	On March 31, John Frederick Lewis Joseph La Farge born in New York City.
1841	First drawing lessons from maternal grandfather, Louis Binsse de Saint-Victor (1778-1844).
1848	Graduates Columbia Grammar School, New York City.
1848-53	Attends Saint John's College, New York City (now Fordham University) and Mount Saint Mary's College, Emmitsburg, Maryland. Receives B.A. from Mount Saint Mary's in June 1853.
1854	Works for a law firm in New York; studies painting as a sideline with François Régis Gignoux (1816-1882).
1855	Awarded Master's Degree from Mount Saint Mary's College for two years of independent study, presumably in law.
1856-57	On April 7, 1856, departs for France on Steamship *Fulton*. Stays at Paris with relatives; travels to Belgium and Brittany. Brief stint in Parisian studio of Thomas Couture; travels to Denmark, Germany, and Switzerland. In November 1857, called back to New York by father's illness. Visits London and Manchester Art Treasures Exhibition on way through England. Arrives home around Christmas.
1858	Father dies on June 26. Rents studio in new Tenth Street Studio Building.
1859	During spring, moves to Newport to study with William Morris Hunt. By fall, romantically linked to Margaret Mason Perry.
1860	In April, visits Louisiana where Perrys have gone to winter. Becomes engaged. Suffers bout of malaria. Married on October 15 in Newport. Margaret converts to Roman Catholicism in New York on November 7.
1861	In March, purchases house at 24 Kay Street. Begins to frequent Paradise.
1862	On January 5, birth in Newport of first son, Christopher Grant (1862-1938), later a successful architect.
1863	Works at Paradise with John Chandler Bancroft (1835-1901); imports Japanese prints through Abiel Abbott Low (1811-1893) with Bancroft. On October 28, birth at Glen Cove of first daughter, Emily Maria Louisa (1863-1919).
1864	On April 14, flees Kay Street domicile after going bankrupt; lives for a year in Roxbury, Massachusetts. Studies anatomy in Boston with William Rimmer. In October, returns to Newport to sell Kay Street house. Works at Paradise on illustrations for Tennyson's *Enoch Arden* with Elihu Vedder.
1865	Moves to Paradise; rents space at Hessian House from Stephen P. Barker, who also lives there. On September 23, birth at Hessian House of John Louis Bancel (1865-1938; known as Bancel), later an artist and his father's studio assistant. In late October, stricken by hand paralysis and serious illness believed to be lead poisoning.
1866	Rents from Stephen P. Barker in Paradise Hills, living in house formerly on site of present Orchard Lea. Begins *Paradise Valley* (Private Collection). First illustration in series intended for *The Riverside Magazine for Young People*.
1867	Rents Grayledge Farm at 532 Paradise Avenue from E. Truman Peckham. Begins *The Last Valley* (Private Collection). On September 16th, birth at Grayledge Farm of Margaret Angela (1867-1956).

Margaret Mason Perry,
late 1850s
Photograph
6 x 4 in. (15.2 x 10.2 cm.)
Private Collection
The photograph dates from the years just before Margaret's marriage to John La Farge in 1860.

The La Farge Children
with their Grandmother,
c. 1873
Photograph from a lost tintype
5 3/8 x 4 in. (13.5 x 10 cm.)
(size of photograph)
Private Collection
From left to right:
Nonna (Mrs. Christopher Grant Perry,
Margaret's mother, 1817-1903), Bancel
(1865-1938), Joseph Raymond (1872-
1874), and Emily (1863-1919). The
fence was in the backyard of the home
at 10 Sunnyside Place, Newport, where
the La Farge family moved in August
1873.

1869	Rents at Isaac Barker house at 478 Paradise Avenue. On July 10th, birth at house of fourth son, Oliver Hazard Perry La Farge (1869-1936).
1870	Publishes "Essay on Japanese Art" in Raphael Pumpelly's *Across America and Asia*. Spends much of summer in Shrub Oak, New York, visiting mother.
1871	Lives at farm belonging to General John Alfred Hazard on west side of Paradise Avenue just above Maidford River crossing. Appointed lecturer on composition in art at Harvard College.
1872	Rents residence and studio from Mrs. Lovie on the corner of Mann Avenue and Kay Street in Newport. Illustrates Abby Sage Richardson's *Songs from the Old Dramatists*. Lectures on Ruskin at Harvard College; talks interrupted by illness. Before April, birth of Joseph Raymond (1872-1874).
1873	In March, Margaret purchases 10 Sunnyside Place, Newport. In July, takes *The Last Valley* to London for exhibition. Meets with Pre-Raphaelites. Re-visits Paris and Brittany.
1874	In January, returns from Europe; death of infant son, Joseph Raymond. On January 10, birth of third daughter, Frances Mary Aimée (1874-1951). First stained glass designs for Memorial Hall at Harvard.
1875	Helps organize exhibition at Daniel Cottier's gallery in New York, protesting jury policies of National Academy of Design (organization becomes the Society of American Artists).
1876	During summer, begins work on decorations for Trinity Church, Boston. Plans Edward King Tomb; completed with Augustus Saint-Gaudens and installed in Newport's Island Cemetery in 1878. Birth of third daughter Marie Aimée (1876-1877).
1877	In February, completes major phase of work at Trinity Church; continues work for a year on secondary nave mural panels. During spring, receives commission for altarpiece in chancel of Saint Thomas Church, New York.
1878	In April, completes Saint Thomas commission. In November, holds one-man auction at Peirce and Co., Boston. Takes a studio at 28 Prospect Hill Street on the corner of Corne Street in Newport.
1879	In June, first large opalescent window for residence of Dr. Richard Henry Derby, Huntington, Long Island. During summer, wins commissions for stained glass and murals in new Vanderbilt mansions on Fifth Avenue in New York. In December, one-man auction at Leonard's Gallery, Boston; announces that he will henceforth devote himself to decoration. Establishes window manufacturing concern at 39 West Fourth Street, New York.
1880	Between January and June, designs murals and stained glass for the United Congregational Church, Newport. February 13, birth of last child, John La Farge (1880-1962), later a Jesuit priest and eminent Catholic theologian. Receives commissions for two memorial windows at Channing Memorial Church, Newport. From this point forward, lives primarily in New York and carries out hundreds of decorative commissions in self-made atelier.
1881	In summer, moves atelier to 33 East 17th Street, top floor of Century Building overlooking Union Square.
1883	In October, forms La Farge Decorative Art Company to bail himself out of debt. Split in company leads former partners to form Decorative Stained Glass Company for manufacturing windows.
1884	In April, first forced auction at Ortgies and Co., New York, as dispute with partners augments. In May, second forced auction at Ortgies and Co.
1885	In March, forced auction at Moore's Art Gallery, New York. On May 19, La Farge arrested for Grand Larceny by partners. Legal action dropped on July 1. On October 31, dissolution of La Farge Decorative Art Company.

1886	On June 3, leaves for Japan with Henry Adams. On October 20, arrives back in San Francisco. In December, arrives back in New York.
1887	Installation of *The Angel of Help*, Helen Angier Ames Memorial Window, Unity Church, North Easton, Massachusetts (project begun in 1883 and delayed by dispute with La Farge Decorative Art Company).
1888	Works on articles on Japanese travels for *Century Magazine* (published in 1890 and 1893 in ten installments). Completes mural of *The Ascension* in the Church of the Ascension, New York, a project dating back to 1884.
1889	Exhibits stained glass in London and Paris. Awarded French Legion of Honor.
1890	In January, first of many exhibition/sales held at Doll and Richards in Boston. In August, departs for San Francisco with Henry Adams for start of tour of the South Seas. On August 29, arrives in Honolulu. On October 5, arrives in Samoa.
1891	On January 28, leaves Samoa. On February 4, arrives in Tahiti. On June 4--leaves Tahiti. On June 16, arrives in Fiji. On July 15, leaves Fiji. In August, visits Ceylon on way to Paris. Visits Brittany in fall and returns to New York in December.
1893	Appointed instructor in color and composition at Metropolitan Museum of Art; in November, begins six lectures, "Considerations on Painting" at the museum. Receives commission for *Athens*, mural for Walker Art Building, Bowdoin College, Brunswick, Maine (completed in 1898).
1894	Visits Italy for first time. Lectures on Ruskin in Buffalo.
1895	Records of Travel exhibition organized for showing in Boston (February), New York (February), and Paris (March). Repeats "Considerations on Painting" lectures in Philadelphia and publishes book of same title. Lectures in Boston. Wife and family spend year with him in New York at 65 Clinton Place, a house rented from the editor Richard Watson Gilder. La Farge's mother dies.
1897	*An Artist's Letters from Japan* published by the Century Company. Works on *Japanese Fantasies* based on Chinese legend and Zen Buddhist philosophy.
1899	Visits France with Henry Adams, including trip to Chartres Cathedral. Delivers commencement address at Yale University.
1900	Receives commission from William Collins Whitney for a pair of allegorical windows representing the seasons of *Spring* (Philadelphia Art Museum) and *Autumn* (French Cultural Embassy, New York) (commission completed in 1902).
1901	Receives honorary LL.D. from Yale University. Awarded medal at the Pan-American Exposition, Buffalo.
1902	Receives commission for four murals representing the history of Law; installed in 1904 and 1905 in the Supreme Court Chambers, Minnesota State Capitol, St. Paul, Minnesota.
1903	Delivers six Scammon Lectures on the Barbizon School at Art Institute of Chicago. Receives commission for spandrel murals representing the history of Law; installed in 1906 and 1907 in the Baltimore Court House.
1905	Receives commission for John Harvard Memorial Window, Southwark Cathedral, London (shattered by bomb in 1941 and since reconstructed).
1908	Receives commission for *Welcome*, allegorical staircase window for the New York townhouse of Mrs. George T. Bliss (now in Metropolitan Museum of Art).
1910	In April, suffers nervous collapse but denies in the press that he is seriously ill. On November 14, dies from heart failure in Butler Hospital, Providence, Rhode Island. Buried in Greenwood Cemetery, Brooklyn, in La Farge family mausoleum.
1911	In January, retrospective exhibition at the Museum of Fine Arts, Boston. On March 29-31, Estate Sale at the American Art Galleries, New York. Royal Cortissoz's biography, *John La Farge: A Memoir and a Study*, published by Houghton Mifflin.

Margaret Mason Perry La Farge
at the Chateau of Amboise, 1903
Snapshot photograph
3 3/8 x 5 in.
(8.7 x 12.7 cm.)
The Preservation Society of Newport
County, Newport
For Easter 1903, Margaret traveled to Europe with her daughter, Margaret Angela. Her son, John, then was attending the Jesuit seminary at Innsbruck University in Austria. The three met in Rome for a general audience with Pope Leo XIII, and later joined up in Paris to tour nearby cathedrals and the Loire Valley.

DICTIONARY OF PEOPLE AND PLACES

Ridge numbers refer to the classification of the Paradise Hills devised in 1884 by T. Nelson Dale, illustrated in map 3. Entries on the Barker and Peckham families have been compiled by Natalie N. Nicholson, a great-granddaughter of Stephen P. Barker. Entries on the La Farge and Perry families have been provided by Mrs. Henry A. La Farge, whose late husband was a grandson of John La Farge. All other entries are by James L. Yarnall.

ARMSTRONG, DAVID MAITLAND (1836-1918). Armstrong was born near Newburgh, New York, on April 15, 1836. He graduated from Trinity College in Hartford in 1858, studied law, and passed the bar in 1862. During the next five years while practicing law in New York City, he summered in Newport. On December 6, 1866, he married Helen Neilson, sister of John Neilson who summered at Paradise, and they had seven children. In 1867, Armstrong received an appointment as consul-general to the Papal States, and while in Rome, he took up painting seriously. He became Luc Olivier Merson's first pupil in Paris in 1878, the same year that he directed the American art department at the Paris Exposition of 1878. He was made a chevalier of the Legion of Honor by the French government for this work. In 1879, Armstrong moved to New York and took up stained-glass design, remaining there for the rest of his life, and joined in the business by his daughter, Helen Maitland Armstrong. He helped found the Metropolitan Museum of Art, was a pioneer member of the Century Club, and was instrumental in the development of the World's Columbian Exposition at Chicago in 1893. He died on May 26, 1918, aged 82 ("Maitland Armstrong, Artist, Dies at 82," *New York Times* [27 May 1918], p. 13). Two years later, his autobiography *Day before Yesterday: Reminiscences of a Varied Life* was published with the help of his daughter, Margaret. His son, Edward Maitland Armstrong, married Maud Gwendolyn King in 1901; hence, many of his paintings are in their house Kingscote, bequeathed in 1972 to the Preservation Society of Newport County.

BANCROFT, JOHN CHANDLER (1835-1901). John Chandler Bancroft was the son of George Bancroft (1800-1891), an ambassador to England and later a historian, teacher, and writer. His mother died when he was two. With his younger brother George, Bancroft grew up in boarding schools in Roxbury, Massachusetts and Switzerland. He entered Harvard in 1849, graduated with the class of 1854, and went to Europe to study drawing and painting in Düsseldorf and Paris. After the outbreak of the Civil War, he returned to this country, taking up residence at Newport at his father's summer house called Rosecliff, formerly on the site of the present Rosecliff just off Bellevue Avenue. Chronic ill health at first disqualified him for military service, but he also turned down two commissions after his health had improved. He probably met La Farge in 1862 but they seem to have become close friends in 1863 when, according to the latter, they studied color theory and experimented with painting optical effects. They also imported Japanese prints with the help of another Newport summer resident, Abiel Abbott Low (1811-1893), who headed a leading East Asian trade company in New York. In 1864, Bancroft married and moved to Milton, Massachusetts, maintaining a painting studio at Cambridge. He gave up art in 1869 to join the brokerage firm of Lee, Higginson and Company in Boston. After a year and a half, he resigned and, for the rest of his life, lived off his father's wealth. In 1895, Bancroft built a large shingle-style residence on Tuckerman Avenue, next to Purgatory Chasm, which remains one of the prominent landmarks on Easton's Point. Throughout his life, Bancroft collected Japanese art and his outstanding collection of over three thousand prints was given by his son to the Worcester Art Museum.

BARKER, ISAAC (1813-1903). A brother of Stephen P. Barker, Isaac Barker first married a cousin, Frances S. Barker (1813-1868). After her death, he married her sister, Laura A. Barker (1831-1925). He resided in a large house, now 478 Paradise Avenue (see fig. 49), probably built by E. Truman Peckham for Stephen P. Barker after the Civil War. The La Farges lived in this house with Isaac Barker and his wife in 1869, and Oliver H.P. La Farge was born there on July 10th of that year.

BARKER, IRVING (1838-1892). The eldest son of Stephen P. Barker and Betsey Barker, Irving lived with his wife Elvira (1846-1915) in the Paradise Hills (see fig. 159). The house was on the site of the present Orchard Lea, and the foundations of the original house are enclosed in the present foundations of Orchard Lea. The La Farges apparently lived in this house with Irving and Elvira in 1866, but La Farge's daughter Margaret Angela recalled that the La Farges went to buy eggs and milk from Irving and Elvira for many years afterwards. Sarah Chauncey Woolsey, writing under the pseudonym Susan Coolidge, gave Irving Barker the name "Mr. Bacon" in her fictional version of life at Paradise, *A Little Country Girl* (Boston: Roberts Brothers, 1887). After 1890, Irving Barker's house was moved "over the rocks" to 400 Paradise Avenue (see fig. 158), where it remains today. This move evidently was linked to the sale of sixty acres of land in 1891 by Irving's uncle Isaac Barker to O.H.P. Belmont, or to the death of Irving in 1892.

BARKER, STEPHEN P. (1815-1898). Stephen Peckham Barker was born on July 18, 1815 on Paradise Avenue. He was a grandson of Isaac Barker, a spy for the American cause during the Revolution. In 1837, he married Betsey Gardiner Barker, daughter of "Judge" Peter Barker, for whom Peter's Rock is named. They had eight children, seven boys and a girl, with six of the boys reaching adulthood. In 1841, he was elected Collector of Taxes of Middletown, a post he held by re-election until 1855 when he moved to Massachusetts for at least five years. When he moved back to Middletown, he engaged in farming the family lands, and thereby grew wealthy. "By strict economy and untiring industry as a farmer, he acquired a comfortable fortune," one obituary noted, "and observing how frequently disposal of property by will

breeds contention he resolved to execute his own will, and several years ago divided his real estate and between his five sons [who survived at the time of his death], retaining only a life lease." ("Middletown," *Newport Daily News* [4 Mar. 1898], p. 5). From 1867 to 1879, Barker served as assessor of taxes for Middletown. In 1865, and probably from 1861 to 1864, Barker leased space in the Hessian House to La Farge, evidently in separate edifice attached to the north side of the house (see figs. 39, 44-45). Sometime during the 1860s, he built another house across and down the street at 426 Paradise Avenue (see figs. 47-48).

BERKELEY, REVEREND GEORGE (1684/5-1753). Born in Ireland on March 12, 1684 or 1685, Berkeley was of English descent. He graduated from Trinity College, Dublin in 1700, and went on to earn different degrees, including an M.A. in 1707. His interest in philosophy led him to write *Essay towards a New Theory of Vision* in 1709 and *Treatise concerning the Principles of Human Knowledge* in 1710. Disappointed with the reception of his work, he wrote *Dialogues between Hylas and Philonous* in 1713. Throughout, he remained an instructor and lecturer at Trinity College. In 1713, Berkeley went to England and received an enthusiastic reception among English scholars. He became chaplain to Lord Peterborough, ambassador to Sicily, spending the next seven years in Paris, Rome, Naples, and Ischia before returning to London in 1720. After his return to Ireland in 1721, he eventually became the Dean of Derry and acquired the wealth that would lead to his scheme to found a college in the Bermudas. Returning to England, he obtained a charter for the college in June 1725 and had himself named first President. In September 1728 he sailed from Greenwich to continue the promotion of his plan, arriving at Newport in January 1729. He stayed until the autumn of 1731, buying ninety-six acres of land in Middletown and building his small house, Whitehall, which still stands off Berkeley Avenue. During his tenure, he read and meditated, supposedly seated much of the time in the cleft of the Hanging Rocks. Here he produced the *Alciphron or Minute Philosopher*, filled with descriptions of the scenery. When the financing of his scheme for the college fell through in England, Berkeley returned to London. He presented his farm at Whitehall to Yale as a means to found scholarships, and gave his library to Yale and Harvard. He also donated an organ to Trinity Church, Newport. The *Alciphron* enjoyed great success in England, eventually leading to his appointment as the Bishop of Cloyne in 1734. He spent the rest of his life at Cloyne.

BERKELEY AVENUE. See **Paradise Avenue**.

BISHOP BERKELEY'S ROCK (known also as Bishop's Seat, Berkeley's Chair, and Hanging Rocks). The termination of a long ridge of the Paradise Hills (Ridge VI) takes the form of an unusually shaped rock cleft reputed to be the site of Bishop Berkeley's meditations. According to legend, Berkeley actually set up a writing desk in the cleft so that he could compose *The Alciphron, or Minute Philosopher* in comfort. The rock juts out into a salt marsh and faces directly onto the nearby Atlantic Ocean. Today, a cattail marsh and brambles have surrounded the base of the rock. Ever since Newport became a fashionable watering-place in the early nineteenth century, Bishop Berkeley's Rock has been a favorite spot for tourists and artists alike.

DALE, T. NELSON (1845-1937). Thomas Nelson Dale was born in New York City on 25 Nov. 1845 and received his general education in Europe and Williston Seminary, Massachusetts. He received geological training under the German paleontologist and geologist Karl Alfred von Zittel (1839-1904) and Raphael Pumpelly. He married Margaret Brown in 1874 and had seven children, residing in Pittsfield, Massachusetts. From the time of the founding of the Newport Natural History Society by his mentor Pumpelly in 1883, Dale was an active member. In 1883-1884, he served as Librarian; in 1885, he was listed as a Corresponding Member from Toronto, Canada, with the official title of "Professor," presumably indicating that he was teaching at the University of Toronto. He took part in the U.S. Geological Survey between 1885 and 1920 and was an instructor in geology and botany at Williams College in Williamstown, Massachusetts from 1893 to 1901. He was the author of various books and articles on geology. He died 16 Nov. 1937.

EASTON'S BEACH. The preferred name for First Beach during the nineteenth century.

EASTON'S POINT. The land mass jutting into the ocean between First and Second Beaches. It includes on its west side Purgatory Rocks, Purgatory Chasm, The Bluff, and Long Rock. It is now circumambulated by Tuckerman Avenue. One of the largest houses on this point is that built by John Chandler Bancroft next to Purgatory Chasm.

EASTON'S POND. The tidal basin across from First Beach, extending from Memorial Boulevard (formerly Bath Road) to Green End Avenue. There are actually two ponds partially divided by dikes; the north is smaller and shallower than the south pond. George H. Norman was responsible for incorporating this into the Newport Water Works system.

FIRST BEACH (also called Easton's Beach). The main bathing beach of Newport located at the base of Memorial Boulevard, formerly Bath Road. The cliff walk begins here and ends at Ledge Road, the former location of the "Old Boat House," a gathering-place for men much like a clubhouse that was torn down on March 19, 1883.

FLINT POINT. The curl of Third Beach along the Sakonnet River ends at its southern extremity in Flint Point. A mirror image of Sachuest Point, Flint Point is covered with heavy brambles and occasional spruce trees. An unusual elevation or small ridge running parallel to Sachuest Point Road may contain underlying puddingstone. A small squarish unnamed pond to the north of this ridge is just behind Third Beach.

GARDINER'S POND. Named for Benjamin Gardiner who purchased a farm on the site of the Norman Bird Sanctuary's headquarters in 1783, and whose family cemetery lies near Third Beach Road. Originally, Gardiner's Pond was little more than a series of rivulets related to the Maidford River that coalesced into a pool just to the east of Bishop Berkeley's Rock. Beginning in 1889 and continuing well into this century, the pond was dredged and greatly expanded by a dike to serve as a component in the Newport Water Works system. Much of the former "east side" of Paradise has been submerged by the refashioned Gardiner's Pond.

GLEN COVE. La Farge's father was one of the first New Yorkers to choose Glen Cove, Long Island as the site of a country home when he built a large brick house there around 1835. The house was south of the town's landing in the present Morgan Park, on a hill that is now McLoughlin Street. A barn that stood on McLoughlin Street until recently traditionally has been called the young John La Farge's studio. After the death of La Farge's father in 1858, the house remained a place where the family gathered during the Thanksgiving and Christmas holidays for at least four or five years. La Farge's second child, Emily, was born at Glen Cove on October 28, 1863. The property remained in the family until 1868, when it was purchased by Charles Edgar Appleby. The house was torn down in the 1930s, but the site remains undeveloped and is now part of Garvie's Point Park.

GRAY CRAIG (formerly known as Gray Crag). The present mansion with its gardens and outbuildings is on land purchased by O.H.P. Belmont from Isaac Barker in 1891, formerly part of the Barker family's Paradise Farm. Belmont named the estate Gray Crag after the gray ledges of puddingstone and slate that protrude from the ground throughout the estate. Belmont sold the land to Sarah Wood Clark in 1901. Her husband, J. Mitchell Clark (1847-1913), was the brother of Mrs. Eugene Sturtevant and son of Rt. Rev. Thomas M. Clark, D.D., Episcopal Bishop of Rhode Island. In 1902, the J. Mitchell Clarks erected a castellated mansion designed by Abner J. Haydel and built from the gray rock on the estate. In 1916, after Sarah Wood Clark remarried following her husband's death, Mr. and Mrs. Jordan L. Mott purchased Gray Crag and renovated it for five years for the own use. The house burned to the ground the day before the Motts moved in ("Paradise Rocks Burned," *Newport Mercury* [5 Jun. 1919], p. [1]). They sold the property to Mary and Michael M. van Beuren who built the present house in 1926, changing the name to Gray Craig. The architect was Harrie T. Lindeberg of New York, who designed matching stables, a gate house, and a gardener's cottage in the valley to the north of the main house, that have been sold off as separate properties.

GRAY CRAIG POND. Among local residents, the name Gray Craig Pond is another name for Nelson's Pond, derived from the twentieth-century name of the mansion found near the head of the pond.

GRAYLEDGE FARM. A large farmhouse dating from before 1860, now at 532 Paradise Avenue (see fig. 67, 160-162), Grayledge Farm originally was a typical but comfortable farmhouse, built by **E. Truman Peckham** for his own use. Peckham was a house builder and constructed many of the residences of the Barkers and others along Paradise Avenue. As early as 1862 when John Neilson leased it for the season, the house was being used as an alternative to renting in Newport proper. The house was especially convenient, then being the first house on the right along Paradise Avenue from Second Beach. The backyard of the house contains several prominent puddingstone outcroppings and is readily accessible to the ledges of Ridge II, overlooking Nelson's Pond. Paradise Court runs along the north side of this property. The La Farges rented Grayledge Farm from Peckham in 1867, and Margaret Angela was born there on September 16th of that year. She later told her brother Bancel that La Farge put a north window into this house to "paint by." This apparently refers to the north windows in a long, narrow building with just one room that served as La Farge's studio, perhaps throughout the decade of the 1860s when he frequented Paradise.

GREEN END AVENUE (formerly Green End Road). Green End Avenue today defines the north end of Paradise, though by some accounts Paradise continues for another mile north to Wyatt Road. Until the 1870s, Green End Avenue stopped at Third Beach Road, but now continues further east until meeting up with Indian Avenue just before the Sakonnet River.

HANGING ROCK (or Hanging Rocks). See Bishop Berkeley's Rock.

HANGING ROCKS ROAD. The road connecting Purgatory Avenue to Indian Avenue that winds around Bishop Berkeley's Rock heralded the conversion of Paradise from agrarian to other uses. When Eugene Sturtevant "rented a cottage" in the Paradise Hills in 1872 (supposedly from John Neilson), he realized the potential of nearby Indian Avenue for residential use. His wife, Mary Clark Sturtevant, told the sometimes amusing story in the *Bulletin of the Newport Historical Society* ("The East Shore of Middletown, R.I.," no. 54 [Jul. 1925], pp. 13-18) of her husband's manipulations to obtain the rights to build a roadway that he regarded as essential to the real-estate ventures along Indian Avenue. The *Newport Daily News* carried a story on the completion of the road, which took over seven years to build due to legal impediments ("A New Road in Middletown" [15 May 1883], p. [2]).

HAZARD, GENERAL JOHN ALFRED (1806-1880). Hazard was born January 29, 1806, descended from two old Rhode Island families. His father was Dr. Enoch Hazard; his mother Mary Easton, daughter of Nicholas Easton, a large land-holder in Paradise. Hazard graduated from Trinity College in Hartford and studied law in the office of Hon. Benjamin Hazard, but he never practiced law. He married Benjamin Hazard's daughter, Nancy, on June 11, 1855. Their only child, a son, died at age seventeen. Hazard spent most of his time managing his large tracts of his real estate. He owned the land fronting on Second Beach running from Paradise Avenue to Sachuest Point, as well as the land to the west of Paradise Avenue between the beach and the beginning of Easton Farm. He also owned a large part of Newport on Ocean Drive, including Almy's Pond and the Lily Pond. Near the latter was his residence, Rocky Farm. Hazard was renowned for his strong convictions and quirky personality. He was said to love litigation. At the time of his death, several important lawsuits against the town of Newport defending his property rights around Second Beach were pending. (see obituary, *Newport Mercury*, 29 May 1880, p. [2].) According to maps, the only edifice on his large tracts of land in Middletown was a farmhouse on the west side of Paradise Avenue, just above the place where the Maidford River crosses the road. The La Farges rented this farm in 1871. From descriptions of a lost painting of the farm by La Farge, it is known that from Paradise Road, an orchard was to the right in front of the house. Hazard may also have owned the odd timbered building seen in one of La Farge's watercolors that was painted near the eastern boundary of his beachfront properties (see fig. 140).

HESSIAN HOUSE (see figs. 39, 44-45). The name Hessian House stems from its occupation for fourteen months by British and Hessian troops during the American Revolution, beginning in August 1778. The British allowed the owner, Isaac Barker (1752-1834), to remain at the house with his wife and infant daughter. Barker pretended to be a Tory sympathizer and ingratiated himself with a British colonel to such an extent that he gained access to the nearby British camp and even convinced the British to let him visit the "rebel" American camp across the Sakonnet River in Little Compton to gather intelligence. Instead of helping the British, Barker spied on them, taking advantage of his friendly relations with the British to both gain information and disseminate it. Tradition maintains that his method for alerting the Americans to pick up communiques was to arrange crotches in a fence running through the gap behind Peter's Rock and up to its summit. He would leave the messages in a cave at North Point, jutting out into the Sakonnet River (see Edward Field, "Isaac Barker's Signal," *Newport Mercury* [28 Nov. 1903], p. 7). The Hessian House had been in the Barker family for at least four generations when Stephen P. Barker moved there after returning from Massachusetts in the early 1860s. He apparently kept boarders such as the La Farges in a separate building attached to the north of the house. The Hessian House was razed not long after Stephen P. Barker's death in late February 1898, and today a storage shed for "Bridge House" at 485 Paradise Avenue stands just behind the place where the Hessian House once stood. The old rough-hewn pillars that marked the driveway to the house in La Farge's time remain beside the driveway today.

INDIAN AVENUE. The continuation of Hanging Rocks Road, and the reason for its existence. When Eugene Sturtevant and a partner purchased the land along the shore from Third Beach Road north in

1872, he financed a five-mile road called Indian Avenue, named after the many American Indian artifacts found in the area. The area was built up in the mid-1880s, including the erection of the Berkeley Memorial Chapel, now called St. Columba's, and the nearby summer house of the actor Edwin Booth, called Boothden.

LA FARGE, BANCEL (1865-1938). John Louis Bancel La Farge, known as Bancel, was born in the **Hessian House** on September 23, 1865. He attended the University of Pennsylvania School of Medicine in 1885-86 but was unable to continue medical studies after losing an eye, reportedly as a result of a laboratory accident. By the late 1880s, and perhaps as early as 1885, he was working in his father's studio and began performing the functions of painting assistant and studio manager for La Farge when the latter went to the South Seas in the summer of 1890. On September 8, 1898, he married Mabel Hooper (1875-1944), daughter of La Farge's friend and patron, Edward William Hooper (1839-1901). Around 1900, faced with the costs of maintaining a new family, Bancel had a falling-out with his father over outstanding loans and wages. To get out of his father's shadow, and to continue his artistic career independently, he took his family abroad to live, first settling in Paris and then moving to Switzerland because of his wife being treated for a nervous breakdown in a Swiss sanitorium (1906-1907). Bancel and Mabel had four children: Louis Bancel (17 May 1900-2 Jul. 1989), Edward Hooper (6 Jun. 1901-28 Jan. 1981), Henry Adams (27 May 1902-27 May 1985), and Thomas Sergeant (5 Sept. 1904-17 Dec. 1942). Bancel died on August 14, 1938, at his home in Mount Carmel, Connecticut, where he and his family had lived since returning to the United States from Switzerland in 1915.

LA FARGE, CHRISTOPHER GRANT (1862-1938). Christopher Grant La Farge, known as Grant or C. Grant, was the first child of John and Margaret La Farge. He was born on January 5, 1862, in the couple's first house, now at 24 Kay Street in downtown Newport. At the age of fourteen, Grant began helping his father in making tracings and putting in colors. During the late 1870s, he traveled to Spain and, inspired by visits to cathedrals, decided to become an architect. He attended the Massachusetts Institute of Technology 1880-881, worked in the office of Henry Hobson Richardson in Cambridge in 1882, and then served as an architectural assistant to his father for two years. From 1884-86, he was joined in his father's studio by George Heins, an MIT classmate who married La Farge's youngest sister, Aimée, in 1896. In 1886, Grant and Heins founded the architectural firm of Heins and La Farge, which lasted until 1910. George Heins died in 1907 and, from 1910-15, Grant was a partner in the firm of La Farge and Morris. In 1931, he and his eldest son from his marriage to Florence Bayard Lockwood on September 5, 1895, also named Christopher Grant, formed the firm of La Farge and Son. Among the many projects undertaken by the firm of Heins and La Farge were the interior of the Church of St. Paul the Apostle in New York City (1888-1899), the Church of the Blessed Sacrament in Providence (c. 1899), St. Matthew's Cathedral in Washington, D.C., the Catholic Chapel at West Point, the Seattle Cathedral, numerous mausoleums, and stations for the New York City IRT subway system (1900-1904). In 1892, Heins and La Farge won a competition for the building of the Cathedral of St. John the Divine in New York City. After the building of the apse on a Romanesque plan and design, a change of bishops led to the abandonment of the firm's plan. In 1912, a Gothic design by Ralph Adams Cram was substituted, a discouraging blow that dampened Grant's remaining career. He died at his home in Saunderstown, Rhode Island, on October 11, 1938.

LA FARGE, MARGARET ANGELA (1867-1956). Margaret Angela, La Farge's second daughter, was born September 16, 1867 at **Grayledge Farm**. She never married, living with her mother in Newport until the latter died in 1925, and frequently serving as her companion in travel, concerts, or other activities. Margaret designed book covers and also wrote an article on "Old Newport" illustrated by

240.
Unidentified Photographer
The La Farge and Perry Families
at Glen Cove, Long Island, 1861
Photograph
3 x 2 1/2 in. (6.9 x 6.2 cm.)
Private Collection
Left to right:
Margaret Mason Perry La Farge (1839-1925),
Mrs. Louis (Georgianna Perry Browne)
La Farge (1837-1909),
Louis La Farge (1836-1888),
John La Farge (1835-1910, seated),
Thomas Sergeant Perry (1845-1928), and
Aimée La Farge (1852-1938, in foreground
with dog).
This photograph was taken on the porch of
the La Farge family country home at Glen Cove
when the family assembled for the holidays in
November 1861.

Bailey for *Scribner's Magazine* (vol. 62, no. 5 [Nov. 1917], pp. 542-53). She died in Newport on May 25, 1956, and is buried next to her mother in St. Columba's Roman Catholic Cemetery in Middletown.

LA FARGE, MARGARET MASON PERRY. See Perry, Margaret Mason.

LA FARGE, OLIVER H.P. (1869-1936). Oliver Hazard Perry La Farge, the third son and fifth child of John and Margaret La Farge, was born in the Isaac Barker house at 478 Paradise Avenue (see fig. 49) on July 10, 1869. Oliver attended the Columbia School of Mines in New York in 1887, studying civil engineering and architecture. He began working in the sugar refinery business in 1891, first in New York and then in Philadelphia, but after just a couple of years became seriously ill from the working conditions. He returned to New York and became involved in railway construction, fire-proofing, and fire insurance. His primary employer, the Tariff Association of the New York Board of Fire Underwriters, was disbanded in 1898 and, on the advice of doctors, he went west. After a year in the Klondike, he settled in Seattle and spent the rest of his career in insurance, real estate, and banking. He died in New York City on May 29, 1936. A brief autobiography by Oliver appears in the book of his writings privately published by his daughter, Margaret La Farge Hamill (*The Gold Rush and Other Stories* [1990], p. 123).

THE LAST VALLEY. The valley between Ridges V and VI of the Paradise Hills. In the nineteenth century, the valley floor was a meadowland and popular picnic spot. Today, cattail marshes fill the valley, rendering the floor inaccessible. The valley includes Paradise Pond, a body of muddy water fed by the Maidford River (formerly Paradise Brook). Ridge V is the less dramatic of the two ridges, with sides composed of splintered boulders and only a couple of high promontories along the ridge. Ridge VI is a long, narrow ridge with many high points, including one promontory some seventy feet above sea level. It terminates in Bishop Berkeley's Rock at the southern end.

MAIDFORD RIVER. The ribbon-like river formerly called Paradise Brook. It originates near East Main and Oliphant Roads in Bailey's Pond, runs to the west of Berkeley and Paradise Avenues, crosses the road, connects to the pool in the Last Valley, and exits south of Gardiner's Pond and under Third Beach Road to the Sakonnet River. The course of the river was changed during construction of the Water Works. It once entered and exited both Nelson's and Gardiner's Ponds.

NEILSON, JOHN (1837-1903). Neilson belonged to a prominent and wealthy New York family. His father was Dr. John Neilson Jr. He was the grandson of Colonel Nicholas Fish, one of the first members of the Society of the Cincinnati, the patriotic and charitable military society formed after the American Revolution. Neilson resided in Newport for many years and was a charter member of the Newport Reading Room. He married Augusta Balch, the daughter of a local Newport minister, on January 17, 1861 ("Married," *Newport Mercury* [19 Jan. 1861], p. [3]). The next year, they rented Grayledge Farm from E. Truman Peckham. On December 6, 1866, his sister Helen married David Maitland Armstrong, then a New York lawyer and later a successful artist. According to Mary Clark Sturtevant, Neilson owned a house in the Paradise Hills by 1872 ("East Shore of Newport," p. 14) but, if so, nothing is known about this house or its precise location. Late in life, Neilson spent most of his time the South and died in Hibernia, Florida ("Obituary Notes," *New York Times* [29 Dec. 1903], p. 9).

NELSON'S POND. The pond was named for an unidentified "J. Nelson" whose house was at the end of Paradise Court, according to the 1870 map of Middletown (map 4). The pond has two basins separated by a peninsula that extends into the north side of the pond from the Gray Craig front lawn. The "Small Basin" to the east is fed by a river from the north, now called Paradise Brook but nameless in La Farge's day. A peninsula of rock boulders juts into the water from the north, now the lawn of the Gray Craig estate. The "Large Basin" lies on the other side of the peninsula, now skirting the base of the cliff-like puddingstone ledge that lines the west wall of the pond. Beginning in 1882, the pond was converted for use of the Newport Water Works, changing it from a shallow, marshy pond to a deeper body of water with strong currents. At that time, the southern end of the pond was regularized and slightly extended, while the west side was dredged so that in wet season the water floods over a stretch of land and rocks that served as a small beach in La Farge's day. A dike surrounds the southern end of the pond, meeting up with the paths that come from Ridge IV of the Paradise Hills. A small island often accessible over dried land is in the southeast corner of the pond. A pumping station is located near the southwest corner of the dike.

NEWPORT WATER WORKS. Taken as a whole, the reservoirs in Newport and Middletown that supply drinking water for the area, including Easton's Pond. In Paradise, Nelson's Pond and Gardiner's Pond became part of the Water Works system in the 1880s under the guidance of George H. Norman.

NORMAN BIRD SANCTUARY. A 450-acre bird sanctuary maintained by the Rhode Island Audubon Society that opened to the public in 1950. The sanctuary consists of land formerly belonging to two farms, divided roughly along a north-south axis formed by the center of Ridge V of the Paradise Hills. A brick wall running along the crest of the ridge still testifies to this division. To the west of the axis, the land belonged to the Barker Family until its sale in 1891 to O.H.P. Belmont as part of the estate that became the present Gray Craig. To the east of the axis, the land belonged to the Gardiner Family. Benjamin Gardiner had purchased this land in 1783 from Isaac Smith, who in turn had purchased it in 1871 from William Taggart. The barn serving as the headquarters of the sanctuary was built by the Gardiner family in the 1780s, and their family cemetery is nearby. George H. Norman (1827-1900), owner of the *Newport Daily News* and developer of the Newport Water Works, purchased Gardiner's Farm around the turn-of-the-century. This, in combination with land that he had previously purchased for the Newport Water Works, became the bird sanctuary upon the death in 1949 of his youngest child, Mabel, wife of Dr. George Cerio.

ORCHARD LEA. A house dating from the 1920s just behind the present Gray Craig. Originally the gardener's cottage for the Gray Craig estate when owned by the van Beurens, it is now a separate residence. The house is on a ledge formerly occupied by the house of Irving and Elvira Barker, which was moved "over the rocks" to 400 Paradise Avenue around the time O.H.P. Belmont purchased the land from Isaac Barker in 1891. Part of the foundation originally under the Irving Barker house was incorporated into the foundation for Orchard Lea.

PARADISE AVENUE. A 1.5 mile stretch of road beginning at the base of the Purgatory Rocks, where Purgatory Avenue ends, and running to Green End Avenue. Until 1865, it went by the name Swamp Road. After that, it was called Paradise Road. Most of La Farge's time on Paradise Avenue was spent on the half mile stretch between Prospect Avenue and the place where the Maidford River crosses under Paradise Avenue. The continuation of Paradise Avenue after the intersection with Green End Road is called Berkeley Avenue. Just beyond this intersection is Whitehall, the residence of Rev. George Berkeley during his stay in Middletown from 1829 to 1831.

PARADISE BROOK. An estuary emptying into Nelson's Pond, running north along Ridge IV and through Paradise. In the nineteenth century, this brook was not named and "Paradise Brook" referred to what is now called the Maidford River. The Paradise Brook Watershed is the area covered roughly by the Norman Bird Sanctuary.

PARADISE COURT. A small road between Grayledge Farm and the Isaac Barker house. In La Farge's day, the house of an unidentified "J. Nelson" was at the end of the court to the right, near the present driveway entrance of a modern house built near the ledge overlooking Nelson's Pond.

PARADISE HILLS. The term Paradise Hills, interchangeable with Paradise Rocks, is generally used to refer to the three ridges enclosed by the Norman Bird Sanctuary. It also applies to the other ridges of Paradise, especially that of **Peter's Rock** that runs parallel to Paradise Avenue.

PARADISE LOST. The view east over the Paradise Hills from Peter's Rock, with Sachuest Point, Flint Point, Third Beach, the Sakonnet River, Little Compton, and the southern coast of Massachusetts in the distance.

PARADISE POND. A small pool of water within the Last Valley, fed by the Maidford River. In the nineteenth century, this was set off clearly from the verdant valley floor. Today, it is surrounded by a cattail marsh that obscures the pond except when seen from above on the ridges of the Last Valley.

PARADISE ROCKS. See **Paradise Hills**.

PECKHAM BROTHERS QUARRY. The quarry sits on land purchased by William Peckham and William Francis Peckham from Peter Barker on March 2, 1844, and on land purchased by William Francis Peckham from the Barker family on April 18, 1861. In 1867, a stone wall was built from Peter's Rock (or Great Rock) to Paradise Avenue in order to separate the Peckham lands from Paradise Farm (see figs. 6-7, 9, 83, 109, 117-18). By 1883, a crushing plant had been begun on this land; in March 1893, the Peckham family was operating the quarry and had set up a stone crusher near Peter's Rock, a crusher operating until 1954 when replaced with a new stone crusher. The operation has remained in the family for four generations, providing bedrock for roads on Aquidneck Island, private driveways, and state roads. Because of its attractive bluish color, the rock is especially sought by the large estates in Newport for use in landscaping (see Phillip Michael O'shea, *Peckham Bros. Quarry, Middletown, R.I.* [published by Middletown Historical Society, 1986]).

PECKHAM, E. TRUMAN (1831-1903). Edward Truman Peckham was the builder of many houses in and around Newport, including those on Paradise Avenue owned by the Peckham and Barker families. He owned Grayledge Farm (see fig. 67), which he built around 1860 and rented out for the season beginning in 1862, when John Neilson lodged there shortly after his marriage. La Farge lived in Grayledge Farm in 1867, and his daughter Margaret Angela was born there in September of that year. Peckham apparently renovated the small edifice at the back of the house as a studio that facilitated La Farge's work on *Paradise Valley* and other paintings.

PERRY, MARGARET MASON (1839-1925). Margaret Mason Perry was the sister of La Farge's Newport friend, **Thomas Sergeant Perry**. She was born in the Oliver Hazard Perry mansion on Washington Square (then the Parade) on February 26, 1839, the daughter of Christopher Grant Perry (1812-1854) and Frances Sergeant (1817-1903). Her grandfather was Oliver Hazard Perry, naval hero of the Battle of Lake Erie in the War of 1812. She was also the great-niece of Matthew Calbraith Perry, who opened Japan to western trade in 1853. Margaret's family lived year-round in Newport until her father's death in 1854, after which their winter residence was in her mother's native city of Philadelphia. She met La Farge not long after he arrived in Newport, and their relationship grew serious rather quickly. Her mother disapproved of her daughter being courted by a Roman Catholic, and arranged for Margaret to spend the winter of 1859-1860 at "Oaklawn," the estate of their friends, the Porters, in Louisiana. La Farge, enamored of Margaret, joined them in the spring of 1860, leading to a deepened romantic involvement and ultimately to his betrothal to Margaret. She married La Farge on October 15, 1860, about eighteen months after he came to Newport to study painting. Episcopalian by upbringing, she converted to Roman Catholicism not long after their marriage. Margaret had ten pregnancies, including one still-born child at an unknown date and two children who died in childhood (Joseph Raymond, early 1872-Jan. 1874 and Mary Aimée, 1876-1877). Her other seven children were **Christopher Grant** (1862-1938), Emily Aimée Marie (28 Oct. 1863-23 Dec. 1919), **Bancel** (1865-1938), **Margaret Angela** (1867-1956), **Oliver** (1869-1936), Frances Aimée (10 Jan. 1874-28 Feb. 1851), and John (13 Feb. 1880-24 Nov. 1963; a famous Jesuit theologian). Using money inherited from her grandmother, Mrs. Oliver Hazard Perry, Margaret purchased a house in her own name in 1873 at 10 Sunnyside Place in Newport, not far from where she grew up. She lived there for the remainder of her life, her primary company being her unmarried daughter Margaret Angela. She died on May 2, 1925 at home, and was buried in St. Columba's Roman Catholic Cemetery in Middletown after a funeral mass from St. Mary's Roman Catholic Church.

PERRY, THOMAS SERGEANT (1845-1928). Thomas Sergeant Perry was the younger brother of **Margaret Mason Perry**. He was a friend of the James brothers during the years the latter spent in Newport. Perry received his B.A. from Harvard in 1866, then studied in France and Germany for two years. He mastered Greek, Latin, German, French, and Sanskrit. Late in life, at the age of 60, he learned Russian. Returning from Europe in 1868, he became a tutor of French and German at Harvard, receiving his M.A. in 1869. He left Harvard in 1872 to become assistant editor of the *North American Review* from January 1873 through January 1874. In 1874, he married Lilla Cabot (1848-1933), a poet and painter, and settled in Boston. From 1871 to 1881, Perry wrote all of the reviews of foreign books and numerous articles for the *Atlantic Monthly*. From 1871 to 1878, he was also in charge of fiction reviews for *The Nation*. He additionally translated several books, including Turgenev's *Virgin Soil* (1877), and published five scholarly books, the last and most notable being a *History of Greek Literature* (1890). When his books brought little financial or popular success, he ceased writing for the public except for occasional articles and a brief biography of his friend, John Fiske, a historian and philosopher (1906). Perry was a witty conversationalist and letter writer, corresponding with many leading continental scholars. He was a friend of such prominent Bostonians as William Dean Howells, Henry Lee Higginson, James Russell Lowell, Ralph Waldo Emerson, Oliver Wendell Holmes, Jr., John Fiske, Edward William Hooper, and William Sturgis Bigelow. In the art world, his friends included Bernard Berenson, Walter Gay, Camille Pissarro, and Claude Monet, the latter a neighbor and instructor in painting for his wife during their many summers spent in Giverny. He was also a friend of the architect, Henry Hobson Richardson, and the poet, Edward A. Robinson. Perry and his wife spent much of their time abroad from 1887 until 1909. From 1898 to 1901, Perry was a professor of English Literature at Keiogijiku University in Tokyo, having refused a post at the University of Tokyo that would have committed him to five years there. From 1902-05, he worked regularly every morning at the Boston Public Library as the expert in modern literature. In 1903, Lilla Cabot Perry bought a farm in Hancock, New Hampshire to serve as their summer residence in this country. Their three daughters all had musical talents. The youngest, a pianist, became the wife of diplomat Joseph Grew, to whom Perry became greatly attached.

PETER'S ROCK. The spine of the Paradise Hills the furthest from Second Beach, lying just north of the triple ridges now enclosed by the Norman Bird Sanctuary. This is the highest spine in Paradise and offers the finest views on Aquidneck Island. From Peter's Rock one can see Little Compton across the Sakonnet River and even the entrance to Vineyard Sound at Martha's Vineyard. Looking towards Newport, many mansions lining the cliff walk are visible. In 1893, a stone crusher was set up at the north end of Peter's Rock and became the heart of the Peckham Brothers Quarry operations. In the intervening century, Peter's Rock has been consumed until just the high point on the rock remains untouched. Peter's Rock was named for Peter Barker (1787-1875), known as "Judge Peter," who owned this part of the Paradise Hills until 1844 when he sold it to William Peckham and William Francis Peckham.

PURGATORY CHASM. The most dramatic rupture in puddingstone rock at Paradise. Like similar ruptures, the chasm resulted from glacial pressure on puddingstone. A favorite tourist spot in the nineteenth century, and part of the National Park system today, Purgatory Chasm is one of the most famous spots in Paradise, and has been the subject of innumerable illustrations and postcards.

PURGATORY ROCKS. The cliffs at the west end of Second Beach that include Purgatory chasm, Long Point, and The Bluff go by the name Purgatory Rocks. This large puddingstone mass is on Easton's Point and is part of Ridge I running to Honyman's Hill and beyond.

SACHUEST BAY. The inlet enclosed by the Purgatory Rocks and Sachuest Point, giving onto Second Beach.

SACHUEST BEACH. The preferred name in the nineteenth century for Second Beach.

SACHUEST POINT. The curving finger of land bordered on the west by Sachuest Beach and on the east by the Sakonnet River. During the nineteenth century, there were two farms along the point. Today, this is part of a nature preserve operated by the National Fish and Wildlife Service. The point is covered with thick brambles punctuated by occasional spruce trees.

SAKONNET RIVER (also spelled Seaconnet). The river defining the east side of Aquidneck Island. It runs from north of Tiverton, at its joining with Narragansett Bay, to Sachuest Point, where it meets the Atlantic. On the east side of the river is the Rhode Island community of Little Compton.

SECOND BEACH (also Sachuest Beach). The curving expanse of beach beginning at the Purgatory Rocks and running to Sachuest Point.

SMITH BEACH. See Third Beach.

STADTFELD, MAURICE (active in New York, c. 1860-1880). Little can be learned of Maurice Stadtfeld, aside from the fact that he had a studio at 711 Broadway in New York City. Several photographs of La Farge family members are stamped on the back with his logo, but he probably took many of the photographs that La Farge used as aids for painting during the 1860s and 1870s. In 1863, and perhaps at other times, he came to Paradise and taught La Farge to use a camera, as proven by caricatures of Stadtfeld by La Farge and his brother Frank.

THIRD BEACH (also called Smith Beach). Bordering the Sakonnet River, Third Beach offers calmer and warmer waters than the neighboring Second Beach. The Maidford River empties into Third Beach through a culvert running under the road. According to Mary Clark Sturtevant, "parties of fashionable people sometimes found their way to fish for crabs from a bridge back of Third Beach, under which ran a brook, the waters mingling with the incoming tide. Here also the farmers washed their sheep and sometimes the Baptists brought their converts for immersion" ("East Shore of Middletown," p. 13). Watercolors by Louisa C. Sturtevant owned by the Preservation Society of Newport County shows the bridge and surrounding rivulets that ran from Gardiner's Pond to Third Beach.

THIRD BEACH ROAD. The road begins at the intersection of Mitchell Lane and Wapping Road, and then runs to the parking lot at the end of Third Beach. In the 1860s, this continued down to Sachuest Point where there were at least two residences. According to Mary Clark Sturtevant, this was also called Wet Lane, an appropriate name given the propensity of the road to flood, even today.

WHITNEY, MARY (1855-1940). Mary Whitney was the granddaughter of one of the founding fathers of Binghamton, New York. In 1878, she married Henry (Harry) Lawrence of Mooers, New York, in the northeast corner of the state. From all indications they chose to live apart within a year of being married; he died in 1890. She apparently came to New York in 1879 as a writer of verse for the *New York Ledger*. First as a model and then as a painting assistant, she joined La Farge's atelier around 1880. In 1882, they became romantically involved. When La Farge went bankrupt in 1883 and became embroiled in legal problems, it strained the relationship. Mary lost her job in the fall of 1884, no doubt as a retaliatory move by La Farge's partners. In serious financial distress, she returned to Broome County even while La Farge speculated that he and Mary might right the firm and lead it in a new direction. The formal demise of the La Farge Decorative Art Company in October 1885 dashed this hope but, even so, Mary returned to work for La Farge not long after. Her name appears alongside his on the mural representing Christ's Ascension in the Church of the Ascension in New York, executed between 1886 and 1888. In Broome County, where she settled at the Whitney homestead on Conklin Road just south of Binghamton after the death of her mother in 1892, tradition maintains that she also posed for the figure of the Madonna in the mural. With Bancel La Farge, Mary helped run the New York studio during La Farge's prolonged absence in the South Seas from August 1890 through late November 1891. Her correspondence with La Farge continued until the artist's death. Mary Whitney claimed to have several hundred letters from La Farge, but only about fifteen of these have been located, along with several other letters to a confidante.

Mary Whitney Lawrence,
Self-Portrait,
c. 1878
Oil on linen, 20 x 16 in.
(50.8 x 40.6 cm.)
Broome County
Historical Society,
Binghamton, New York
*There are no known
photographs of Mary
in her youth.*

241.
William A. Williams
Bancel La Farge, c. 1885
Photograph
6 1/4 x 4 1/4 in. (15.5 x 9.9 cm.)
Private Collection
Bancel sits on the porch at 10
Sunnyside Place. The photographer
William A. Williams was a son of
Newport photographer Joshua
Appleby Williams.

242.
William A. Williams
Bancel La Farge with Drum,
c. 1876
Photograph
6 1/4 x 4 in. (15.5 x 10 cm.)
Private Collection

243.
Unidentified Photographer
Margaret Angela La Farge,
c. 1900
Photograph from glass-plate
negative
5 x 3 3/4 in. (12 x 9.4 cm.)
Newport Art Museum, Newport,
Gift of Sal Lopes, courtesy of
Ethel T. Storer
The brick house in the back-
ground cannot be identified.

244.
Unidentified Photographer
Oliver Hazard Perry La Farge, c. 1890
Photograph
3 15/16 x 2 3/4 in. (9.9 x 7 cm.)
Private Collection
Oliver appears to be dressed in a
school sweater. He attended the
Columbia School of Mines in New
York beginning in 1887.

APPENDIX I:
"PARADISE VALLEY," AN UNPUBLISHED MANUSCRIPT

Bancel La Farge (fig. 241), the third child of John and Margaret La Farge was born in the Hessian House on Paradise Avenue on September 23, 1865. He died at his home in Mount Carmel, Connecticut, on August 14, 1938, after an illness of some eight months. This essay, written in the month before his death, was found among the papers of Bancel's late wife, Mabel Hooper La Farge, in the house of their late son, Henry A. La Farge, at New Canaan, Connecticut. It apparently was the only part completed of a much longer memoir about his childhood that Bancel contemplated writing before his death.

"PARADISE VALLEY"
Early July 1938

To have been born in Paradise was a distinction; to return there eventually remains a hope. For us Paradise became an ideal and the precious memories of it still exist. To what extent the association with it dominated our feelings I can not say; but its beauty still remains, though much has been ruthlessly destroyed. Like Fitzgerald's beloved spot: "In those meadows far from the world, it seemed as Salamans Island before an Iron Railway broke the heart of that Happy Valley whose Gossip was the Mill-wheel, and Visitors the Summer Airs that momentarily ruffled the sleepy stream that turned it as they chased one another over, to lose themselves in whispers in the copse beyond." That was also the story of our enchanted Valley, except that instead of a Railway we had ugly waterworks to flood the scenes of our enchantment. There we had played, pic-nicked and dreamed while my father painted his immortal impressions of the Sacred Groves. Those were the happiest days of our lives, for both young and old. My father's joy in his surroundings was reflected in his paintings; which are an eternal record of the spirit of the Happy Valley. "Paradise trees" and Paradise Rocks became by-words with us, expressing our yearning for those poetical backgrounds before which my parents in my memories pass as figures in a dramatic setting—my father, long and thin painting or contemplating his idyllic surroundings; my mother graceful and pensive melting into the silver-grey rocks in the Valley, or emerging to be silhouetted against the distant sea and sky. Though for many subsequent years I frequented these Elysian places with their unfortunate changes, these figures continued to dominate the memories of it. There I could now still feel my mother leading me by the hand through the high and waving grasses toward the beaches; or across the rivulets of rushing sea-water to safety in the deep beach sand. It has always been my hope that the memory of that guiding hand may yet lead me into that other Everlasting Paradise.

The whole of that Valley possessed its attractions for us, whether it were the rising Northern slope to the "Clumps", from where my father painted his famous "Paradise Valley",[1] or whether it were the gentle descent, from there, which led the eye down through the sacred groves across Nelson's pond to the swampy meadows and the beach, to the shining sea and the silvery Purgatory rocks, and cliffs beyond, it was all equally precious and endeared to us, and all equally familiar. Nelson's pond with its wild surroundings, reeds, rushes and swamp—in summer the blooming beds of water-lilies, destined as models for my father's watercolors, perfumed the air in gentle breezes—in the fall wild and melancholy calls drifted across the marshes as plover or yellow legs passed on their way to the South, or the honk of the wild goose rose from the boggy edges of the pond mingled with the splashing rhythm of the surf on the beach. With these as a chorus the Sacred Grove was complete. There our interests were centred [*sic*]. The little lichen-covered cliff of pale silvery rocks out of which grew the groups of old hickory trees emerging like spirits from a classic past created for my father an enchanting setting for his compositions. "Noli me tangere"[2], "The Three Marys"[3], "Virgil Writing,"[4] The Golden Age"[5] were inspired by the beauty and significance of the "Sacred Grove". Its classical enchantment came from an indescribable sense of remoteness or abstraction.

Here my mother posed sometimes for the figures in these religious paintings in classical draperies, flecked by the sunlight and shadows of the overhanging hickories.

That strange grove is long ago gone, together with all the rest of the Valley, and the actors in the Drama. All its beauties and its mysteries are now but a memory buried beneath the waters of that aimless commercial enterprise. However, in its place cheap snobbishness might have been equally disastrous.

---

1. Now running from the Peckham Brothers' Quarry, along the east side of the ridge of Peter's Rock, down the lawn of Gray Craig, and to the Sacred Grove on the northwest side of Nelson's Pond. The "clumps" were clumps of cedars that stood across the valley near the site of the present Gray Craig mansion.
2. The left panel of the altarpiece in the Church of St. Thomas, New York, destroyed by fire in 1905 (see fig. 223).
3. The right panel of the altarpiece in the Church of St. Thomas, New York, destroyed by fire in 1905 (see fig. 218). Bancel footnoted at this point: "Decorations in the Church of St. Thomas's in New York, since burned down."
4. *Virgil*, 1874, Fogg Art Museum, Harvard University Art Museums, Cambridge, Massachusetts (see fig. 224).
5. *Eve, or the Golden Age*, 1878-79, National Museum of American Art, Smithsonian Institution, Washington, D.C. (see fig. 226).

APPENDIX II:
EXTRACT FROM AN UNPUBLISHED LETTER

Margaret Angela La Farge (fig. 242), the fourth child of John and Margaret La Farge, was born on September 16, 1867 at Grayledge Farm. This letter from Margaret to her brother Bancel, dated July 14, 1938, and written on stationery printed with the address "Sunnyside Place, Newport, R.I.," responded to questions evidently asked by him while working on his memoir of life at Paradise (Appendix I). Along with the memoir, this letter turned up in the papers of Bancel's wife, Mabel Hooper La Farge.

Dear Bancel,

What a pleasure to see your handwriting on an envelope addressed to me! It was a surprise indeed and a great satisfaction to know that you were really gaining in health & strength. . . . I think your idea of writing your boyhood memoirs is a splendid one. I had thought of suggesting [it] to you when it seemed as if an inactive convalescence was ahead of you and nothing will give me more pleasure than to help you any way that I can. Yesterday I looked for all the photos that I can find of Paradise & am sending them all to you.[1] Do not return them. As some are badly torn I am mounting them as best I can, so there will be a little delay. The "mounts" that I am using are one of the many duplicate photographs we have of, I suppose, Glen Cove.[2] Included in the package are some old ones that may amuse you and the children. I have always loved the one of you with the drum [fig. 243]. Of your four boys, only Henry[3] resembles you at all as you looked when the drum picture was taken.

I don't think Helen Hunt ever became a Catholic.[4] I can only remember her very vaguely, but then I have a *very* poor memory for personalities. About the Barkers, *Irving* Barker & his wife owned the house that was in Paradise. I remember them both well. He was tall & rather nice looking & I think Mother used to buy eggs from him long after we left going out there. The house they lived in no longer remains & the property all now belongs to the van Beurens.[5] The first house on Paradise Rd on the right now owned by the Henry Howards (she was the youngest Sturtevant & very nice simple people)[6] was called the Chase house. *There* I first saw the light of day [September 16, 1867]. On the north side of the house is a large window put in by Father to paint by. The Howards who let me go over the house a few years back were much interested when I told them about it. On the left *stood* (for it was long ago pulled down) the house where *you* were born [September 23, 1865].[7] The Isaac Barker house still stands farther along on the right hand side & there Oliver was born [July 10, 1869]. Mrs. Isaac Barker lived on for *years* & only died a few years before Mother [1925]. We used to see her sitting all hunched up on her piazza as we drove by. Mother often said she would love to go into the house again, but she remembered it as not *very* pleasant & did not want to attempt it. The house now belongs to the van Beurens too.[8] I have not as yet been able to find out anything about George Rose[9] as you asked me to when I saw you this Spring.

I came across several photographs of Bartholdi & Madame. Do you remember their marriage in the parlor here?[10] And how kind they were to us children?

The letter goes on to discuss other family news and members before concluding.

1. Regrettably, these photographs of the La Farges at Paradise have yet to turn up.
2. Several oversized photographs on cardboard of the large brick house that La Farge's father built at Glen Cove, Long Island, around 1835 were found at Shrub Oak after the death of LaFarge's sister Aimée Heins in 1938. These presumably were copies of those mentioned by Margaret Angela. Mrs. Henry A. La Farge donated these photographs to the Local History Room of the Glen Cove Public Library in 1994.
3. Henry A. La Farge (1902-1985), founder in 1933 of the La Farge Catalogue Raisonné.
4. Helen Maria Hunt (1831-1885), also called by her married name Helen Jackson, an American poet and novelist, best known for her novel *Ramona* (1884). Early in her career, she used the pseudonym *Saxe Holm*.
5. The house "in Paradise" was on the site of the present Orchard Lea, once the gardener's cottage for the estate of Gray Craig. Mary and Michael M. van Beuren owned this land beginning in 1920. The house was moved to 400 Paradise Avenue around 1890, probably when the land was sold by the Barkers to O.H.P. Belmont in 1891. Irving Barker was the oldest son of Stephen P. Barker.
6. Alice Sturtevant (1878-1945), the youngest daughter of Eugene and Mary Clark Sturtevant, married the chemist, inventor, and yachtsman Henry Howard (1858-1951). The house in question is Grayledge Farm, now at 532 Paradise Avenue.
7. The Hessian House once occupied what is now 485 Paradise Avenue. The property of the Barker family since the time of the American Revolution, the house was razed around 1898 following the death of Stephen P. Barker that year. As Margaret Angela's statement implies, the La Farges rented there in 1865, apparently living in a small cottage-like addition at the west end of the house.
8. The house is now at 478 Paradise Avenue, and remains largely as it was in La Farge's time when Isaac Barker, a brother of Stephen P. Barker, lived there. Isaac kept the house in 1891 when he sold much of the land behind the house to O.H.P. Belmont. The van Beurens, who built the nearby Gray Craig mansion in 1926, still own the Isaac Barker house today.
9. George Rose was one of the main assistants who worked for La Farge in his decorative art ventures from at least 1881 until the end of the artist's life.
10. Through his connections to Richard Morris Hunt, La Farge helped French sculptor Auguste Bartholdi (1834-1904) to obtain the commission for the Statue of Liberty during the early 1870s. In late 1876, Bartholdi and his mistress, Jeanne-Emilie Baheux de Puysieux, one of his models, came to visit the La Farges in the house on Sunnyside Place. According to John La Farge S.J., his father discovered that the couple were not married, due to Bartholdi's being sure that his mother, a "strong-minded and imperious" woman "would not countenance a marriage with a girl who worked as a model." However, Bartholdi and Jeanne agreed to be married by Dr. Ellery Channing, a Unitarian minister, in the parlor of the La Farges' house on December 20, 1876, and "the bride was properly given in marriage" by the artist "as her American 'relative' and when the story reached France, it was accepted even by Madame Bartholdi sr. [*sic*], who became firm friends with her daughter-in-law." (LaFarge, *Manner is Ordinary*, p. 14).
    In a letter to his mother at the end of October 1876, Bartholdi, in an elaborate fictional account, had spoken of Jeanne as a cousin of Mrs. La Farge, and Jeanne in a letter to Madame Bartholdi before the marriage, also spoke of Mrs. La Farge as her cousin. A French newspaper account of the wedding spoke of her as a "niece" of John La Farge (see Andre Gschaedler, *True Light on the Statue of Liberty and its Creator* [Narberth, Pennsylvania: Livingston Publishing Company, 1966], pp. 52-57). Of course, as Father La Farge says, these rumored relations were just part of a story with no basis in fact.

APPENDIX III:
EXTRACT FROM *THE GOLD RUSH OF 1898 AND OTHER WRITINGS*

Oliver La Farge (fig. 244), the fifth child of John and Margaret La Farge, was born on July 10, 1869, in the Isaac Barker House at 478 Paradise Avenue. These extracts come from a chapter entitled "Reminiscences of John La Farge's Home Life in Newport" in a book of Oliver's writings compiled and privately published in 1990 by his daughter, Margaret La Farge Hamill: The Gold Rush of 1898 and Other Reminiscences. *The extract below, taken from pp. 88-89, begins after a discussion of the family's move into the house at 10 Sunnyside Place, which took place in August 1873.*

During the earliest period of our occupancy of this home, my Father was painting a great deal at Paradise Valley, about three miles from our home, in fact for a few years prior to moving into this house, we had lived in the summers at Paradise Farm with the Barkers, a place chosen for the family by Mr. William James. I and two of my brothers and sisters were born there. Mr. Barker was a venerable old man with a white beard and very kind to all of us.[1]

For several years we regularly drove to Barker's on Saturdays and Sundays, in an old fashioned wide embracing phaeton, the rumble of which sometimes contained two or even three children.

Barker's farm was always a place of great joy to us, because it had all the freedom of a farm with the aspects of a tired mother and an absorbed Father. There were chickens, ducks, cows and sheep, and besides woods, brooks and a wonderful pond full of pond lilies, reached only by an ancient leaky boat. The pond always seemed to belong to us, as well as the pond lilies, as we were continually picking them for father to paint.

We never could forgive in later years the desecration of this beautiful spot, by the coming of the water works and the flooding of the wonderful valley so dear to us all. It was the second blow to that, which was dear to us children. Father loved the pond lilies and also the apple blossoms, and as I look back on it now, it seemed as if we lived in a continuous spring and summer, I suppose because we went so often to paint the apple blossoms. We also painted the apple blossoms in the orchard back of our house in the lane. I say *we*, because with Father it was impossible not to assist in some manner. One of my earliest recollections of a severe punishment, the flat back of a hair brush, was on one spring day, when, Father having been called to his usually belated lunch, my sister and I carefully squeezed innumerable little colored worms over the surrounding grass from endless oil tubes. Today I never see an orchard in full blossom, without smelling the delightful odor of oil paints.

All the memories of our very happy childhood are wrapped up in the pleasures of those pleasant fields and the old house, while through it all I seem to see my mother, serenely acquiescing in all our interruptions of her own quiet moments, but carefully guarding Father from our invasions of those frequent days, when he worked in the house, writing it seems to me, innumerable letters and telegrams, and drawing and painting a profusion of things.

1.   Stephen Peckham Barker (1815-1898) (see fig. 40).

Margaret Angela La Farge in a Model T,
1918
Snapshot Photograph
Private Collection

SELECTED BIBLIOGRAPHY

This selected bibliography cites only sources referenced in the notes to the essay and within the captions or dictionary. A more complete bibliography and a full listing of La Farge's exhibitions is found in the first book listed below.

General Books on John La Farge

Adams, Henry et al., *John La Farge* (New York: Abbeville Press, 1987). Essays by Henry Adams, Kathleen A. Foster, Henry A. La Farge, H. Barbara Weinberg, Linnea H. Wren, and James L. Yarnall.

Cortissoz, Royal, *John La Farge: A Memoir and a Study* (Boston and New York: Houghton Mifflin and Co., 1911).

Waern, Cecilia, *John La Farge: Artist and Writer* (London: Seeley and Co. and New York: Macmillan and Co., 1896).

Weinberg, H. Barbara, *The Decorative Work of John La Farge* (New York: Garland Press, 1977; Ph.D. dissertation, Columbia University, 1972).

Yarnall, James L. *Nature Vivante: The Still Lifes of John La Farge* (New York: Jordan-Volpe Galleries Inc., 1995).

_____, *John La Farge: Watercolors and Drawings* (Yonkers, New York: Hudson River Museum, 1990).

Newport and Vicinity Residency Lists, 1859-1873

(arranged chronologically)

"Local Intelligence," [Houses and Cottages Rented for the Season of 1859], *Newport Daily News* (19 May 1859), p. [2].

_____, *Newport Daily News* (26 May 1859), p. [2].

"Local Items. Furnished Houses, Rented for the Season of 1860," *Newport Daily News* (23 Jun. 1860), p. [2].

"List of Cottages, Reported for the Daily News and Newport Mercury, By Alfred Smith. Summer Cottages and Villas Rented for the Season of 1861," *Newport Daily News* (15 Jul. 1861), p. [2].

[List of Cottages, Reported Rented for the Season of 1861], *Newport Mercury* (20 Jul. 1861), p. [2].

"Summer Cottages and Villas Rented for the Season of 1862," *Newport Daily News* (14 Jul. 1862), p. [2].

_____, *Newport Daily News* (15 Jul. 1862), p. [1].

[No residency list has been located for 1863.]

"Summer Cottages and Villas Rented for the Season of 1864," *Newport Daily News* (19 Jul. 1864), p. [2].

"List of Rentals for the Season of 1865," *Newport Daily News* (22 Jul. 1865), p. [2].

"Newport Cottages and Villas Rented for the Season of 1865 [reported by Alfred Smith]," *Newport Daily News* (18 Jul. 1865), p. [2].

"Summer Cottages and Villas Rented for the Season of 1865," *Newport Daily News* (5 Aug. 1865), p. [2].

"Summer Cottages and Villas Rented for the Season of 1866," *Newport Daily News* (17 Aug. 1866), p. [2].

"Our Watering Places," *New York Times* (22 Aug. 1866), p. 5.

List of Cottages in Newport, Summer," *New York Times* (22 Aug. 1866), p. 5.

Hazard, Ford & Co., *List of Families Residing in Newport, R.I.*, 1867.

"Cottages and Villas Rented for the Season of 1867," *Newport Daily News* (5 Jul. 1867), p. [2].

"Summer Residents," *Newport Daily News* (11 Jul. 1868), p. [2].

"Cottages and Villas Rented for the Season of 1868," *Newport Mercury* (18 Jul. 1868), p. [2].

Newport and How to See It (Newport: Davis & Pitman, 1869).

"Summer Residents," *Newport Daily News* (12 Jul. 1869), p. [2].

"Cottages and Villas Rented for the Season of 1870," *Newport Mercury* (9 Jul. 1870), p. [2].

Newport and How to See It (Newport: Davis & Pitman, 1871).

"List of Cottages, Season of 1871," *Newport Daily News* (8 Jun. 1871), p. [2].

Boyd, Andrew, comp., *Boyd's Newport City Directory for 1871-72* (Newport: A.T. Ward, 1871).

Books on Related Topics

Agassiz, Prof. and Mrs. Louis, *A Journey in Brazil* (London: Trubner & Co., 1868).

Armstrong, David Maitland, *Day Before Yesterday: Reminiscences of a Varied Life* (New York: Charles Scribner's Sons, 1920).

Baker, Paul, *Richard Morris Hunt* (Cambridge, Massachusetts and London: The MIT Press, 1980).

Bayles, Richard M., *History of Newport County, Rhode Island* (New York: L.E. Preston & Co., 1888).

Black, Mary, *Old New York in Early Photographs* (New York: Dover Publications, 1976).

Boutroux, É. et al., *Les États-Unis et la France, leurs rapports historiques, artistiques et sociaux* (Paris: Librarie Félix Alcan, 1914).

Cahoone, Sarah S., *Visit to Grand-papa; or, A Week at Newport* (New York: Taylor and Dodd, 1840).

Cate, Curtis, *George Sand* (Boston: Houghton Mifflin Company, 1975).

Coolidge, Susan, *A Little Country Girl* (Boston: Little, Brown and Company, 1885).

Edel, Leon, *Henry James Letters*, 2 vols. (Cambridge, Massachusetts: The Belknap Press of Harvard University Press, 1974).

Foster, L.H., *Newport Guide, 1876* (Newport: J.P. Sanborn, 1876).

Gerdts, William H. and Russell Burke, *American Still-Life Painting* (New York: Praeger, 1971).

Hamill, Margaret La Farge, comp., Oliver H.P. La Farge, *The Gold Rush of 1898 and Other Reminiscences* (Princeton, New Jersey: Privately Published, 1990).

Harris 1879 Guide to Newport (Newport: Harris and Co., 1879).

Higginson, Mary Thacher, ed., *Letters and Journals of Thomas Wentworth Higginson 1846-1906* (Boston and New York: Houghton Mifflin Company and The Riverside Press, 1921).

Jackson, Charles T., *Report on the Geological and Agricultural Survey of the State of Rhode Island made under a resolve of Legislature in the Year 1839* (Providence: B. Cranston and Co., 1840).

Janson, Anthony F., *Worthington Whittredge* (Cambridge, England: Cambridge University Press, 1989).

Keats, John, *The Complete Poetical Works of Keats* (Boston: Houghton Mifflin Company, 1899).

La Farge, John, *Considerations on Painting* (New York: Macmillan and Company, 1895).

_____, *Great Masters* (New York: McClure, Phillips and Co., 1903).

_____, *Hokusai: A Talk about Hokusai, The Japanese Painter, at the Century Club, March 28, 1896* (New York: William C. Martin Printing House, 1897).

La Farge, John, S.J., *The Manner is Ordinary* (New York: Harcourt, Brace and Co., 1954).

McSpadden, J. Walker, *Famous Painters of America* (New York: Thomas W. Crowell and Company, 1907).

Middletown Historical Society, *Middletown, Rhode Island: Houses, History, Heritage* (Middletown, Rhode Island: Middletown Historical Society, 1990).

Middletown Historical Society, *The Story of Our Town, Middletown, Rhode Island* (Middletown: Middletown Historical Society, 1993).

Morse, John Torrey, *Thomas Sergeant Perry: A Memoir* (Boston: Houghton Mifflin Company, 1929).

The Newport Natural History Society 1883 (Newport: Davis and Pitman, 1883).

Norman Bird Sanctuary History (Middletown, R.I.: Norman Bird Sanctuary, c. 1994).

O'Shea, Phillip Michael, *Peckham Bros. Quarry, Middletown, R.I.* (Middletown, R.I.: Middletown Historical Society, 1986).

Reid, Forrest, *Book Illustrators of the Sixties* (London: Archibald Constable and Co., Ltd., 1897).

Rossetti, William, comp., *Rossetti Papers 1862 to 1870* (London: Sands & Co., 1903).

Saint-Gaudens, Homer, ed., *The Autobiography of Augustus Saint-Gaudens*, 2 vols. (New York: The Century Co., 1913).

Sainte-Beuve, Charles-Augustin, *Étude sur Virgile* (Paris: Michel Lévy Frères, 1870).

Soria, Regina, *Elihu Vedder* (Rutherford, N.J.: Farleigh Dickinson Press, 1970).

Spassky, Natalie et al., *American Paintings in the Metropolitan Museum of Art, Volume II, A Catalogue of Works by Artists Born Between 1816 and 1845* (New York: Metropolitan Museum of Art, 1985).

Story, William W., *Reports of the United States Commissioners to the Paris Universal Exposition, 1878*, 2 vols. (Washington, D.C., 1880).

Tennyson, Alfred Lord, *Enoch Arden* (Boston: Ticknor and Fields, 1865).

_____, *The Poetic and Dramatic Works of Alfred Lord Tennyson* (Boston and New York: Houghton, Mifflin and Company, 1899).

Van Rensselaer, Mrs. John King, *Newport: Our Social Capital* (Philadelphia and London: J.B. Lippincott Company, 1905).

Walker, Francis A., ed., *United States Centennial Commission, International Exhibition, 1876: Reports and Awards Group XXVII* (Philadelphia, 1877).

Webster, Sally, *William Morris Hunt 1824-1879* (Cambridge, England: Cambridge University Press, 1991).

Whiting, Lilian, *Kate Field: A Record* (Boston: Little, Brown and Company, 1899).

Wilkins, Thurman, *Clarence King: A Biography* (New York: Macmillan Company, 1958).

Workman, Robert G., *The Eden of America: Rhode Island Landscapes, 1820-1920* (Providence: Museum of Art, Rhode Island School of Design, 1986).

Articles

Adams, Henry, "A Fish by John La Farge," *Art Bulletin*, vol. 62 (Jun. 1980), pp. 269-80.

_____, "John La Farge's Discovery of Japanese Art," *Art Bulletin*, vol. 67 (Sept. 1985), pp. 449-85.

_____, "Winslow Homer's 'Impressionism' and Its Relation to His Trip to France," in *Winslow Homer: A Symposium, National Gallery of Art Studies in the History of Art*, vol. 26 (1990), pp. 61-90.

"Art. American Art and Artists," *Round Table* (23 Sept. 1865), pp. 36-37.

"Art. Art Notes," *Round Table* (9 Sept. 1865), p. 7.

_____, *Round Table* (14 Jul. 1866), p. 7.

"Art. La Farge and Vedder," *Aldine*, vol. 6 (Aug. 1873), p. 167.

"Art Notes," *Boston Evening Transcript* (20 Feb. 1885), p. 2.

"Artist La Farge Arrested," *New York World* (20 May 1885), p. 2.

Ballou, Ellen B., "Horace Elisha Scudder and the *Riverside Magazine*," *Harvard Library Bulletin*, vol. 14 (Winter 1960), pp. 426-52.

Caffin, Charles H., "The Beginning and Growth of Mural Painting in American," *The Bookman*, vol. 28 (Oct. 1908), pp. 127-39.

Cook, Clarence, "Recent Church Decoration," *Scribner's Monthly*, vol. 15 (Feb. 1878), pp. 569-77.

Dale, T. Nelson, "The Geology of the Mouth of Narragansett Bay," *Proceedings of the Newport Natural History Society*, no. 3 (Jul. 1885), pp. 5-14.

_____, "The Geology of the Tract Known as 'Paradise,' Near Newport," *Proceedings of the Newport Natural History Society*, no. 2 (Jul. 1884), pp. 3-5.

_____, "Remarks on Some of the Evidences of Geological Disturbances in the Vicinity of Newport," *Proceedings of the Newport Natural History Society*, no. 2 (Jul. 1884), pp. 5-8.

Danes, Gibson, "William Morris Hunt and His Newport Circle," *Magazine of Art* 43 (Apr. 1950), pp. 144-50.

de Kay, Charles, "A Notable Gift to the Metropolitan Museum: La Farge's 'Muse of Painting,'" *Harper's Weekly*, vol. 54 (12 Mar. 1910), p. 7.

"Dimensions of Purgatory," *Newport Daily News* (12 Aug. 1893), p. [1].

Field, Edward, "Isaac Barker's Signal," *Newport Mercury* (28 Nov. 1903), p. 7.

"The Fine Arts. Exhibition of the National Academy of Design," *New York Times* (8 Apr. 1876), p. 7.

"Fine Arts in Newport," *Boston Evening Transcript* (11 Aug. 1868), p. 1.

"The Fine Arts: Mr. La Farge's Pictures," *Boston Daily Advertiser* (18 Dec. 1879), p. 2.

"Fine Arts. What the Artists are Doing," *New York Evening Post* (14 Jan. 1867), p. 1.

"Gen. John Alfred Hazard," *Newport Mercury* (29 May 1880), p. [2].

"The Grist Mill" [Purgatory Legends by E.E.E.], *Newport Mercury* (1 Jun. 1934), p. [3].

Howe, Bruce, "Early Days of the Art Association," *Newport Historical Society Bulletin*, no. 110 (Apr. 1963), pp. 3-29.

James, Henry, "Art," *Atlantic Monthly*, vol. 34 (Sept. 1874), pp. 375-79.

_____, "Art," *Atlantic Monthly*, vol. 37 (Jun. 1876), pp. 759-62.

_____, "Art," *Atlantic Monthly*, vol. 38 (Aug. 1876), pp. 250-52.

La Farge, Henry A., "The Early Drawings of John La Farge," *American Art Journal*, vol. 16, no. 2 (Spring 1984), pp. 4-39.

_____, "John La Farge and the 1878 Auction of his Works," *American Art Journal*, vol. 15, no. 3 (Summer 1983), pp. 4-34.

La Farge, John, "The Son of Bancroft" [Letter to the Editor], *New York Times Saturday Review of Books and Art* (17 Aug. 1901), p. 581.

La Farge, Margaret [Angela], "Old Newport" *Scribner's Magazine*, vol. 62, no. 5 (Nov. 1917), pp. 542-53.

Lathrop, George Parsons, "John La Farge," *Scribner's Monthly*, vol. 21 (Feb. 1881), pp. 503-16.

"Local Affairs," *Newport Journal* (16 Sept. 1875), p. [2].

[Local Affairs], *Newport Mercury* (11 Sept. 1858), p. [2].

"Maitland Armstrong, Artist, Dies at 82," *New York Times* (27 May 1918), p. 13.

Margaux, Adrian, "My Best Picture. No. VII.—The Choice of Eminent American Painters," *Strand Magazine*, vol. 32 (Dec. 1906), pp. 497-504.

"Married" [John La Farge], *Newport Mercury* (27 Oct. 1860), p. [3].

"Married" [John Neilson], *Newport Mercury* (19 Jan. 1861), p. [3].

McCormick, Richard C., "Our Success at Paris in 1878," *North American Review*, vol. 129 (Jul. 1879), pp. 1-22.

"Middletown," *Newport Daily News* (4 Mar. 1898), p. [5].

_____, *Newport Mercury* (26 Aug. 1876), p. [2].

"Mr. La Farge's Pictures," *The American Architect and Building News*, vol. 4 (30 Nov. 1878), pp. 182-83.

"The National Academy of Design. (Second Notice)," *Art Journal* [New York], vol. 2 (Jun. 1876), p. 189-91.

"New Pictures at Williams & Everett's," *Boston Evening Transcript* (9 Feb. 1864), p. 1.

"A New Road in Middletown," *Newport Daily News* (15 May 1883), p. [2].

"Newport" [by W.E.A.], *The Family Magazine*, vol. 6 (1838-1839), pp. 381-87.

"Newport and How to See It," *Newport Daily News* (20 Jun. 1870), p. [2].

"Obituary Notes," *New York Times* (29 Dec. 1903), p. 9.

"Our Watering Places—The Empty Sleeve at Newport," *Harper's Weekly*, vol. 9 (26 Aug. 1865), p. 1.

"Paradise Rocks Burned," *Newport Mercury* (5 Jun. 1919), p. [1]

"Pictures at the National Academy," *Round Table* (18 May 1867), p. 310.

"The Purgatory," *Appleton's Journal*, vol. 3 (22 Jan. 1870), pp. 100-02.

[Real Estate Notes], *Newport Observer* (28 Aug. 1891), p. 8.

_____, *Newport Observer* (31 Oct. 1891), p. 8.

"Real Estate Sales," *Newport Mercury* (10 Oct. 1864), p. [2].

Richards, T. Addison, "Newport," *The Knickerbocker*, vol. 54 (Oct. 1859), pp. 337-53.

Richardson, Charles F., "A Book of Beginnings," *The Nation*, vol. 91 (1 Dec. 1910), pp. 520-21.

Riordan, Roger, "A Pilgrimage Down East," *Lippincott's Magazine*, vol. 31 (Apr. 1883), pp. 345-57.

Riverside Magazine for Young People, vol. 1, no. 12 (Dec. 1867), pp. 552-53; vol. 2, no. 19 (Jul. 1868), pp. 289-91; vol. 2, no. 24 (Dec. 1868), pp. 528, 576; vol. 3, no. 39 (May 1869), pp. 193-94; vol. 4, no. 44 (Aug. 1870), pp. 336, 380-81.

"Sale of the La Farge Collection," *New York Times* (18 Apr. 1884), p. 5.

"Seasonal Notes," *Newport Daily News* (15 Sept. 1894), p. [3].

Senter, Oramel S., "Scenic and Civic New England—Newport 1877," *Potter's American Monthly*, vol. 9 (Jul. 1877), pp. 1-15.

Sloan, Julie L. and James L. Yarnall, "Art of an Opaline Mind: The Stained Glass of John La Farge," *American Art Journal*, vol. 24, nos. 1-2 (1992), pp. 4-43.

Stanley, J.N., letter to the editor, *Newport Mercury* (14 Feb. 1852), p. [3].

Stillman, William J., "The Paris Exposition—XI," *Nation*, vol. 27 (3 Oct. 1878), pp. 210-11.

Sturtevant, Mary C., "The East Shore of Middletown, R.I.," *Bulletin of the Newport Historical Society*, no. 54 (Jul. 1925), pp. 13-18.

Sturgis, Russell, "John La Farge," *Scribner's Magazine*, vol. 26 (Jul. 1899), pp. 3-19.

Swinton, Elizabeth de Sabato, "John Chandler Bancroft: Portrait of a Collector," *Worcester Art Museum Journal*, vol. 6 (1982-1983), pp. 53-64.

Williams, Joshua Appleby, letter to the editor from his "Daguerreotype Rooms," *Newport Daily News* (8 May 1854), p. [2].

_____, [Gallery Advertisement], *Newport Daily News* (13 Apr. 1859), p. [4].

Yarnall, James, "John La Farge and Henry Adams in the South Seas," *American Art Journal*, vol. 20, no. 1 (1988), pp. 51-109.

_____, "John La Farge's *Bishop Hatto and the Rats* and *The Pied Piper of Hamelin Town* in the Chicago Sketchbook," *Master Drawings*, vol. 29, no. 2 (Summer 1991), pp. 115-44.

_____, "John La Farge's 'New England Pasture Land,'" *Bulletin of the Newport Historical Society*, vol. 55, pt. 3, no. 187 (Summer 1982), pp. 79-91.

_____, John La Farge's 'Paradise Valley Period,'" *Bulletin of the Newport Historical Society*, vol. 55, pt. 1, no. 182 (Winter 1982), pp. 1-25.

_____, "John La Farge's *Portrait of the Painter* and the Use of Photography in His Work," *American Art Journal*, vol. 18, no. 1 (1986), pp. 4-20.

_____, "John La Farge's 'The Last Valley,'" *Bulletin of the Newport Historical Society*, vol. 55, pt. 4, no. 188 (Fall 1982), pp. 130-42.

_____, "New Insights on John La Farge and Photography," *American Art Journal*, vol. 19, no. 2 (1987), pp. 52-79.

_____, "Tennyson Illustration in Boston, 1864-1872," *Imprint: Journal of the American Historical Print Collectors Society*, vol. 7 (Autumn 1982), pp. 10-16.

Exhibition and Auction Catalogues

American Art Association (at Mendelssohn Hall), New York, *A Descriptive Catalogue of Paintings, Pastels, and Water Colors collected by the late Mrs. S. D. Warren of Boston*, 8-9 Jan. 1903.

Doll and Richards, Boston, *Catalogue of Drawings, Watercolors, and Paintings by Mr. John La Farge on Exhibition and Sale*, 25 Jan.-6 Feb. 1890.

_____, *Exhibition and Private Sale of Paintings in Water Color Chiefly from the South Sea Islands and Japan*, 18-30 Mar. 1898.

Exposition Universelle Internationale, Paris, *Catalogue Officiel* 3 vols. (Paris: Imprimerie Nationale, 1878).

Kende Galleries at Gimbel Brothers, New York, *Representative Paintings by Famous XIX Century Artists*, 4 May 1945.

Leonard's Gallery, Boston, *The Drawings, Water-Colors, and Oil-Paintings by John La Farge. To Be Sold at Auction*, 18-19 Dec. [1879].

London Society of French Artists, *Seventh Exhibition of the Society of French Artists*, [Summer] 1873.

Manchester Art Treasures Exposition, *Catalogue of the Art Treasures of the United Kingdom collected at Manchester in 1857* (Manchester, England: Bradbury and Evans, 1857).

Metropolitan Museum of Art, *An Exhibition of the Work of John La Farge* (New York: Metropolitan Museum of Art, 1936).

Moore's Art Gallery, New York, *Catalogue of a Collection of Oil and Water Color Paintings by John La Farge*, 26-27 Mar. [1885].

National Academy of Design, New York, *Catalogue of the Forty-Second Annual Exhibition*, 1867.

_____, *Catalogue of the Fifty-First Annual Exhibition*, 1876.

_____, *Catalogue of the Fifty-Third Annual Exhibition*, 1878.

_____, *Catalogue of the Second Summer Exhibition*, 1871.

Ortgies and Co., New York, *Catalogue of Stained Glass, Classic and Illustrated Art Books, Stuffs and Bric-a-Brac*, 23 May 1884.

_____, *Important Collection of Oil and Water Color Paintings, by John La Farge of This City. To Be Sold at Auction*, 14-17 Apr. [1884].

_____, *Supplementary Catalogue of Water Colors, by John La Farge. To Be Sold at Auction*, 14-17 Apr. [1884].

Peirce and Company, Boston, *Catalogue. The Paintings of Mr. John La Farge, to Be Sold at Auction*, 19-20 Nov. [1878].

Philadelphia, Centennial Exposition, *Official Catalogue, Art Gallery, Annexes and Out-Door Works of Art*, 1876.

Royal Palace, Munich, *Illustrirter Katalog der Internationalen Künstaustellung*, 1 Jul.-15 Oct. 1883.

Somerville Auctioneers, New York, *The Collection of over Five Hundred*

Unpublished Material

Adams, Henry, "John La Farge, 1830-1870: From Artist to Amateur" (Ph.D. dissertation, Yale University, 1980).

Covell, Virginia Galvin, "A Critical Examination of the Town and Country Club of Newport, Rhode Island" (Master's Thesis, University of Rhode Island, 1964)

Doll and Richards, Boston, "List of Pictures by Mr. John La Farge sold by Doll & Richards, Inc., Boston" (Typescript, Vose Gallery Papers, Boston).

La Farge, Bancel, "Paradise Valley" (Manuscript: Henry A. La Farge Papers, Jul. 1938; published here in Appendix I).

La Farge, Henry A., "Catalogue Raisonné of the Works of John La Farge" (unpublished manuscript, Henry A. La Farge Papers, New Canaan, Connecticut, 1974-1985; an earlier version of this catalogue [1932-1934] is housed in the La Farge Family Papers, Yale).

La Farge, John, "Autobiographical Notes, Memoranda, and Other Material by and about John La Farge: Recorded to Aid in Writing His Biography [1905]," Royal Cortissoz Correspondence, Beinicke Manuscript Library, Yale University, New Haven, Connecticut.

Wren Linnea Homer, "The Animated Prism: A Study of La Farge as Author, Critic, and Aesthetician," (Ph.D. dissertation, University of Minnesota, 1979).

Yarnall, James L., "The Role of Landscape in the Art of John La Farge" (Ph.D. dissertation, University of Chicago, 1981).

Manuscript Collections

Boston, Museum of Fine Arts, Loan Card Files (Department of American Painting; Department of Prints, Photographs, and Drawings).

Brimmer, Martin, Letters for Years 1880-1895, Archives of American Art, Smithsonian Institution, Washington, D.C.

Cortissoz, Royal, Correspondence, Beinicke Rare Book and Manuscript Library, Yale University, New Haven, Connecticut.

Gilder, Richard Watson, Papers, New York Public Library, New York.

Gilder, Richard Watson and Helena de Kay Gilder Correspondence, in the collection of descendants of the Gilders.

La Farge Family Papers, Division of Manuscripts and Archives, Sterling Memorial Library, Yale University, New Haven, Connecticut.

La Farge Family Papers, The New-York Historical Society, New York.

La Farge, Henry A., Papers, New Canaan, Connecticut.

Macbeth Papers, Archives of American Art, Smithsonian Institution, Washington, D.C.

Middletown Town Hall, Middletown, Rhode Island, Plat Maps and Public Land Records.

Newport Historical Society, Newport, Rhode Island, Library and Archives.

Newport City Hall, Newport, Rhode Island, Land Evidence Books.

_____, Newport Marriage Records.

Perry, Thomas Sergeant, Papers, Colby College, Waterville, Maine.

Private Archives.

Private Archives, New Canaan, Connecticut.

Private Archives, Princeton, New Jersey.

Rhode Island Historical Society, Providence, Rhode Island, Library and Department of Graphic Arts.

Saint Mary's Roman Catholic Church, Newport, Rhode Island, Archives.

INDEX

See specialized place subheadings under
NEWPORT, NEW YORK CITY, and PARADISE.
Titles in italic refer to works by John La Farge
unless otherwise indicated.

Addison Gallery of American Art, Phillips
Academy
  collection of: fig. 51 (p. 32)
Afterglow. Evening Study. Newport, R.I.
  128
Agassiz, Alexander
  17, 117
Agassiz, Louis
  117
Alciphron, or The Minute Philosopher
  (Reverend George Berkeley)
  2, 135, 196
Alman & Co.
  96; fig. 143 (p. 96)
Amberley, Lord and Lady
  109
Angel at the Tomb; Panel from *Resurrection*
  Altarpiece, Church of St. Thomas,
  New York
  155-60; fig. 222 (p. 158)
Appleby, Charles Edgar
  197
Aquidneck Island, Rhode Island
  2, 120, 176 (note 3), 201-02
Arabian Nights Entertainments
  (Eastern Folklore)
  144, 149
Armstrong, David Maitland
  42, 80, 96-97, 103, 116, 195, 200;
  paintings by: figs. 145-46
  (p. 97); portrait by Gessford
  Studios: fig. 144 (p. 96)
Armstrong, Edward Maitland
  195
Armstrong, Helen Maitland
  195
Armstrong, Helen Neilson
  see Neilson, Helen (later Mrs. David
  Maitland Armstrong)
Armstrong, Margaret
  195
Atlantic Monthly (Boston Periodical)
  21, 114
*Autumn Study. View over Hanging Rock,
  Newport, R.I.*
  121; fig. 173 (p. 122)
Avery Architectural and Fine Arts Library,
  Columbia University
  collection of: figs. 64 (p. 41), 66 (p.
  41), 127 (p. 84) and 169 (p. 118)
Bailey, Vernon Howe
  199-200
Balch, Augusta
  42, 200
Bancroft, George
  43, 195
Bancroft, John Chandler
  42-43, 48, 78, 113, 195; fig. 68 (p. 43)
Barbizon, France
  21, 24
Barker, Adelia
  figs. 47-48 (p. 30)
Barker, Alden P.
  fig. 239 (p. 196)
Barker, Alden P., Mrs.
  fig. 45 (p. 29)
Barker, Amy
  8; fig. 10 (p. 8)
Barker, Ashton C.
  fig. 239 (p. 196)
Barker, Betsey Gardiner (Mrs. Stephen P.
  Barker)
  195-96; figs. 45 (p. 29) and 239 (p.
  196)
Barker, Elvira (Mrs. Irving M. Barker)
  103-07, 195, 201, 206
Barker, Frances S.
  196
Barker, Francis S.
  fig. 239 (p. 196)
Barker, Irving M.
  107, 195-96, 201, 206; fig. 239 (p. 196)

Barker, Isaac (brother of Stephen P. Barker)
  29, 177 (note 48),
  195, 201, 206 (note 8), 207
Barker, Isaac (Revolutionary War Era)
  8, 27, 102-03, 195, 198
Barker, Laura A.
  195
Barker, Louisa
  fig. 47 (p. 30)
Barker, Lyman H.
  figs. 48 (p. 30) and 239 (p. 196)
Barker, Peter ("Judge Peter")
  6, 195, 201-02
Barker, Stephen P.
  27, 30, 63, 74, 103, 195-96, 198, 206
  (note 7), 207 (note 1); fig. 239
  (p. 196); photograph by H.W.
  Rankin and Co.: fig. 40 (p. 27)
Barker, Stephen P., Jr.
  fig. 239 (p. 196)
Barnes, Grace Edith
  121
Bartholdi, Auguste
  206 (text and note 10)
A Bather (Woman Bathing)
  124; fig. 178 (p. 125)
The Battle Hymn of the Republic
  (Julia Ward Howe)
  96
Bellows, George Wesley
  202
Belmont, O.H.P.
  9, 30, 53, 103, 177 (note 48), 195, 197,
  201, 206 (notes 5 and 8)
Berenson, Bernard
  202
Le Berger et La Mer (La Fontaine Fable)
  164
Berkeley, George, Reverend
  2, 135, 196, 201
*Berkeley's or Hanging Rock, Paradise. North
  Wind. Autumn*
  128; fig. 184 (p. 129)
Bigelow, William Sturgis
  202
Bishop Berkeley's Rock (William Morris Hunt)
  fig. 35 (p. 24)
Bishop Berkeley's Rock, From the North
  121; fig. 175 (p. 123)
Bishop Berkeley's Rock, Looking at the Crown
  121; figs. 182-83 (p. 127)
Bishop Berkeley's Seat (Gabrielle De Veaux
  Clements)
  12, 65; fig. 19 (p. 12)
Bishop Hatto and the Rats (The Riverside
  Magazine for Young People)
  181 (note 201)
Bishop's Rock, Newport
  121; fig. 174 (p. 123)
Bixby, William Kenney
  181 (note 208)
Blake, William
  151
Blue Iris. Study
  154; fig. 216 (p. 154)
*Boat House beneath the Cliff,
  West Side of Nelson's Pond*
  33; fig. 51 (p. 32)
Booth, Edwin
  199
Boston
  Athenaeum: 56; Doll and Richards
  Gallery: 67, 179 (note 108), 180
  (note 163); Harvard College: 21,
  43, 117, 151, 195; Hurd and
  Houghton: 57, 151; Lee,
  Higginson and Company: 195;
  Ticknor and Fields: 57; Tilton
  and Company: 178 (note 89);
  Trinity Church: 151
Bowdoin College Museum of Art
  collection of:
  figs. 80 (p. 50), 142 (p. 95),
  193-94 (p. 137) and 225 (p. 162)
The Bridge on Third Beach Road (Louisa C.
  Sturtevant)
  14, 85; fig. 23 (p. 14)

Brimmer, Martin
  19, 176 (note 20), 179 (note 114)
Broome County Historical Society,
  Binghamton, NY
  collection of: 203
Brown, Margaret (Mrs. T. Nelson Dale)
  197
Browning, Robert
  109, 180 (note 149)
Cabot, Lilla (Mrs. Thomas Sergeant Perry)
  202
Camelot
  34
The Carnegie Museum of Art
  181 (note 213)
Centaur
  178 (note 85), 181 (note 198)
Cerio, Mabel Norman (Mrs. George Cerio)
  201
Channing, Ellery, Dr.
  206 (note 10)
Chapman, George
  121
Chassériau, Théodore
  144
Chevreul, Michel-Eugène
  (Color Theory and Optics)
  22, 43, 113
Chicago
  World Columbian Exposition: 195
Civil War
  25, 43, 151, 177 (note 43)
Clark, J. Mitchell, Mr. and Mrs.
  9, 197
Clark, Sarah Wood
  109, 197
Clark, Thomas M., Rt. Reverend
  176 (note 15), 197
Clark, Willard G., Mr. and Mrs.
  collection of: fig. 69 (p. 44)
Clements, Gabrielle de Veaux
  fig. 19 (p. 12)
Clouds over Sea; From Paradise Rocks
  44-45, 48; fig. 69 (p. 44)
Coleman, Charles Caryl
  179 (note 128)
Cook, Clarence
  160
Coolidge, Susan (pseudonym of
  Sarah Chauncey Woolsey)
  195
Corcione, Francine
  178 (note 75)
The Corcoran Gallery of Art
  collection of: fig. 41 (p. 28)
Corot, Camille
  23
Cortissoz, Royal
  20, 180 (note 145)
Courbet, Gustave
  19
Couture, Thomas
  19
Cram, Ralph Adams
  5, 199
Cross, Gorham and Beatrice
  179 (note 114)
Crucifixion Triptych (St. Peter's Roman
  Catholic Church, New York)
  36, 44, 138
Cumulus Cloud. Late Afternoon in Summer
  47
Cupid and Psyche
  181 (note 198)
Dale, T. Nelson
  4-5, 17, 149, 170, 197
Dana, Charles A., III
  collection of: fig. 124 (p. 83)
Darley, Octavius Carr
  178 (note 88)
Daubigny, François Charles
  23
Davis Museum and Cultural Center,
  Wellesley College
  collection of: fig. 180 (p. 126)
Davison Art Center, Wesleyan University
  collection of: fig. 153 (p. 101)

de Chavannes, Puvis
  138
*Decorative Panel. Seated Figure in Yellow.
  Study for The Muse of Painting*
  135-38, 151, 160, 181 (note 198);
  fig.192 (p. 136) and frontispiece
de Kay, Charles
  121, 135, 181 (note 186)
de Kay, Helena (later Mrs. Richard Watson
  Gilder)
  151
Delacroix, Eugène
  19, 120, 144, 162, 177 (note 55), 180
  (note 179)
de Puysieux, Jeanne-Emilie Baheux
  (Mrs. Auguste Bartholdi)
  206 (note 10)
Dewing, Maria Oakey
  see Oakey, Maria
Drapery of the Muse;
  Study for *The Muse of Painting*
  135; fig. 194 (p. 137)
Dupin, Amantine Lucile Aurore (George Sand)
  139
Durand-Ruel, Paul
  120
Düsseldorf, Germany
  43
Early Spring. Sun Struggling Through Clouds
  53-54, 62, 67, 117; fig. 84 (p. 52)
Easton, Mary
  198
Easton, Nicholas
  198
Elaine (versions by Dante Gabriel Rossetti
  and Henry Wallis)
  177 (note 55)
Ely Cathedral
  47
Emerson, Ralph Waldo
  202
Enoch Alone
  58, 168; figs. 90 (p. 58), 91 (p. 59) and
  232 (p. 170)
Enoch Arden (Alfred Lord Tennyson)
  57-62, 102, 138, 178 (note 88)
Enoch's Supplication
  62; fig. 96 (p. 62)
Eve, or The Golden Age
  see *The Golden Age*
*Evening; Barker's Rocks, Paradise Farm,
  September*
  74
*Evening. October. Corner of Old Orchard,
  Paradise Farm*
  47
Evening Study. Newport, R.I.
  (From Hazard's Farm, Paradise)
  131; fig. 189 (p. 132)
Field, Kate
  109, 178 (note 90), 179 (note 128)
*Figure in Purple Dress.
  Landscape Background; Afternoon*
  48, 60; fig. 76 (p. 48)
Fish, Nicholas, Colonel
  200
The Fisherman and the Afrite
  (The Riverside Magazine for Young
  People)
  144; fig. 202 (p. 145)
Fiske, John
  202
Flowering Tree and Well at Paradise
  78; fig. 121 (p. 81)
*Flowers. Blue Iris, with Trunk of
  Dead Apple-Tree in the Background*
  133; fig. 191 (p. 133)
Flowers on a Window Ledge
  25, 29; fig. 41 (p. 28)
Fogg Art Museum, Harvard University Art
  Museum
  collection
  figs. 84 (p. 52) and 224 (p. 161)
Fogg Art Museum Conservation Laboratory,
  Harvard University Art Museums
  fig. 155 (p. 105)

Fontainebleau Forest, France
78
Freeland, Charles (Dining Room Decorations)
102
French Impressionism
23, 113, 165
From the Puddingstone Ledge over Nelson's Pond
44; fig. 72 (p. 45)
From the Studio at Grayledge Farm
107-09; fig. 163 (p. 110)
The Gap behind Peter's Rock
72; fig. 110 (p. 73)
Gardiner, Benjamin
177 (note 47), 197, 201
Gardiner's Pond and Paradise Farm
(Louisa C. Sturtevant)
12, 30; fig. 21 (p. 13)
Gargilesse, France
139
Gay, Walter
202
Gessford Studios
fig. 144 (p. 96)
The Giant (The Giant and the Travelers)
(The Riverside Magazine for Young
People)
149; figs. 207 (p. 148) and 208 (p. 149)
Gifford, Robert Swain
153
Gignoux, François Régis
19, 176 (note 22)
Gilder, Helena de Kay
see de Kay, Helena (later Mrs. Richard
Watson Gilder)
Girl leaning Against Tree.
Study of Blue Sky in Sunlight
72-73
Giverny, France
202
Glen Cove, Long Island
25, 197, 206 (text and note 1)
The Golden Age
162, 205 (text and note 5); fig. 226
(p. 163)
Grayledge Farm at Sunset
107; fig. 160 (p. 108)
Grew, Joseph
202
A Grey Day--Newport
40; fig. 61 (p. 40)
Griffith, P.T.
182 (note 244)
The Halt of the Wise Men (The Three Wise Men)
144; fig. 204 (p. 146)
Hanging Rock (George Quincy Thorndike)
16, 65, 138; fig. 25 (p. 16)
The Hanging Rock, near Newport, R.I.
(Joshua Appleby Williams)
17; fig. 26 (p. 17)
"Happy Valley"
10, 116
Happy Valley (Engraving)
10; fig. 17 (p. 10)
Harper's Weekly (Boston Periodical)
98; fig. 149 (p. 98)
Haydel, Abner J.
197
Hazard, Benjamin, Hon.
198
Hazard, Enoch, Dr.
198
Hazard, John Alfred, General
16, 63, 93-94, 128, 154, 179
(note 105), 198
Hazard, Nancy
198
Hecker, Isaac Thomas, Reverend
35
Heins and La Farge
199
Heins, Aimée La Farge
see La Farge, Aimée
(Mrs. George L. Heins)
Heins, George L.
199
The Heliograph Company, New York
fig. 2 (p. 3)

Hennessey, William John
178 (note 88)
Higginson, Henry Lee
202
Higginson, Thomas Wentworth
109
Hill-Side with House. Paradise Farm,
Afternoon Sky, Autumn
27-28; fig. 38 (p. 26)
Hokusai
78, 144, 149, 179 (note 119)
Hollyhocks
47, 133, 155; fig. 74 (p. 46)
Holmes, Oliver Wendell, Jr.
202
Homer (Greek Epic Poet)
121
Homer, Winslow
98-99; fig. 149 (p. 98)
Homer, Winslow, Attributed to
99; fig. 151 (p. 100)
Honyman's Hill
5
Hooper, Alice Sturgis
180 (note 163)
Hooper, Edward William
199, 202
Hooper, Mabel (Mrs. Bancel La Farge)
199, 205
Howard, Henry, Mr. and Mrs.
206 (text and note 6)
Howe, Julia Ward
96, 120; photograph by Alman & Co.:
fig. 143 (p. 96)
Howells, William Dean
202
Hudson River School
37, 86, 96, 114
Hunt, Helen Maria
206 (text and note 3)
Hunt, Richard Morris
19, 206 (note 10)
Hunt, William Morris
19-22, 40-41, 56, 176 (note 24);
figs. 35 (p. 24) and 63 (p. 41)
Hut in The Last Valley
116; fig. 168 (p. 116)
Impressionism
23, 113, 165
An Impromptu Lecture on Art: Winslow Homer
and his Man-Servant Lewis (Photograph)
98; fig. 148 (p. 98)
Ingres, Jean-Auguste-Dominique
19
Inness, George
176 (note 22)
Irving Barker House, Paradise Hills
107; fig. 159 (p. 106)
The Island Home
57-58; fig. 89 (p. 58)
Jackson, Helen
206 (note 3)
James, Henry
8, 21, 54, 67-69, 113-14, 202
James, William
21, 23, 30, 202, 207; as model: 36
Japanese Prints
43, 47, 78, 195
Jordan-Volpe Gallery Inc.
collection of: fig. 216 (p. 154)
Keats, John
121
Kensett, John Frederick
38, 96, 117, 180 (note 172); fig. 58
(p. 37)
Kimball, Benjamin
fig. 147 (p. 98)
King, Clarence
117-19
King, Maud Gwendolyn
195
The Lady of Shalott
34, 138; fig. 52 (p. 34)
La Farge and Morris
199
La Farge and Son
199

La Farge, Aimée (Mrs. George L. Heins)
199, 206 (note 1); fig. 240 (p. 199)
La Farge, Bancel
30, 33-34, 36, 63, 76, 102-03, 124, 155,
179 (note 136), 199, 202-203,
205; as child, in family photograph: 193; as model: 151; photographs by William A. Williams:
figs. 241-42 (p. 204); writings
by: 205
La Farge, Christopher Grant
25, 199, 202; photograph with nurse by
Maurice Stadtfeld: fig. 37 (p. 25)
La Farge, Edward H.
199
La Farge, Emily Aimée Marie
197, 202; as child, in family photograph:
193
La Farge, Frances Aimée
202
La Farge, Francis
49-50; fig. 79 (p. 49)
La Farge, Henry A.
72-73, 199, 205, 206 (text and note 2)
La Farge, John (artist)
figs. 31 (p. 20) and 240 (p. 199);
posing for self-portrait: fig. 78 (p. 49);
self-portrait in an illustration: 148
La Farge, John Frederick (father of artist)
19, 153, 197
La Farge, John S.J. (son of artist)
202, 206 (note 10)
La Farge, Joseph Raymond
202; as child, in family photograph: 193
La Farge, L. Bancel
199
La Farge, Louis
fig. 240 (p. 199)
La Farge, Louis, Mrs. (Georgianna Perry Browne)
fig. 240 (p. 199)
La Farge, Mabel
see Hooper, Mabel (Mrs. Bancel La Farge)
La Farge, Margaret Angela
30, 63, 107, 109, 198-201, 206;
fig. 243 (p. 204); writings by: 206
La Farge, Margaret Mason Perry
(Mrs. John La Farge)
21-22, 107, 151, 166, 179 (note 136),
199-202; figs. 32 (p. 21), 211 (p.
152) and 240 (p. 199); as model:
34, 36, 48, 60, 73, 76, 102, 124,
151; in early photograph: 192; in
late photograph: 193; see also
Perry, Margaret Mason (Mrs. John
La Farge)
La Farge, Mary A. (Mrs. Henry A. La Farge)
206 (note 1)
La Farge, Mary Aimée
202
La Farge, Oliver H.P.
30, 36, 63, 93, 195, 200, 202, 206-07;
fig. 244 (p. 204); writings by: 207
La Farge, Thomas Sergeant
199
La Fontaine, Jean de
164
Landscape (Peter's Rock and Paradise Farm,
Looking Northeast)
72; fig. 109 (p. 72)
Landscape (View of the Puddingstone Ledge
above Nelson's Pond)
54; fig. 86 (p. 55)
Landscape, Newport, 1865
(Near Nelson's Pond, Man Plowing)
78; fig. 127 (p. 84)
The Last Valley
10, 97, 116-20, 180 (notes 181 and 182)
figs.167 (p. 115) and 172 (p. 119)
The Last Valley--Paradise Rocks
(David Maitland Armstrong)
97, 116; fig. 146 (p. 97)
The Last Water Lilies
39-40, 156; fig. 59 (p. 38)
Lathrop, George Parsons
139
Lawrence, Henry (Harry)
203

Lawrence, Mary Whitney
see Whitney, Mary (Mrs. Henry Lawrence)
Lee, Charles Carroll
105; collection of: fig. 156 (p. 105)
Légendes Rustiques (George Sand)
139
Le Strange, Henry Styleman
47
Lindeberg, Harrie T.
197
Little Compton, Rhode Island
8, 33, 93, 198, 101, 201-02
A Little Country Girl (Susan Coolidge)
195
Lockwood, Florence Bayard
199
"Lost Valley"
10, 116
Louisiana
22; Porter Plantation: 177 (note 32), 201
Lovie, Mrs.
181 (note 217)
Low, Abiel Abbott
195
Lowell, James Russell
202
The Magi; Alternative Study for
The Wise Men Out of the East
148; fig. 206 (p. 147)
Man Standing Before a Landscape
(The Last Valley)
117; fig. 171 (p. 119)
Manchester Art Treasures Exhibition
54, 178 (note 83)
Manga (Hokusai)
144, 149
Margaret Mason Perry La Farge
fig. 116 (p. 76)
Marsh, Henry
57, 181 (note 201)
Martha's Vineyard, Massachusetts
33, 202
Martin, Homer Dodge
176 (note 22)
The Martyrdom of Saint Peter Martyr (Titian)
139
Mather, Frank Jewett, Jr.
181 (note 186)
Meadow with Goose
35-36; fig. 55 (p. 36)
Men and Women (Robert Browning)
180 (note 149)
Merson, Luc Olivier
195
The Metropolitan Museum of Art
collection of: figs. 173 (p. 122), 192
(p. 136 and frontispiece) and 233
(p. 171); *Portrait of the Painter*:
49 (caption)
Middletown, Rhode Island
history: 3, 16, 93
Middletown Historical Society
collection of: figs. 7 (p. 6), 28 (p. 18) and
236 (p. 172)
Midsummer Evee
(The Riverside Magazine for Young
People)
150-51; fig. 209 (p. 150)
Millais, John Everett
57, 177 (note 55)
Millet, Jean François
21
Monet, Claude
120, 202
Morning Study--Newport, R.I.
117
Mother and Child
102; fig. 156 (p. 105)
Mott, Jordan L., Mr. and Mrs.
9, 197
Mount Saint Mary's College, Emmitsburg,
Maryland
105
Mountain Study: Cloud
45, 48; fig. 71 (p. 45)
Moxon Tennyson
177 (note 55), 178 (note 92)

Moxon, Edward
    57
Munich, Germany
    International Exposition: 166
Muse of Painting, The
    135-38, 151, 160, 181 (note 198); fig. 192
        (p. 136) and frontispiece
Museum of Fine Arts, Boston
    collection of: figs. 38 (p. 26), 61 (p. 40),
        63 (p. 41), 88 (p. 56), 99 (p. 64),
        108 (p. 72), 175 (p. 123), 204 (p.
        146) and 235 (p. 172)
Narragansett Bay
    3, 202
Narragansett Indians
    15
National Academy of Design
    collection of: fig. 128 (p. 84)
National Museum of American Art,
    Smithsonian Institution
    collection of: fig. 226 (p. 163)
Neilson, Helen
    (later Mrs. David Maitland Armstrong)
    42, 195, 200
Neilson, John
    42, 96, 195, 198, 200-01
Nelson's Pond from the Peninsula, Paradise
    85; fig. 135 (p. 90)
*Nelson's Pond from the Puddingstone Ledge,
    at Paradise*
    78; fig. 124 (p. 83)
Nelson's Pond from the Sacred Grove
    33; fig. 50 (p. 32)
*Nelson's Pond, Looking West toward
    Puddingstone Cliff*
    34; fig. 54 (p. 35)
The New Britain Museum of American Art
    collection of: fig. 52 (p. 34)
New England Pasture Land (Paradise Valley)
    113
Newport Art Museum
    collection of: figs. 82 (p. 51), 149 (p. 98),
        211 (p. 152) and 243 (p. 204)
*Newport. Bishop Berkeley's Rock.
    From the East, 1865*
    63-65; fig. 101 (p. 65)
Newport; From Paradise Rocks
    99; fig. 150 (p. 100)
The Newport Historical Society
    collection of: figs. 25 (p. 16),
        39 (p. 27), 44-45 (p. 29)
Newport Natural History Society
    17, 117-20, 197
Newport, Paradise, 1862
    (Looking Southwest across Nelson's
    Pond toward Purgatory Rocks)
    41; fig. 64 (p. 41)
Newport, Rhode Island
    3, 16; Almy's Pond: 198; Bailey's Beach:
        21; Bath Road: 197; Belcourt
        Castle: 9; Bellevue Avenue: 21,
        43, 107, 195; Boat House Beach:
        23; Brenton's Cove: 23; Castle Hill:
        117; Catherine Street: 22, 63, 177
        (note 32); Church Street: 21; Cliff
        Walk: 33; Easton's Beach: 197;
        Eustis House: 109; First Beach:
        6, 16, 197; fig. 7 (p. 6); Fort
        Adams: 23; Greenough Place:
        107, 177 (note 32); Hill Top Cot-
        tage: 21; Kay Street: 25, 54, 109,
        151, 178 (note 104), 199; fig. 36
        (p. 25); La Farge's arrival in:
        19-21; Ledge Road: 23, 197; Lily
        Pond: 23, 198; Long Wharf: 23;
        Mann Avenue: 151; Memorial
        Boulevard: 197; Mill Street: 107;
        Mount Vernon Street: 25; Ocean
        Drive: 21, 117, 198; Old Boat
        House Beach: 181 (note 186),
        197; Perry Mansion: 22, 201;
        Rocky Farm: 198; Rosecliff: 43,
        195; Spouting Horn: 21, 23; St.
        Mary's Church: 177 (note 34),
        202; Sunnyside Place: 151, 166,
        174, 182 (note 220), 199, 206 (text
        and note 10), 207; figs. 213-15 (p.
        153); Thames Street: 109, 172,

182 (note 244); Touro Street: 22,
    107; Town and Country Club: 96,
    120, 179 (note 124); Trinity
    Church: 196; Washington Square
    (The Parade): 22, 172, 182 (note
    244), 201
Newport. The Rocks of the Last Valley, Paradise
    117; fig. 169 (p. 118)
New York City
    25, 35-36; Broadway: 49, 178 (note 75),
        202; Cathedral of St. John the Di-
        vine: 199; Century Club: 195;
        Church of St. Paul the Apostle:
        199; Church of St. Thomas:
        155-60, 205 (text and notes 2, 3);
        figs. 217 (p. 155), 218 (p. 156),
        222 (p. 158) and 223 (p. 159);
        Church of the Ascension: 203;
        Jefferson Market Court: 167;
        Kende Galleries: 181 (note 208);
        La Farge Decorative Art Company:
        165, 167-68, 203, 206 (note 9); La
        Farge's upbringing in: 19; Metro-
        politan Museum of Art: 49, 97,
        195; Montross Gallery: 121; Na-
        tional Academy of Design: 113,
        179 (note 108), 179 (note 136),
        180 (note 171); O'Connor Galler-
        ies: 181 (note 208); Paulist Or-
        der: 35; Society of American Art-
        ists: 180 (note 181); St. Peter's
        Roman Catholic Church: 36; figs.
        56-57 (p. 37); Tenth Street Studio
        Building: 19, 49, 56, 98, 167, 174
New York Ledger
    203
Noli me tangere; Panel from *Resurrection*
    Altarpiece, Church of St. Thomas,
    New York
    155-60, 205; fig. 223 (p. 159)
Norman, George H.
    177 (note 47), 197, 201
Norman, Mabel
    see Cerio, Mabel Norman
        (Mrs. George Cerio)
Oak Leaves and Branches
    163; fig. 225 (p. 162)
Oakey, Maria (later Mrs. Thomas Wilmer Dewing)
    151
*The Obliging Disposition of Maurice
    Stadtfeld* (Francis La Farge)
    49-50; fig. 79 (p. 49)
O'Connor, Patrick
    181 (note 208)
Old Farm-House, and Orchard on Hill-Side
    133
On the West Bank of Nelson's Pond
    164; fig. 229 (p. 166)
On Third Beach Road at Paradise
    85; fig. 132 (p. 88)
Ophelia (versions by Eugène Delacroix and
    John Everett Millais)
    177 (note 55)
An Orchard in Bloom at Paradise
    78; fig. 120 (p. 80)
*Our Watering Places--The Empty Sleeve
    at Newport* (Winslow Homer)
    98; fig. 149 (p. 98)
The Painter and the Muse;
    Study for *The Muse of Painting*
    135; fig. 193 (p. 137)
The Palace of Art (Alfred Lord Tennyson)
    51, 178 (note 80)

PARADISE

Atlantic Ocean
    8, 16, 33, 58, 196, 202
Barker, Irving, House
    30, 106-07, 195, 206 (text and note 5);
        fig. 158 (p. 106)
Barker, Isaac, House
    28, 30, 63, 178 (note 104), 195, 200-01,
        206 (text and note 8), 207; fig.
        49 (p. 30); baseboard of window
        sill: fig. 42 (p. 28)
Berkeley Avenue
    196, 200-01
Berkeley Memorial Chapel
    199
Bishop Berkeley's Rock
    2, 10, 12, 14-18, 23-24, 56, 58, 63-65,
        93, 116, 121, 128, 135-36, 170,
        179 (note 105), 196-98, 200;
        figs. 1 (p. 2), 98 (p. 64), 100
        (p. 64), 102 (p. 65), 176 (p. 123),
        181 (p. 127), 185 (p. 129), 190
        (p. 133) and 195 (p. 137); pho-
        tograph by Joshua Appleby Wil-
        liams: fig. 236 (p. 172)
Boothden
    199
Bridge House
    198
Easton Farm
    179 (note 105), 198
Easton's Point
    5, 33, 41, 99, 195, 197, 202
Flint Point
    6, 18, 33, 85, 101, 128, 131 (caption),
        144, 197, 201; fig. 30 (p. 18)
Four Corners
    102-03
Gardiner's Farm
    30
Gardiner's Pond
    12, 14, 17, 30, 65, 85, 197, 200-01,
        203; figs. 20 and 22 (p. 13); dike:
        12, 14, 17, 138
Gray Crag
    9, 17, 103, 197; postcard by Robbins
        Brothers, Boston: fig. 11 (p. 9)
Gray Craig
    9, 10, 15, 17, 35, 37, 73, 75, 85, 103,
        197, 200, 205 (note 1), 206 (note
        5); fig. 12 (p. 9); "canyon": fig.
        15 (p. 11)
Gray Craig Pond
    197
Grayledge Farm
    28, 30, 42, 63, 78, 96, 107-09, 198-201,
        206 (text and note 6); fig. 67
        (p. 42); baseboard of window
        sill: fig. 43 (p. 28); from the
        backyard: fig. 161 (p. 108); stu-
        dio: 107-09, 198, 201, 206; stu-
        dio exterior: fig. 162 (p. 110);
        studio interior: figs. 164-65
        (p. 111)
Green End Avenue
    3, 5, 16, 102-03, 197-98, 201
Hanging Rocks Road
    16-17, 93, 128, 138, 170, 198; figs. 27
        (p. 17) and 28 (p. 18)
Hessian House
    27-30, 33, 63, 72, 76, 195-96, 198,
        205-06, 206 (note 7); figs. 39
        (p. 27) and 44-45 (p. 29)
Honyman's Hill
    202
Indian Avenue
    16, 85, 176 (note 15), 198-99
Last Valley
    10, 23-24, 58, 63, 93, 99, 101, 149,
        154, 170, 200-01; figs. 16
        (p. 11), 18 (p. 11), 34 (p. 23) and
        170 (p. 118)
Lion's Mouth
    63
Maidford River
    14, 17, 63, 85, 179 (note 105),
        197-98, 200-01, 203

Mitchell Lane
    203
Nelson, J., House
    33, 47, 177 (note 48), 200-01
Nelson's Pond
    9-10, 12, 33, 36-41, 41, 44-45, 56, 60,
        69, 73, 78, 84-85, 103, 139, 148,
        155-56, 170, 174, 177 (note 48),
        197, 200, 205; figs. 200 (p. 142)
        and 228 (p. 165); boat house:
        33; cliff and puddingstone
        ledge: 9-10, 45 (caption), 139;
        figs. 13 (p. 10) and 199 (p. 142);
        cliff and Sacred Grove: 33-36;
        fig. 53 (p. 35); dike: 10, 12, 41,
        45, 65, 200; fig. 73 (p. 45); from
        dike: 174; fig. 238 (p. 175); from
        lawn of Gray Craig: 85; fig. 138
        (p. 92); from puddingstone
        ledge: 45, 78; figs. 70 (p. 44)
        and 125 (p. 83); island: 39-41,
        41, 200; fig. 60 (p. 39); Large
        Basin: 12, 32, 35, 45, (caption)
        78, 83,85, 200; peninsula: 10,
        32, 35, 36 (caption), 39-41, 45
        (caption), 83, 85, 200; figs. 14
        (p. 11) and 62 (p. 40); Small
        Basin: 12, 32, 35, 39, 45 (cap-
        tion), 78, 83, 200; water lily
        patch: 12, 36-38, 207
Newport Water Works
    12, 16, 78, 138, 151, 197, 200
Norman Bird Sanctuary
    10, 30, 45 (caption), 99, 101, 177 (note
        47), 197, 200-01; Gray Craig
        Trail: 99; Valley Trail: 116
Orchard Lea
    30, 63, 105-07, 195, 201, 206 (note 5)
Paradise Avenue
    3, 9, 14, 16, 27-30, 42-43, 63, 102-03,
        107, 128-31, 179 (note 105), 195,
        198, 200-01, 206 (notes 5 and 6)
Paradise Brook
    14, 200-01
Paradise Court
    33, 78, 82, 198, 201
Paradise Farm (Barker's Farm)
    27-30, 48, 53-54, 72-74, 78, 85,
        102-03, 177 (note 48), 197, 201,
        207
Paradise Farm (Paradise Avenue)
    30, 78; fig. 46 (p. 30)
Paradise Farm (Third Beach Road)
    12, 17, 30, 99, 101, 177 (note 47), 197,
        201; fig. 22 (p. 13)
Paradise Hills
    3, 10, 16, 30, 36, 45, 60, 63, 69, 85,
        99, 128-31, 148, 174, 177 (note
        48), 179 (note 128), 195-196,
        198, 200-02; fig. 152 (p. 101)
Paradise Ledge
    75
Paradise Lost
    6, 144, 201; figs. 8 (p. 7) and 205 (p.
        147)
Paradise Pond
    10, 14, 24, 58, 116, 176 (note 12), 201
Paradise Road
    5, 201
Peckham Brothers Quarry
    6, 17, 51 (caption), 77, 103, 107, 172
        (caption), 201-02, 205 (note 1);
        figs. 9 (p. 7) and 157 (p. 105)
Peter's Rock
    6, 30, 33, 51, 69, 74, 76, 105-07, 124,
        201-02; figs. 6 (p. 6), 107 (p. 71),
        112 (p. 74), 115 (p. 75) and 112
        (p. 74), 115 (p. 75) and 118
        (p. 77); gap: 8, 30 (caption), 72,
        198; figs. 10 (p. 8) and 111
        (p. 73)
Prospect Avenue
    102-03, 201
Puddingstone Ledge above Nelson's Pond
    9, 33-34, 45, 47-48, 53-54, 61-62,
        67-69, 85, 148, 151, 168; figs.
        85 (p. 53), 95 (p. 61), 105 (p. 69)
        and 212 (p. 152)

214

Puddingstone Rock
    defined: 5; geological interest: 117-20
Purgatory Avenue
    16, 96, 198
Purgatory Chasm
    4, 66, 176 (note 4), 195, 197, 202; fig.
        3 (p. 4); postcard by Heliograph
        Company: fig. 2 (p. 3)
Purgatory Rocks
    4, 9-10, 18, 33, 41, 58, 66, 69, 85, 99,
        103, 114, 124, 128-31, 164, 168,
        197, 201-02, 205; figs. 65 (p.
        41), 92 (p. 59) and 179 (p. 125)
Sachuest Bay
    18, 85, 202
Sachuest Beach
    202
Sachuest Point
    6, 16, 18, 33, 44, 50, 114, 131 (cap-
        tion), 144, 197-98, 201-02
Sachuest Point Road
    78, 131 (caption)
Sachuest Way
    6, 202
Sacred Grove
    10, 33, 41, 47, 61, 78, 85, 103, 139,
        151, 155-60, 205; figs. 75 (p.
        47), 123 (p. 82), 219 (p. 157) and
        221 (p. 158); cliff and
        puddingstone ledge: fig. 220
        (p. 157)
St. Columba's Chapel
    176 (note 15), 199
St. George's School
    5, 14, 87, 102, 133; fig. 4 (p. 5)
Sakonnet River
    6, 10, 18, 33, 85, 93, 99, 101-03, 131,
        144, 197-98, 200, 202; fig. 141
        (p. 95)
Sea Breeze Farm
    30, 63, 74, 106, 195-96; figs. 47-48
        fig. 30 (p. 30) and 113 (p. 74)
Second Beach
    3, 9, 14, 16, 18, 33, 36, 41, 44, 50, 58,
        69, 73, 78, 93, 96, 114, 124, 128,
        131, 144, 154, 168, 197-98, 202-
        03, 205; figs. 29 (p. 18), 81 (p.
        50), 92 (p. 59), 179 (p. 125) and
        187 (p. 131)
Smith Beach
    203
Swamp Road
    5, 201
Third Beach
    14, 18, 93-94, 197, 201, 203; fig. 30
        (p. 18)
Third Beach "Bridge"
    14, 85, 87
Third Beach Club
    89
Third Beach Road
    3, 14, 16, 85, 87, 197-98, 200, 203;
        fig. 133 (p. 88); looking west
        from overpass: fig. 24 (p. 15)
Tuckerman Avenue
    195, 197
Turner Road
    102-03
Wapping Road
    203
Wet Lane (Third Beach Road)
    85, 203
Whitehall
    196, 201
Wyatt Road
    102-03, 198

Paradise Brook from the Bridge on
        Third Beach Road
    85; fig. 130 (p. 87)
Paradise Brook near the Bridge on
        Third Beach Road
    85; fig. 131 (p. 87)
Paradise Farm and Nelson's Pond, n
        ear the "Canyon"
    85; fig. 136 (p. 91)
Paradise Farm and Nelson's Pond,
        near the Sacred Grove
    85; fig. 137 (p. 92)
Paradise Farm, Levity Place,
        Rhode Island (Elihu Vedder)
    99; fig. 153 (p. 101)
Paradise Near Newport, R.I. (Paradise Avenue)
    5; fig. 5 (p. 5)
Paradise Rocks (James A. Suydam)
    78; fig. 128 (p. 84)
Paradise Rocks, Looking East
        (Photograph)
    170; fig. 234 (p. 171)
Paradise Rocks, near Newport
        (John Frederick Kensett)
    38; fig. 58 (p. 37)
Paradise Rocks, Newport, from the West
    63-65; fig. 99 (p. 64)
Paradise Rocks, Newport, R.I. Faint Sunlight
    74
Paradise Rocks.--Study at Paradise.
        Newport, R.I.
    170; fig. 233 (p. 171)
Paradise Rocks--Study of Orchard and
        Rocks on the Barker Farm
    74
Paradise Rocks Viewed from Top of Ridge
        (Afternoon. Autumn. Paradise Rocks)
    127; fig. 180 (p. 126)
Paradise Valley
    8, 97, 102-11, 128, 144, 201, 205;
        fig. 154 (p. 104); X-ray: fig. 155 (p. 105)
Paris, France
    19, 25, 43, 120; Salon of 1874: 120;
        Universal Exposition of 1878: 113, 195
Parker, Charles H.
    179 (note 114)
Pastoral Study.--Paradise, Newport, R.I.
    54; fig. 87 (p. 55)
Peckham, E. Truman
    29, 42, 63, 96, 107, 109, 195, 198,
        200-01
Peckham, William
    201-02
Peckham, William Francis
    201-02
Peekskill, New York
    128
Perry, Christopher Grant
    22, 201
Perry, Elizabeth Champlin Mason
        (Mrs. Oliver Hazard Perry)
    22, 153, 182 (note 220), 201
Perry, Frances Sergeant
        (Mrs. Christopher Grant Perry)
    22, 201; in family photograph
        with grandchildren: 193
Perry, Lilla Cabot
        see Cabot, Lilla
        (Mrs. Thomas Sergeant Perry)
Perry, Margaret Mason (later Mrs. John La Farge)
    21-22, 177 (note 32), 200-02;
        conversion: 22; marriage: 22;
        see also La Farge, Margaret Mason Perry
Perry, Matthew Calbraith, Commodore
    78, 201
Perry, Oliver Hazard, Commodore
    22, 201
Perry, Oliver Hazard, Mrs.
        see Perry, Elizabeth Champlin Mason
        (Mrs. Oliver Hazard Perry)
Perry, Thomas Sergeant
    21-22, 27, 51, 199; fig. 240 (p. 199);
        as model, in Japanese kimono:
        fig. 82 (p. 51)
Peter's Rock from Paradise Farm
    76; fig. 117 (p. 77)
Philadelphia Centennial Exposition
    120, 180 (note 181)

Philip and Annie in the Wood
    60-61; fig. 94 (p. 61)
Photography
    49-53, 139, 149, 151, 168-70, 182 (note
        244), 203; cliché-verre process:
        180 (note 149); tintype: fig. 205
        (p. 147)
The Pied Piper of Hamelin Town
        (The Riverside Magazine for Young
        People)
    181 (note 201)
Pine Trees near Nelson's Pond at Paradise
    174; fig. 237 (p. 175)
Pissarro, Camille
    120, 202
Porter, Mary (widow of James C. Porter)
    177 (note 32)
Portrait of the Painter (Metropolitan Museum
        of Art, New York)
    photograph showing artist posing
        for self-portrait: fig. 78 (p. 49)
Portsmouth, Rhode Island
    history: 3; The Glen: 23
Pre-Raphaelite Art
    34, 47, 57, 102, 113, 178 (notes 75
        and 83)
The Preservation Society of Newport County
    181 (note 213), 195, 203; collection of:
        figs. 21 (p. 13), 23 (p. 14) and 145
        (p. 97)
Princeton University, The Art Museum
    collection of: figs. 109 (p. 72), 171 (p.
        119), 174 (p. 123) and 186 (p. 130)
Protus (for Robert Browning's Men and Women)
    109, 180 (note 149)
Providence Plantations
    3
Providence, Rhode Island
    Church of the Blessed Sacrament: 199
Puddingstone "Steps" behind Sea Breeze Farm
    75; fig. 114 (p. 75)
Pumpelly, Raphael
    17
Purgatory Chasm
    66; fig. 103 (p. 66)
Purgatory Chasm (David Maitland Armstrong)
    97; fig. 145 (p. 97)
Ramona (Helen Hunt Jackson)
    206 (note 3)
Rankin, H.W., and Co.
    .fig. 40 (p. 27)
The Redwood Library and Athenaeum
    collection of: figs. 68 (p. 43) and 77
        (p. 48)
The Resurrection; Altarpiece formerly in Church
        of St. Thomas, New York
    155-60; fig. 217 (p. 155)
Revolutionary War
    27, 198
Richardson, Abby Sage
    151, 165
Richardson, Henry Hobson
    138, 151, 181 (note 198), 199, 202
Rimmer, William
    56, 178 (note 85)
Riordan, Roger
    165-66
The Riverside Magazine for Young People
    138-51, 168
Robbins Brothers, Boston
    fig. 11 (p. 9)
Robinson, Edward A.
    202
Rocks by the Path in the Sacred Grove at
        Paradise
    78; fig. 122 (p. 82)
Rogers, John
    178 (note 75)
Rogers, William B., Professor
    120
Rose, George
    206 (text and note 9)
Rossetti, Dante Gabriel
    57, 177 (note 55)
Rossetti, William Michael
    57
Rousseau, Théodore
    120, 180 (note 179)

Roxbury, Massachusetts
    56, 178 (note 85)
Rubens
    162
Sacred and Profane Love (Titian)
    166
Saint-Beuve, Charles-Augustin
    160
St. Cecilia Asleep at the Organ; Study for
        Tennyson's The Palace of Art
    51; fig. 83 (p. 51)
St. Columba's Roman Catholic Cemetery,
        Middletown, Rhode Island
    200, 202
St. John the Evangelist at the Foot of the Cross;
        Panel for a Triptych of the Crucifixion
    36; fig. 57 (p. 37)
Saint Paul Preaching at Athens
    35
Saint-Gaudens National Historic Site, U.S.
        Department of the Interior, National Park
        Service collection of: fig. 150 (p. 100)
The Sakonnet River near Flint Point,
        View from Hut
    93, 131; fig. 140 (p. 94)
The Sakonnet River near Flint Point,
        View over Fence
    93, 131; fig. 139 (p. 94)
Sand, George (pseudonym of Amantine Lucile
        Aurore Dupin)
    139
Saxe Holm (pseudonym of Helen Hunt Jackson)
    206 (note 3)
Scudder, Horace Elisha
    57, 138
Sea Side Study
    180 (note 171)
The Seashore
    180 (note 172)
Second Beach (Worthington Whittredge)
    93, 96; fig. 142 (p. 95)
Second Beach and Bishop Berkeley's Rock,
        Sheep Grazing
    78; fig. 126 (p. 84)
Second Beach and Purgatory Rocks, Newport
    69, 124; fig. 106 (p. 70)
Second Beach and Purgatory Rocks;
        from Paradise Farm, Southeast Wind
    69, 124; fig. 177 (p. 124)
Second Beach from Flint Point
    128, 133; fig. 188 (p. 131)
Second Beach, Middletown, R.I.
    50, 144; fig. 80 (p. 50)
The Shepherd and the Sea
    142 (caption), 156, 164-66; fig. 227
        (p. 164)
Shrub Oak, New York
    128
Sisley, Alfred
    120
Sketch. Blue and White Sky.
        Rocks and Pond. Newport
    23; fig. 33 (p. 23)
Smith, Isaac
    177 (note 47)
Snow Storm
    67-69, 128, 168; fig. 104 (p. 68)
Snow Weather. Sketch (Landscape in Snow)
    93, 128, 133; fig. 186 (p. 130)
Society of the Cincinnati
    200
Soderholtz, Eric E.
    178 (note 79)
The Solitary
    58-60; fig. 93 (p. 60)
The Song of the Siren
    165; fig. 230 (p. 167)
Songs from the Old Dramatists (Abby Sage
        Richardson)
    151, 165
Songs of Feeling & Songs of Thought
    151; fig. 210 (p. 152)
Songs of Innocence and of Experience (William
        Blake)
    151
South Seas
    170, 174, 199, 203

Stadtfeld, Maurice
    49-50, 178 (note 75), 203; fig. 37 (p. 25)
Still-Life Painting (La Farge)
    25, 28
The Studio at Grayledge Farm, Paradise
    109; fig. 166 (p. 112)
Study at Berkeley Ridge or Hanging Rock (Rocks at Newport)
    170; fig. 235 (p. 172)
Study at Bishop Berkeley's Rock, Newport
    56; fig. 88 (p. 56)
Study for The Wolf Charmer
    139; fig. 198 (p. 142)
Study of Appletree. Spring
    177 (note 44)
Study of Cloud Movement, Newport
    72; fig. 108 (p. 72)
Study of Hanging Rock, Newport
    63; fig. 97 (p. 64)
Study of Snow
    168; fig. 231 (p. 168)
Study of Spring. Orchard-Trees, with Horse Browsing
    177 (note 44)
Study of Trees (Hickories in the Sacred Grove)
    41; fig. 66 (p. 41)
Sturgis, Russell
    174
Sturtevant, Alice
    206 (text and note 6)
Sturtevant, Eugene
    16, 93, 176 (note 15), 197-98, 206
        (note 6)
Sturtevant, Louisa C.
    14, 18, 30, 203; figs. 21 (p. 13) and 23
        (p. 14)
Sturtevant, Mary Clark
    14, 16, 176 (note 15), 197-98, 200, 203,
        206 (note 6)
Suydam, James A.
    78; fig. 128 (p. 84)
Taggart, William
    177 (note 47), 201
Tall Trees along Paradise Brook, near the Bridge on Third Beach Road
    85; fig. 129 (p. 86)
Tennyson, Alfred Lord
    34, 51, 57-62, 138
Third Beach and Flint Point at Paradise
    85; fig. 134 (p. 89)
Thomas Sergeant Perry
    fig. 77 (p. 48)
Thorndike, George Quincy
    16, 107, 138; fig. 25 (p. 16)
The Three Maries; Panel from *Resurrection* Altar piece, Church of St. Thomas, New York
    155-60, 205; fig. 218 (p. 156)
The Three Wise Men (Halt of the Wise Men)
    144; fig. 204 (p. 146)
Timmins, Mary Ann
    179 (note 114)
Titian
    139, 162, 166, 181 (note 205)
Tiverton, Rhode Island
    203
The Toledo Museum of Art
    collection of: figs. 86 (p. 55), 101 (p.
        65) and 198 (p. 142)
Tonalism
    107
A Tree at Paradise, near Peter's Rock
    78; fig. 119 (p. 79)
Tryon, Dwight William
    107
Turner, Joseph Mallord
    178 (note 83)
Twin Lambs (William Morris Hunt)
    40; fig. 63 (p. 41)
United States Geological Survey
    117, 197
van Beuren, Mary and Michael M.
    9, 197, 201, 206

Vareika, William, Fine Arts
    collection of: figs. 1 (p. 2), 2 (p. 3), 11 (p.
        9), 71 (p. 45), 106 (p. 70), 119 (p.
        79), 122 (p. 82), 129 (p. 86), 131
        (p. 87), 132 (p. 88), 134 (p. 89),
        135 (p. 90), 136 (p. 91), 137 (p.
        92), 139-40 (p. 94), 146 (p. 97),
        156 (p. 105), 160 (p. 108), 184 (p.
        129), 189 (p. 132), 206 (p. 147),
        227 (p. 164) and 237 (p. 175)
Vedder, Elihu
    56-57, 98-99, 109, 131, 178 (notes 88
        and 90); fig. 153 (p. 101); photo-
        graph by Benjamin Kimball: fig.
        147 (p. 98)
Virgil
    160-61, 205 (text and note 4); fig. 224
        (p. 161)
Virgil (Roman Epic Poet)
    33, 160
The Virgin at the Foot of the Cross; Panel for a Triptych of the Crucifixion
    36; fig. 56 (p. 37)
von Zittel, Karl Alfred
    197
Vose, Robert C.
    121
Wallis, Henry
    177 (note 55)
Wampanoag Indians
    15
Ward, Sam
    109
Warren, Samuel Dennis, Mrs. (Susan
    Cornelia Clarke)
    128
Washington, D.C.
    St. Matthew's Cathedral: 199
Washington University, Saint Louis
    144, 181 (note 208)
Watercolor Techniques
    54, 75-76, 168-70
Wheelwright, Andrew Cunningham, Mrs.
    177 (note 70)
Wheelwright, Edward
    21
Wheelwright, Mary Cabot
    177 (note 70)
Whitman, Sarah Wyman
    176 (note 20)
Whitney, Mary (Mrs. Henry Lawrence)
    165-66, 203; as model: figs. 226 (p. 163)
        and 227 (p. 164); self-portrait:
        203
Whitney, William Collins
    144
Whittredge, Worthington
    93, 96; fig. 142 (p. 95)
Williams, Joshua Appleby
    170, 182 (note 244); figs. 26 (p. 17) and
        236 (p. 172)
Williams, William A.
    204; figs. 241-42 (p. 204)
The Wise Men Out of the East
        (The Riverside Magazine for Young People)
    144, 148, 156; fig. 203 (p. 146)
The Wolf Charmer (Oil Painting)
    144; fig. 201 (p. 143)
The Wolf Charmer
        (The Riverside Magazine for Young People)
    139, 142 (caption), 144, 151, 156, 164;
        figs. 196-97 (p. 140)
Woman Bathing (A Bather)
    124; fig. 178 (p. 125)
Woodland Nymph
    162, 182 (note 231)
Worcester Art Museum
    195; collection of: fig. 178 (p. 125)
Yale University Art Gallery
    collection of: figs. 78-79 (p. 49), 87
        (p. 55), 110 (p. 73), 130 (p. 87),
        163 (p. 110), 172 (p. 119) and 182
        (p. 127)

John La Farge
Portrait of the Painter, 1859
Oil on wood
16 x 11 1/2 in. (40.6 x 29.2 cm.)
The Metropolitan Museum of Art,
New York, Samuel D. Lee Fund,
1934 (34.134)

John La Farge
Margaret Mason Perry La Farge, c. 1860
Oil on canvas
16 x 13 in. (40.6 x 33 cm.)
William Vareika Fine Arts, Newport